MARKETING TO **HISPANICS**

A Strategic Approach to Assessing and Planning Your Initiative

TERRY J.
SOTO

KAPLAN PUBLISHING

DEDICATION

This book is dedicated to Cesar and Teresa Soto, my mom and dad, who came to this country over 35 years ago and whose sacrifice, efforts, and encouragement led to the opportunity of writing this book.

This publication is designed to provide accurate and authoritative information in regard to the subject matter covered. It is sold with the understanding that the publisher is not engaged in rendering legal, accounting, or other professional service. If legal advice or other expert assistance is required, the services of a competent professional should be sought.

President, Kaplan Publishing: Roy Lipner
Vice President and Publisher: Maureen McMahon
Senior Acquisitions Editor: Michael Cunningham
Development Editor: Karen Murphy
Director of Production: Daniel Frey
Production Editor: Caitlin Ostrow
Creative Director: Lucy Jenkins
Typesetter: Todd Bowman

© 2006 by Teresa J. Soto

Published by Kaplan Publishing,
a division of Kaplan, Inc.

Printed in the United States of America

06 07 08 10 9 8 7 6 5 4 3 2 1

Library of Congress Cataloging-in-Publication Data

Soto, Teresa J.
    Marketing to Hispanics : a strategic approach to assessing and planning your initiative / Teresa J. Soto.—1st ed.
        p. cm.
    Includes bibliographical references and index.
    ISBN 1-4195-0278-6
    1. Hispanic American consumers. 2. Marketing—United States. I. Title.
    HF5415.33.U6S66 2006
    658.80089'68073—dc22

                                                                2005033589

Kaplan Publishing books are available at special quantity discounts to use for sales promotions, employee premiums, or educational purposes. Please call our Special Sales Department to order or for more information at 800-621-9621, ext. 4444, e-mail kaplanpubsales@kaplan.com, or write to Kaplan Publishing, 30 South Wacker Drive, Suite 2500, Chicago, IL 60606-7481.

"Ms. Soto's ability to help us see ourselves from a competitive worldview, her use of case studies that lay out the strategic thought processes successful companies go through, and her way of getting down to the brass tacks of internal assessment and program implementation elevates this work far above the typical marketing how-to."
Rick Moss
President and Founder, RetailWire.com

"Terry Soto's book is a conscientious and strategic approach to evaluating and entering the greatest 'foreign' market within our own borders. All the resources necessary to get started marketing to Hispanics are here in one place. Read this book with a highlighter and a notebook by your side. In every chapter you will find tools that apply to your business and that you can use to successfully serve, and sell to, the Latino market."
Russell A. Bennett
Vice President, Latino Health Solutions, PacifiCare Health Systems

"Marketing to Hispanics is fast becoming a corporate mandate. But not all firms are ready to actually service the Latino customers they attract. It is critical to ensure that you are able to 'walk the walk' before you begin to 'talk the talk.' Terry Soto's book provides a practical, systematic approach to preparing your company to target and serve Hispanic America and to setting realistic goals by which to measure your success. Buy it. Read it. Use it."
Carl J. Kravetz
Chairman/Chief Strategic Officer, cruz/kravetz:IDEAS; Chairman, Association of
    Hispanic Advertising Agencies (AHAA)

"Terry Soto's work is penetrating and groundbreaking. *Marketing to Hispanics* builds on current business cases and research in this practical, comprehensive, and seminal book. I recommend it not only to companies interested in the Hispanic market but to anyone engaged in a business relating to any minority culture in the U.S. and abroad."
Kurt Motamedi, PhD, MBA, MSEE
Professor of Strategy and Leadership, Pepperdine University; CEO and President,
    Executive Alliance, Inc.

"Terry Soto's gift as a multicultural strategist and years of successful hands-on experience working with corporate America are clearly captured in her new book. In *Marketing to Hispanics,* Terry skillfully shares her in-depth market knowledge in the context of the real business world in a no-nonsense, step-by-step approach. Terry's book is a must-read for committed, seasoned executives and students alike."
M. Isabel Valdes
Principal/IVC, Isabel Valdes Consulting; Author of *Marketing to American Latinos: A
    Guide to the In-Culture Approach, Parts I & II*

"*Marketing to Hispanics* is the first to address Hispanic market strategy within a business planning framework that considers both the realities of the external environment in which companies compete for a piece of this market, and the need for internal alignment consistent with a company's business model. This book is a must read across all levels of the organization."
E. Martin Heldring
President and CEO, Harris Bank–Glencoe Northbrook

"It's no secret that the Hispanic/Latino population is the fastest growing minority group in the U.S. But the magic of Soto's book is that she takes you beyond the numbers, providing American businesses with a strategic blueprint for connecting with the Latino consumer. A must-read, especially for U.S. retailers."
Don Longo
Editorial Director, Retail Group, VNU Business Media, and Hispanic Retail 360
  Conference

"Business is rightfully focused on the incredible opportunity that lies in serving and satisfying the Hispanic market. The key lies in understanding the complexity of this vast population segment and defining the strategic fit within your organization. Terry Soto walks you through the research, assessment, planning, and strategy development frameworks that are necessary before any company can truly say: 'se habla Español.'"
Michael Sansolo
Senior Vice President, Food Marketing Institute

"In *Marketing to Hispanics*, Terry Soto has skillfully distilled her extensive experience working with many of America's top companies, helping them to effectively reach Hispanics. It is a great 'how-to' guide and gets into the nitty gritty of Hispanic marketing that many marketing books overlook. *Marketing to Hispanics* is a must-read for anyone looking to avoid the pitfalls that can befall the most well-intentioned marketer in the rewarding but tricky multicultural marketplace."
David R. Morse
President & CEO, New American Dimensions

"*Marketing to Hispanics* is important because it argues that Hispanic marketing initiatives must be based on sound strategy. It treats Hispanic marketing as another key strategy within the broader context of a company's overall corporate objectives and strategies. This is the only approach that will ensure that Hispanic marketing efforts are effective and enduring."
Lou Nieto
President, ConAgra Meats and Deli Group

"Terry Soto's book reflects a growing trend towards maturity in Hispanic marketing. Her strategic perspective and her case studies take the understanding of the Hispanic market to a higher level of sophistication."
Felipe Korzenny, PhD
Author of *Hispanic Marketing: A Cultural Perspective*; Director of the Center for Hispanic
  Marketing Communication at Florida State University; Cheskin Co-Founder

"This book gives a clear and complete roadmap that companies can follow to successfully market to Hispanics. Soto combines a deep knowledge of the subject with a rigorous process that will help marketers create greater value through their Hispanic initiatives."
Bill Bishop
President, Willard Bishop

Contents

As a business owner and strategic planning consultant who has worked with a number of *Fortune* 500 companies to successfully market their products to U.S. Hispanics, it never ceases to amaze me how business and marketing principles go out the window when companies decide to target the Hispanic market. So, when I agreed to write this book, I was inspired by the opportunity to share the basic principles and thinking used in my company when we consult on Hispanic market strategy development to capture profitable Hispanic market share. I didn't think the world needed another book on marketing to Hispanics, per se, but rather some insights on how companies need to organize to pursue this market opportunity in a well-thought-out, methodical, disciplined, and strategic manner. I wanted to share some critical perspectives of market assessment and strategy development that can mean the difference between corporate-wide integration that can positively impact the business and the less-than-favorable alternative. Why? Because I believe this is the only way that companies today can optimize their competitive advantages to capture the rewards that come from accurately delivering value to their consumers.

Another motivator was a desire to dispel a mystery that seems to come with accessing this huge and diverse marketplace. I want to show that the same basic approaches and tools already used in everyday business analysis not only apply, but also are critical components. The key to successfully leveraging a new segment opportunity, Hispanic or otherwise, depends on having a thorough understanding of the environment in which you will compete for it, identifying which of those consumers will allow you to generate profit, and defining how well an organization and its environment and target consumer are aligned. Mission, goals, culture, products, and infrastructure must be in sync in order to deliver profitable growth. That's it. There is no mystery. What often feels mysterious is a company's unfamiliarity with a different culture and how that culture interacts with its product category. The "mystery" of this culture is about nothing more than understanding behavioral context and drivers. Once you see it for what it is and apply the business frameworks, you will know if being "culturally relevant" within your organization's existing strategies and goals is possible, and if not, you will have the "situation intelligence" to determine if it makes business sense to adapt and how.

While it is important to point out some of the fundamental differences between U.S. Hispanics and mainstream Americans—including the vast differences that exist among U.S. Hispanics in terms of race, ethnicity, country of origin, and acculturation level—try to look at these areas as behavioral context thought starters, because the purpose of this book is not to provide "everything you ever wanted to know about Hispanics but were afraid to ask." The intention of this book is to aid you in applying a proven and effective process for assessing the Hispanic market as a viable growth opportunity and for developing a Hispanic market strategy for your company founded on: (1) assessing the macro environment, industry trends, the competition, and the consumer; and (2) assessing your own company's alignment with the Hispanic market and its current readiness so your organization can leverage internal strengths to capitalize on the environmental market opportunities, and do so by addressing identified weaknesses and by being conscious of and averting environmental threats. Only by completing this assessment in a rigorous and disciplined manner will you know where you stand with this marketplace vis-à-vis your organization's business model and long-term direction—its vision. The assessment process and outcome are the starting points for creating the strategies that align with the rest of the organization, including how your organization will implement them, how implementation will be controlled, how risk will be managed or mitigated, and how you will create and monitor relevant metrics.

It is a process that most companies across many industries utilize, but one that is severely underused when it comes to assessing the Hispanic market as a potential growth opportunity. There are several case study examples of companies that have candidly shared their experiences on this journey. Just as each company is unique, so too are their approaches. While enormously instructive, keep in mind that their experiences provide lessons, not a blueprint. What this book provides is more like a road map, with customizable directions and a host of tools and research resources to address the needs of your specific situation.

In 2004, the United States was home to more than 40 million Hispanics, over 14 percent of the entire population. By 2050, Hispanics are projected to make up nearly 25 percent of the U.S. population, or more than 100 million people. And while many of us will not be in the positions we hold today, being in sync with a company's vision and the interest of key stakeholders implies having a long-term outlook.

Of late, there is a sense of urgency among many executives to tap into this fast-growing market potential. But I caution you not to rush into execution prematurely, because if you approach this opportunity tactically and in a piecemeal manner, you will produce piecemeal results that will discourage support and raise skepticism that is very difficult to overcome. Targeting the Hispanic market needs to be a well-designed, integrated strategy that considers the company's operating context and connects with its corporate goals.

In the following chapters, you will find the tools and resources you need to craft your Hispanic market strategy. Chapter 1 provides an overview of the U.S. Hispanic market. It breaks down the demographic numbers, showing the trends over the past 20 years and predicting the likely growth over the next 50. In addition, it touches on some elements of culture to help you understand the beliefs, attitudes, and values that are likely to influence behavior. This is an excellent place to start, particularly if you are new to this territory. For others, some of this material may already be familiar and an experienced Hispanic marketer may find great value in obtaining a deeper understanding of Hispanic culture from two of the industry's pioneers: *Marketing to American Latinos: A Guide to the In-Culture Approach, Parts I and II* by M. Isabel Valdes and *Hispanic Marketing: A Cultural Perspective* by Felipe Korzenny, PhD, and Betty Ann Korzenny.

Chapter 2 begins the process of self-diagnosis. It presents some scenarios of how companies decide to pursue the Hispanic market, while also addressing some of the challenges and barriers involved in that pursuit. It provides some key considerations, steps, and caveats to keep in mind as you prepare to take on the assessment, planning, development, and implementation of your Hispanic market strategy.

In Chapter 3, we look at three real-world case studies in three distinctly different industries—grocery retail, financial services, and health care services. The processes undergone by the companies profiled—Carnival Food Stores, Wells Fargo Bank, and PacifiCare Health Systems—are prime examples of three different organizational approaches. They provide a preview of some of the processes outlined in this book.

Chapters 4, 5, and 6 cover the external assessment, including the macro forces and industry trends that create the environment in which your company competes or will compete for the Hispanic market and to which it constantly will need adapting. We look at the competitive environment, starting with the fact that your company's Hispanic market competitive set may look very different from how you currently define it. And finally, we look at target definition and the building blocks to achieve a multidimensional understanding of the consumer. These chapters cover critical questions and provide specific resources and tools to help answer them. There are further case study examples within these and the following chapters to help broaden your perspective and learn from companies in other regions and industries that have gone through the process.

The internal assessment is the focus of Chapter 7, and we turn attention inward to the organization itself. We identify the areas your company will need to assess, the people and operational areas that may be impacted or that may impact the strategy development and implementation, and suggest ways in which corporate and operational alignment ought to be considered.

Chapter 8 delves into some analytical approaches to market sizing. It provides some insights on segmentation approaches and hypotheses development. The chapter also covers some considerations for building your SWOT (strengths, weaknesses, opportunities, and threats) analysis and for identifying critical success factors that ought to be considered in your business and operational strategies.

Chapter 9 works to help crystallize your critical issues and success factors and presents a variety of approaches for developing strategic alternatives, deciding on the corporate strategy, and developing operational strategies. It also touches on considerations for the implementation plan, the control plan, change management, and risk mitigation.

Finally, Chapter 10 focuses on defining and monitoring the metrics and aligning internal resources to generate and disseminate them in a meaningful and relevant way, and most important of all, in a way that ties it all back to corporate strategies and goals. Throughout, it will become clear that the steps involved are not discrete parts, but overlapping, interdependent elements that need to be kept front of mind at all times.

The process of developing and implementing a Hispanic market strategy requires a disciplined approach. The systems in place to measure success must align with and deliver on industry and corporate benchmarks and averages in order to be meaningful to key stakeholders. Keep in mind that there isn't one standard for how your company does business with Hispanics and one for the rest of the company's customers. The success and overall growth of your organization depends upon how you ultimately deliver—alignment is the only way to deliver well.

Done conscientiously, developing a Hispanic business strategy requires a great deal of work and learning—both statistical and in-market intelligence gathering, and a little number crunching. It also necessitates a large commitment from upper management of time, resources, money, and dedication. Depending on the focus of your organizational structure, it might be best to create a stand-alone Hispanic Strategy business group. In others, it may need to be a fully integrated part of every business group and department. Only the specific needs and circumstances of your particular situation can determine what will work best for your company. The important thing to understand from the start is that the process for developing and implementing a Hispanic market strategy is not a quick one; the payoff may not come for two or three years. But the revenues—and the profits—are there, and if you do the hard work of creating a strategy now, you will be working to ensure the long-term viability and profitability of your company well into the future. After all, the most successful companies are those that can leverage market opportunities by building new competencies, capabilities, products, and markets through an established capacity for focused flexibility and adaptability.

While the thought of writing this book didn't seem daunting at first, I quickly learned what a huge undertaking I had signed up for. Fortunately, I had lots of support, understanding, and encouragement from family and friends, many of whom I neglected during this endeavor, but who I know will take me back with open arms. I want to thank the various syndicated research companies and organizations that so graciously allowed the use of their knowledge and provided examples of their products and tools to help illustrate some of the concepts discussed in this book. I thank the Kaplan Publishing staff for originally approaching me about writing this book and for being open to the direction I wanted to take it. Their patience on what may have seemed like endless deadline extensions, their valuable feedback, and their direction on the manuscript is appreciated. I'm also grateful to the Prologue Publishing Services staff for their constructive critique and an editing process that ensured a focused delivery of the subject matter. And importantly, I want to honor, acknowledge, and thank colleagues, current and past clients, and especially case study companies who so willingly and openly shared their companies' strategies, tactics, and experiences to help ground the ideas in this book in the real world of Hispanic strategic planning.

1

AN OVERVIEW OF THE HISPANIC MARKET AND CULTURE IN THE UNITED STATES

HISPANIC OR LATINO?

In starting an overview of any ethnic or cultural group, it's important to understand the terminology used to describe the group and its underlying meanings. Your company's documents may use the terms *Hispanic* or *Latino* exclusively, or as is often the case, interchangeably. It may not seem to matter much, but it does help to know a little bit about where these terms come from before establishing a consistent policy on usage.

Many people are confused about the use of the terms *Hispanic* and *Latino*. Even Spanish speakers are in disagreement as to how these terms should be applied. In the United States, *Hispanic* is used interchangeably with *Latino*. *Hispanic* is an English-language term not generally used in Latin America. *Latino* is a Spanish-language term used increasingly since the introduction of the term *Hispanic* by the U.S. Census in 1970. There is strong preference for one or the other by some, while others reject both terms, insisting on being identified by their national origin. Still others use both situationally.

Those who have a preference for *Latino* argue that the term embodies the essence of national origin and the political connection between

1

the United States and Latin America. It is also suggested that *Latino* is more culturally neutral and racially inclusive of all groups in Latin America, with less connection to Europe. In addition, some propose that *Latino* is most commonly used in Spanish and English publications.

Others argue that *Hispanic* should be used because it is the official label used to collect data on this population. Because of its scientific alignment with market data, it is often used in business and within academic contexts, while *Latino* is a localized term used among Spanish speakers. The term *Latino* includes those from Spain, although it does not cover those from Brazil.

Al Sosa, a historian with the Hispanic Genealogy Forum, suggests that the matter can be addressed simply by tracing the words back to their roots. Sosa indicates that the first time the word *Latin* was heard was in the time just prior to the Roman Republic, in what is now Italy. A tribe of people called Latins appeared in Italy. Their country was Latium, their capital city was Rome, and the language they spoke was Latin. When the Romans invaded Iberia, they found many different tribes there and eventually conquered most of the peninsula, including a city in the south called Hispalis (Seville). The Romans later made it a province they called Hispania. It should be understood, then, that the word *España*, the Spanish word for Spain, comes from the Latin word *Hispania*, and not the other way around. *Hispania*, in ancient times, referred to the people and eventually to the culture of the Iberian Peninsula. As Rome added more territory to its empire, the language became imposed on the conquered people, eventually leading to the creation of several new languages, now called Latin or Romance languages. Several Latin countries were also created—France, Portugal, Spain, Italy, Albania, and Romania.

In Europe, Latins are generally accepted to be individuals coming from these Latin countries where a Latin-based language is spoken. Today, the European view of the term *Hispanic* is fairly precise. It refers to Spain, its culture, the Spanish-speaking people of Latin America, and/or their culture. Today, the word *Hispanic* has been adopted by the U.S. government to categorize the growing Spanish-speaking population. This use, however, has led to additional confusion because the other categories—white, black, Asian, and others—refer to race, while Hispanic was intended to refer to a cultural or ethnic group.

WHO ARE HISPANICS?

Hispanics are members of a very diverse group in terms of socioeconomic positions, religions, racial classifications, and national origins. They now comprise this country's largest minority, but as noted, the term *Hispanic* merely defines a culture.

Consequently, Hispanics are not an easily identified racial group. Using Census terms, Hispanics' race can be white, black, Asian, Arabic, Native Islander, or any other combination of races. For instance, a person could be racially black, yet because his nationality is Cuban or Dominican, he would be considered Hispanic. Culturally, he may self-identify with his Cuban or Dominican heritage, a combination of African, Spanish, and indigenous cultures of the Caribbean. Similarly, a person of Peruvian origin could be ethnically Chinese. He may self-identify with his Peruvian culture, albeit with some influence from his Chinese heritage. You may be wondering, Chinese in Peru? But today there are more than 400,000 multigenerational ethnically Chinese Peruvians resulting from a migration of Chinese that started in 1849 to work in the processing of guano (fertilizer) and on the sugar plantations.

As we know, the conquest, subsequent colonization, and migration well into the 20th century played a significant part in creating a diversity of races and cultures in Central and South America, as well as the West Indies (Caribbean). While Spain and Portugal had the greatest impact on the colonization of Central and South America and the West Indies, Holland, France, Germany, and Great Britain all participated in the colonization of the region. The people of Latin America reflect a variety of ethnic and racial heritages that is unmatched in any other region. Intermarriage among Indians, whites, and blacks created a unique blend of cultures in the region. As such, culture-based traditions borrowed from indigenous people, black slaves, and white immigrants contributed to a rich regional culture. Music, arts and crafts, foods, religion, architecture, and language all reflect the contributions of Native Latin American, African, and European heritage.

Today, the region of Latin America—made up of South America, Central America, Mexico, and the West Indies—is comprised of nearly three dozen independent nations plus some colonies and other political units with special ties to the United States, Great Britain, France, or The Netherlands.

The historical and ethnic influences on their culture created differ-ent societies with different cultures in each of these countries, and even though the universal language (with some exceptions) is Spanish, there are just as many dialects as there are countries of origin.

Suddenly it becomes quite clear why the U.S. Hispanic population, made up of people from more than two dozen Latin American countries, cannot be considered a homogenous group. Along with their history and heritage, each of these groups has also had a unique story in the United States, involving different times of arrival, areas of settlement, and types of migration and reception experiences, which impact the way Hispanics think and how they view life and their place in U.S. society.

This knowledge suggests a need for new ways of thinking about the U.S. Hispanic population and heightens the need to understand the var-ied shared elements and differences of Latin American ancestry and cul-ture.

HOW MANY HISPANICS ARE THERE?

Over the last 100 years, few groups have had as great an impact on the demography of the United States as Hispanics, with the most dramatic im-pact taking place over the last few decades. This significant Hispanic de-mographic shift is considered one of the greatest transformational forces on the 21st century, along with aging baby boomers and a second baby boom that is highly multiracial and multicultural.

According to Census 2000, of the 281.4 million people that resided in the United States, 35.3 million people, or about 13 percent, were His-panic. The Hispanic population grew by 58 percent since 1990. Since 2000, growth has continued at a vigorous pace. In 2004, this number had already increased by 14 percent to 40.4 million, while the non-Hispanic population grew by just 2 percent during the same period.

The impact of this Hispanic population growth is magnified by the fact that the non-Hispanic white and black population is not only stable, but also aging. The "graying" of America is characterized by the fact that non-His-panic white baby boomers, aged 45 and older, make up 40 percent of the U.S. population (Hispanics in the same age groups represent only 19 per-cent). This group is poised to enter retirement within the next 20 years, sig-nificantly draining work forces, and exit as consumers across a variety of product and service categories while creating demand for a whole host of others, many of which will need to be created.

So, as the huge baby boom generation moves toward retirement, a second baby boom is filling in from behind. The largest generation of young people since the 1960s is beginning to come of age. They're called "echo boomers." Born between 1982 and 1995, there are over 80 million of them, and they're already having a huge impact on entire segments of the economy. As the population ages, echo boomers will be become the next dominant generation of Americans.

Not surprisingly, echo boomers are also significantly more racially and culturally diverse than the baby boom generation and the most accepting of diversity. The multicultural segment of the echo boomer market represents 35 percent of people 10 to 23 years old, with most born and educated in the United States. So, not unlike their non-Hispanic white counterparts, Hispanic echo boomers are also a reflection of the sweeping changes in American life over the past 20 years. They are the first to grow up with computers at home, at school, and at work, and they live in a 500-channel television universe. They are multitaskers with cell phones, music downloads, and instant messaging, and Hispanic echo boomers spend approximately $40 billion of the $170 billion a year spent by all echo boomers in the United States.

Will the Hispanic Population Continue to Grow?

The U.S. Census projects that by 2010, the total U.S. population will reach 308.9 million people, of which 47.8 million, or 15.5 percent, will be Hispanics of any race. This will represent a growth of 34 percent between 2000 and 2010. Looking beyond 2010, growth projections reflect double-digit proportions for every ten-year period between 2000 and 2050. The Hispanic population will have the highest growth rate of any ethnic group over the next 25 years—three times faster than the national average. By 2050, Hispanics of any race will reach 102.6 million, representing 24.4 percent of the total U.S. population, a 188 percent increase between 2000 and 2050, from 35.6 million to 102.6 million.

Comparatively, the non-Hispanic white population reached 195.7 million in 2000 and is projected to grow to 201.1 million by 2010, an increase of only 2.8 percent. By 2050, the non-Hispanic, white population is expected to grow to 210.3 million, an increase of 7.4 percent between 2000 and 2050.

Where Will the Growth Come From?

Large-scale immigration from Latin America, especially Mexico, developed in the 1970s, gathered momentum in the 1980s, and surged after the mid-1990s. Immigration drove most of the Hispanic population growth over this time period. Like so many other groups coming to the United States over the last four decades, some groups came mainly as political refugees or political exiles without the benefit of refugee status. Others came as free or contracted laborers, and still others arrived simply as immigrants looking to improve the opportunities in their lives.

Given continuing instabilities in Latin America and continued opportunities in the United States, the foreign-born Hispanic population will continue to grow in the next few decades and is expected to contribute significantly to U.S. Hispanic market growth. According to U.S. Census-based analysis, Goldman Sachs estimates that 700,000 Hispanic immigrants will arrive in the United States every year for the foreseeable future. As such, immigration is expected to account for 50 percent of the total Hispanic population growth through 2030.

However, with the youth of the U.S. Hispanic population (median age is 26, versus 35 for non-Hispanics) and its larger families (2.9 children per couple, versus 2), U.S. births will drive as much of the growth among Hispanics in the future as births in Latin America.

These U.S.-born and U.S.-educated Hispanics have had and will continue to have a very different impact on the country than their immigrant parents. That impact is still to be fully felt, as half of the children of Hispanic immigrants are 11 years old or younger. Their youth, coupled with the expected increase in their numbers, signals a growing presence of Hispanics in the school-age population and in the pool of future entrants to the labor force.

With the aging baby boomers leaving the workforce in droves in the next 20 years and the significant number of Hispanic echo boomers that will enter it, corporations have begun to see the impending dependency on the Hispanic population as a valuable labor resource for this country. Given such significant and continuing demographic shifts,

U.S. institutions will be increasingly impacted by and grow dependent on Hispanics not only as consumers but as employees in the coming decades.

With this in mind, companies like Boeing Corporation, whose future depends on its ability to hire skilled engineers, is involved in strategic planning to that end. Along with a variety of corporations across several industries, Boeing is creating and supporting programs in schools to ensure that young Hispanics are educated and encouraged to excel in math and science. Boeing has a variety of programs in place and continues to develop school and community outreach programs to motivate Hispanic kids to move toward careers in engineering.

What Is Their Income Potential and Purchasing Power?

According to HispanTelligence®, U.S. Hispanic purchasing power surged to nearly $700 billion in 2005 and is projected to reach as much as $1 trillion by 2007, nearly three times the overall national rate over the past decade. Current Hispanic purchasing power is 8.5 percent of total U.S. purchasing power but is projected to reach 11 percent by 2010. While Hispanics have among the lowest median income levels of any population group—$33,000 in 2003, nearly 25 percent below the national U.S. median of $43,300—Goldman Sachs projections indicate that the Hispanic population and their incomes will rise concurrently and continue to converge toward the national average. This rise in income levels is expected to benefit from increased numbers of U.S.-born households whose incomes are significantly higher than those of foreign-born households.

Where Do U.S. Hispanics Live?

Although Hispanics are still migrating to larger cities in California, Texas, Florida, New York, Illinois, and Arizona—states where 66 percent of the population is concentrated and that accounted for 57 percent of Hispanic population growth between 1990 and 2000—a 2002 Pew Hispanic Center study indicates that this population has also begun to disperse across the country. Very fast growth is being seen in states as scattered as Georgia, Colorado, North Carolina, Nebraska, and Washington. Hispanic gateways such as Los Angeles, New York, Miami, and

TABLE 1.1

Ten Metro Areas with the Largest Latino Populations, 2000

	Number of Latinos	Percent of Total Population	Latino Growth, 1980–2000
Los Angeles	4,242,213	45%	105%
New York	2,339,836	25%	60%
Chicago	1,416,584	17%	143%
Miami	1,291,737	57%	123%
Houston	1,248,586	30%	211%
Riverside—San Bernardino	1,228,962	38%	324%
Orange County	875,579	31%	206%
Phoenix	817,012	25%	261%
San Antonio	816,037	51%	67%
Dallas	810,499	23%	324%
Total	15,087,045	31%	130%

Source: "Latino Growth in Metropolitan America: Changing Patterns, New Locations." The Pew Hispanic Center and The Brookings Institution Center on Urban and Metropolitan Policy.

Chicago will continue to house considerable concentrations of Hispanics. (See Table 1.1.) However, the growth rates that slowed in these metros in the 1990s are likely to continue to slow.

The study indicates that 16 of the top 100 major metros constituted a kind of Hispanic heartland in the United States and were home to half of the U.S. Hispanic population in 2000.

But more astonishing was Hispanics' explosive entry into 51 new Latino destinations. (See Table 1.2.) Within these metros, the Hispanic population grew at rates ranging from 147 percent (Knoxville) to 1,180 percent (Raleigh-Durham), albeit from much smaller bases. Nevertheless, this growth reflects an amazing and very rapid entrance of the Hispanic population into new settlement areas and illustrates Hispanics' willingness to settle away from traditional metros. From Wilmington to West Palm Beach, from Little Rock to Las Vegas, the new Hispanic destinations encompass a diverse collection of metropolitan areas scattered across 35 states in every region of the country. It is likely this initial presence will provide the catalyst for continued growth in these areas.

Yet, the study's findings suggest that the Hispanic population will not necessarily stabilize in these metros. Instead, they will experience a continued arrival of new Hispanic immigrants, while other Hispanics will

TABLE 1.2
*"Hypergrowth," * New Latino Destinations, 2000*

	Number of Latinos	Percent of Total Population	Latino Growth, 1980–2000
Raleigh	72,580	6%	1,180%
Atlanta	268,851	7%	995%
Greensboro	62,210	5%	962%
Charlotte	77,092	5%	932%
Orlando	271,627	17%	859%
Las Vegas	322,038	21%	753%
Nashville	40,139	3%	397%
Fort Lauderdale	271,652	17%	578%
Sarasota	38,682	7%	538%
Portland, OR	142,444	7%	437%
Greenville, SC	26,167	3%	397%
West Palm Beach	140,675	12%	397%
Washington, DC	432,003	9%	346%
Indianapolis	42,994	3%	338%
Minneapolis-St.Paul	99,121	3%	331%
Fort Worth	309,851	18%	328%
Providence	93,868	8%	325%
Tulsa	38,570	5%	303%
Total	2,750,564	9%	505%

* Hypergrowth metros had Latino population growth over 300 percent between 1980 and 2000.

Source: "Latino Growth in Metropolitan America: Changing Patterns, New Locations." The Pew Hispanic Center and The Brookings Institution Center on Urban and Metropolitan Policy.

continue to leave in search of better jobs, housing, and quality of life in other U.S. destinations.

This was evidenced by the significant speed in which Hispanics have already exited crowded central cities. The report points to key indicators, which suggest that suburbs, particularly those on the periphery of large metropolitan areas, are becoming ports of entry instead of the old urban *barrios*. Hispanic families in search of the classic American suburban dream are also moving to the outskirts, where housing is cheaper. Accordingly, more Hispanics will be migrating to the suburbs in the coming decades. Fifty-four percent of all Hispanics now reside in suburban areas. This trend contrasts significantly the historical tendency for Hispanics to be urban dwellers, as many still are.

ACCULTURATION

There is a growing body of research that shows a tendency for Hispanics to acculturate rather than assimilate. Historically, immigrants have assimilated into U.S. society by replacing their native customs with the mainstream culture. Hispanics, by contrast, have largely preserved their cultural traits while adopting a complementary set of cultural dimensions from the mainstream and even from other ethnic groups and Hispanic nationalities, a process known as *acculturation*.

Despite expectations that Hispanics would assimilate, factors such as significant continued immigration for the foreseeable future, proximity to Latin America, burgeoning Spanish-language media, accessible and frequent communication with the homeland, and the ever-increasing presence and access to Hispanic products and services lead the market to acculturate rather than assimilate. In many cases, even retro-acculturation among second and third generations is occurring. And importantly, as David Morse of New American Dimensions proposes, many Hispanics don't migrate to the United States because they want to start a new life here like previous generations of immigrants. Rather, many Hispanics who come to the United States leaving family behind do so for the sole purpose of working to send money back home to ensure their family's survival, education, and well being. When they leave home, the move is always considered a "temporary" one. As such, the need to adopt elements of the mainstream culture are of secondary importance. It isn't until many years later, when they realize that working in the United States is the only way to make ends meet, that they send for their wife and kids (or they marry and have children here) and start integrating into mainstream society. This is when they resign themselves to a permanent life in the United States; it is a sacrifice they deem necessary to ensure a better future for their children.

What Is Acculturation?

Otto Santa Ana, PhD, says that acculturation is closely tied to our identities and is a highly individual and unique experience. He states that our identities are fluid and change across time—we have multiple related and unrelated identities, not just one, that correspond to the various roles we play in our daily lives and the setting in which we live them.

In this context, identity can be situational and highly dependent on the social interaction that takes place between people in which each person is playing a role within the situation.

In the context of Hispanics, Santa Ana says that a person might be a mother, a wife, and an employee whose ever-changing identity—one that is based on her life experiences, her place in society (socioeconomic), how she identifies with her various communities (cultural, work, school, family, friends) and wider society (organizations, church, government, business)—contributes to her level and pace of acculturation in the United States. The number of roles, interactions, and experiences a person has in U.S. society, along with the types of groups and environments in which they are carried out, all impact the extent and speed of a person's acculturation process. And as Santa Ana indicates, a person's life dictates the quality and quantity of acculturation accelerators and, therefore, the speed at which one acculturates to an environment and culture.

Imagine two people who arrive in the United States at the same time; one settles in Los Angeles, California, and the other in Nashville, Tennessee. You can quickly imagine the experiences awaiting each person in his respective environment and the need to quickly come up to speed and adapt one's identity to meet given environment and situational demands, as illustrated in Table 1.3.

TABLE 1.3
Acculturation Environments—Los Angeles Metro vs. Nashville Metro

	Los Angeles Metro	Nashville Metro
Hispanic population	6.6 million	40,000
Hispanic-oriented products and services (supermarkets, banks, retail, health care)	Very High	Moderately Low
Spanish-speaking employer or supervisor	Moderately High	Very Low
Spanish-speaking teachers/school administrators	Very High	Very Low
Spanish-language church/mass community	Very High	Moderately Low
Spanish-language media presence	Extremely High	Low

A person's ability to retain, express, utilize, and enjoy his Hispanic cultural traits and behavior will, of course, be much easier in Los Angeles, where the Hispanic population is immense, than in Nashville. Because of this, the culture shock a person experiences will be softened in communities where a person is insulated from the reality of being in another country. The longer a person is able to function easily within this type of insulated environment, the longer a person will adhere to the Spanish language and his Hispanic traditions involving food, music, religion, and sense of family and community.

The person living in Los Angeles is likely to have Hispanic neighbors and friends, so his daily interactions will be within a Hispanic context and his connection to his U.S. Hispanic community will offer comfort and support, if only on a psychological level.

The opposite is likely the case for the person living in Nashville. This person is more likely to feel isolated, fearful, depressed, nostalgic, and completely out of his element. This person's survival mode requires venturing into unfamiliar territory and fending for himself. And by virtue of this, his identity will adapt and his acculturation process in critical areas will be fast-paced. On the other hand, this person will also cling to his Hispanic culture in situations that allow it, and these experiences will be what sustain and comfort him as familiarity with new surroundings grows.

How Do Hispanics Segment Based on Acculturation?

The answer to this question will vary by geography and the drivers experienced by each person. However, many studies, including those conducted by both McKinsey Consulting and Spectra Marketing (see Table 1.4), show that most Hispanics fall into the bicultural (acculturated) segment, which

TABLE 1.4
Cultural Segmentation of Hispanics

Segments	McKinsey (1998)	VNU Spectra (2003)
Assimilated	10%	13%
Bicultural (acculturated)	61%	59%
Monocultural (isolated)	29%	28%

Source: McKinsey Quarterly (1998) and VNU Spectra Marketing, Inc. (2003).

means that they have adopted culture from the mainstream, but what aspects of the mainstream culture have been adopted and to what degree is based on individual experience. These studies, although several years apart, show a consistent depiction of segmentation based on acculturation.

HISPANIC CULTURE'S IMPACT ON CONSUMPTION AND PURCHASE BEHAVIOR

A large and growing Hispanic population leads to ever-evolving and ever-increasing infrastructures that cater to this consumer segment. No one would deny that the private and public sectors in Los Angeles have clearly developed and adapted to serve Hispanics across their various acculturation stages. In fact, in some categories, innovative business models have been created specifically with Hispanic consumption in mind—the market is a veritable laboratory of sorts.

In Nashville, on the other hand, with very few exceptions, it is still business as usual, with less consideration for Hispanic culture and its specific needs and preferences. As such, the consumption behaviors and decisions made in these two environments, driven by social interaction and access to relevant products, will vary greatly.

Shopping and Retail

As the worldwide hub of capitalism, consumerism in the United States is incomparable. Increasing globalization and outsourcing by American manufacturers to Latin America and Asia has led to increasing affordability and access to everything from home electronics and technology (such as computers) to fashion, automobiles, and housewares.

By comparison, in Latin America, access to these items is often cost-prohibitive for many. American brands and workmanship are highly coveted, and those who can afford it wear American brands as status symbols. While retail financing is becoming more widely used to buy high-ticket items, interest rates are high. The retail model in operation in Latin America is primarily "cash and carry." Hispanics bring this mentality and behavior to the United States, with most unacculturated Hispanics shunning credit and opting to pay for their purchases outright. Most often,

TABLE 1.5
Favorite Store

Favorite Store	Total Hispanics
Wal-Mart	36%
Local stores that specialize in serving Hispanic and Latino customers	5%
Target	4%
Sears	4%
JCPenney	4%

Source: 2005 Hispanic OmniTel Retail Study, NOP World Roper Public Affairs, HispanicBusiness.com.

the sentiment is that one ought to live within one's means and not over-extend beyond what one can afford.

In the 2002 Hispanic Yankelovich MONITOR survey, 86 percent of Hispanics said they "pay cash whenever possible." Most save for large-ticket items, and it is not uncommon to hear from auto dealerships that Hispanics will even pay for their cars in full and in cash.

In the past five years or so, auto dealerships, retailers, and credit card companies have been aggressively promoting credit instruments and easy financing to Hispanics, creating an attitudinal and behavioral shift in the marketplace in favor of credit and financing, especially among the more acculturated.

But barring specific consumption attitudes and behavior imported from countries of origin that might impact immediate adoption of certain product categories, accessibility to and consumption of goods and services across categories among Hispanics is strong. The 2003 Consumer Expenditure Survey (see Appendix), published by the Bureau of Labor Statistics, reports that, proportionately, Hispanics spend more of their household income on food at home and in restaurants, apparel and services, transportation, and personal care and products, whereas category development opportunities exist in health care, entertainment, and insurance products.

As a result, retailers of all types continue to adapt the way they do business to attract this consumer, with Wal-Mart being the latest to implement an aggressive push to attract the market. It appears to be paying off, given results from a 2005 Hispanic OmniTel Retail Study by NOP World Roper Public Affairs. The survey indicated that 36 percent of Hispanics considered Wal-Mart their favorite store (see Table 1.5).

TABLE 1.6
Stores Shopped Often

Stores Shopped Often	Total Hispanics
National discount chain stores such as Wal-Mart or Target	61%
Local stores that specialize in serving Hispanic and Latino customers	37%
National home improvement stores such as Lowe's or Home Depot	37%
National midpriced department stores such as Kohl's, Sears, or JCPenney	31%
Specialty clothing stores such as Gap or Old Navy	19%
Electronics, entertainment, or appliance stores such as Circuit City or Best Buy	17%
National upscale department stores such as Macy's, Nordstrom, or Lord & Taylor	10%
Sporting good stores such as The Sports Authority	8%

Source: 2005 Hispanic OmniTel Retail Study, NOP World Roper Public Affairs HispanicBusiness.com.

When considering general merchandise and fashion, Hispanics are shopping a variety of retailers, but the NOP World survey indicates that national mass merchandisers like Wal-Mart and Target are the stores shopped most often by 61 percent of Hispanics (see Table 1.6).

Like their mainstream counterparts, pricing, location, and assortment are top store selection drivers among Hispanics, especially among the un-acculturated foreign-born (see Table 1.7). In comparison, foreign-born, unacculturated Hispanics are much more likely than U.S.-born Hispanics to prefer stores that feature Spanish-language signage, packaging and labeling in Spanish, and employees who speak Spanish. This is an area of tremendous opportunity for retailers hoping to capture a greater share of the unacculturated Hispanic market.

Interestingly, these types of findings are sometimes misunderstood to mean that Hispanics are more demanding in their service expectations. However, if you consider these preferences in a cultural context,

TABLE 1.7

Factors Considered Important for Shopping Locations

	Total Hispanics	U.S.-Born	Foreign-Born	Index Foreign Born to Total Hispanics
Low prices	77%	70%	83%	1.08
Convenient location	72%	67%	75%	1.04
Wide range of merchandising	71%	68%	73%	1.03
Employees who speak Spanish	54%	33%	69%	1.28
Products relevant to Hispanics	52%	35%	64%	1.23
Wide range of payment options	47%	35%	55%	1.17
Signage in Spanish	47%	22%	65%	1.38
Packaging and labels in Spanish	43%	20%	58%	1.35
Owner member of local community	34%	28%	40%	1.18

Source: 2005 Hispanic OmniTel Retail Study, NOP World Roper Public Affairs, HispanicBusiness.com.

you realize that retailers will not fully maximize their operational efforts among foreign-born, unacculturated Hispanics who do not understand their messages through English signage and labeling and employees who only speak English.

From a strategic standpoint, it would behoove a company trying to not only attract but also satisfy and retain this market segment to ensure that this consumer understands the in-store messaging and that the employees can support this understanding on a personal level. In essence, having the same opportunity to impact and motivate a Spanish-speaking customer as you might an English-speaking customer ought to be the goal.

So the question is not about whether unacculturated, Spanish-speaking consumers have higher expectations, it's really about how you align your organization to ensure a positive sales experience, make the sale, ensure satisfaction with the product at home, service that consumer post-sale, ensure that this consumer returns, and ensure that his opinion of your business that he expresses to others is a positive one.

Leisure and Entertainment

If one were to take a typical day in the life of a Hispanic in Latin America on a typical Sunday, the day might go something like this: the family would have breakfast and then rush to get ready for mass. They would then go for a car ride or walk to a park or one of the many squares and stop to chat with friends and acquaintances while the kids run around and play. For a special treat, they might go to the movies or a local street fair. Afterward, around 2:00 PM, they would have the midday meal at a favorite restaurant or at the house of a relative. After the meal, the family would sit and talk, listen to music, watch television and some might even sneak away for a nap. Later in the evening, the family might go visit friends, or if already out with family and friends, they might go home to relax.

When Hispanics come to the United States, many of the people with whom they had spent family and leisure time are no longer available to them. They must recreate a new community of people with whom they can spend time and reminisce. In fact, the 2002 Yankelovich Hispanic MONITOR survey shows that U.S. Hispanics prefer not to go far from their community when looking for people with whom to spend their leisure time. This changes as Hispanics acculturate. For instance, the same study indicates that among the assimilated (Yankelovich's label for the acculturated segment), half divide their leisure time equally between Hispanics and non-Hispanics.

Hispanics' preference for what they consider fun tends to remain very similar to the activities they enjoyed back home. When discussing leisure time with Hispanics in hundreds of focus groups, many miss the social interaction with friends and neighbors in the parks, squares, and even on the street in front of their homes, and they often perceive that non-Hispanics keep to themselves and do not speak to each other, even among neighbors. Yankelovich also reports that the number of Hispanics spending their leisure time mostly or exclusively with other Hispanics has risen from 63 percent in 2000 to 74 percent in 2002, likely due to many being recent arrivals in the United States who have not had a long-term opportunity to establish relationships outside their immediate peers. The study found that the top five ways of relaxing among U.S. Hispanics are: listening to music (63 percent), watching television (53 percent), socializing with friends or relatives (49 percent), reading (41 percent), and napping (36 percent).

Generally speaking, there is also a love for music and, given the opportunity, Hispanics will play music or listen to the radio nonstop. It is no wonder that by the beginning of 2004, there were 678 Spanish-language radio stations in the United States, and many top Hispanic market stations rank in the top five or top ten of all stations in the market, according to spring 2005 Arbitron ratings.

Hispanics love to watch television, and they find it enjoyable to do so as a family. According to ACNielsen media research as of January 2004, Hispanic households watch four more hours of television weekly during prime time than the mainstream (17.17 and 13.21 hours, respectively), 1⅓ more hours during daytime (9.58 and 8.28 hours, respectively), and equally as much late-night television (5.18 and 5.23 hours, respectively). As one would imagine, language of programming watched depends on the viewer's level of acculturation. In general, greater comfort with English means more English-language television viewing, but as expected, preferences for culturally, socially, and demographically relevant programming also impact choices, regardless of language ability.

Not unlike the general market, the Hispanic population enjoys renting movies. Statistics indicate that, proportionately, they own more home entertainment goods and are heavy renters of videos and DVDs, spending $3.4 billion a year on equipment and software. In 2001, recognizing Hispanics' high rental levels, Blockbuster, one of the nation's top renters of VHS tapes and DVDs, set out to create Hispanic-themed "boutique" sections in 1,000 of its 4,412 company-owned stores. These stores stock not only relevant titles in dubbed and subtitled formats, but also direct customers to their targeted snacks and reading material through bilingual signage.

Going to movies is a favorite pastime, especially for Hispanics aged 18 to 34. According to the Motion Picture Association of America (MPAA), Hispanics made up 15 percent of box office receipts in 2003 while accounting for only 13 percent of the population and, according to Scarborough Research, Hispanics are 81 percent more likely than non-Hispanics to see a movie on opening weekend.

Further, Kiser & Associates, Spanish book industry consultants, recently completed a yearlong study to determine the reading habits and media preferences of the growing U.S. Hispanic population at the request of the publishing industry. The 2004 survey conducted among Spanish-dominant Hispanics indicates that 86 percent of households purchased at least one book a year, while 29 percent bought ten or more adult books a year in Spanish, pointing to a Spanish-language book market of more than $350 million annually.

Vacations among Hispanics take on a different purpose—to reunite with family back home. In fact, compared to the national average, Hispanics are 31 percent more likely to say they took five trips or more outside of the United States, with Mexico, South America, and Central America as top destinations, according to a 2004 Scarborough survey. Most Hispanics stay with family when visiting home countries, as to do otherwise would be unthinkable.

Technology and Telecommunications

In Latin America, having a phone in the household is a luxury few can afford. Beyond costs, the bureaucracy involved in obtaining a line is mind-boggling, and some areas, especially in rural communities or on the outskirts of suburbs, simply are not wired for phone service. However, since their introduction, cell phones have overtaken in-home phone service as the primary method of communication, with cell phone rates often less expensive than in-home service. Even homes with phone service are increasingly opting to use their cell phones for day-to-day calls.

Because costs and the process of acquiring and maintaining phone service in the United States makes in-home phone service accessible, the decision to sign up for phone service upon arrival is almost automatic. Beyond functional purposes, the telephone is a catalyst to maintaining close ties to family in countries of origin. As such, Hispanic long-distance spending, along with other technology services, is considerable. U.S. Hispanics will spend more than $21.3 billion on local, long distance, wireless, and Internet services in 2005, representing more than 40 percent of the lucrative ethnic telecommunications consumer market, according to a new report by INSIGHT Research. And according to a Scarborough-sponsored study titled "Internet and Multimedia 11," Hispanics are 87 percent more likely than the non-Hispanic population to spend $100 or more per month on their long-distance service. In addition, the study indicates that 31 percent of Hispanics who own a cell phone use it as their primary phone and 11 percent of Hispanics spend over $100 on cell phones per month, compared to 7.5 percent of the non-Hispanic population. In recognition of this spending, phone service companies spend significant dollars to reach and keep these customers.

On matters of technology, Internet cafes are wildly popular in Latin America, and access to the Internet is quite easy and affordable; however, it is usually skewed to the middle-class to upper-class youth segment. While making an initially slow entrance into U.S. Hispanic households, computers have quickly approached general market levels and, according to a 2005 AOL/Roper Hispanic Survey, half of online U.S. Hispanics now have broadband connections at home. In addition, the study reports that proportionately, more online Hispanics use the Internet to communicate, share, and listen to music than the general online population. The survey also indicates that 47 percent of online Hispanics have children under the age of 18 at home—versus 37 percent for the general online population—and that they are far more confident in the Internet's ability to improve the lives of their children.

Further, the survey shows that Hispanic online consumers have quickly made the Internet part of their everyday lives. They go online at home an average of 9.2 hours per week, for example, compared with 8.5 hours for the general online population, and they now heavily rely on the Internet to learn more about products, share opinions, and improve their lives. In fact, 70 percent now view the Internet as the best source for comparing prices, making it the most powerful information medium for influencing Hispanics throughout the purchase-decision process. Online Hispanic consumers are younger and heavier users of the most cutting-edge features of the Internet as compared to the general online population—56 percent of Hispanics online are between the ages of 18 and 34 versus 34 percent for the general online population.

• • • • •

WHAT'S THE IMPACT?

It is clear that the Hispanic market is not only growing faster than any other segment in the United States, it is constantly evolving in terms of both demographics and acculturation. The Hispanic population has had and will continue to have an impact not only on the demography of the U.S. population, but also on other aspects of U.S. society. This can be seen, for example, in the increasing popularity of Hispanic food and music and in the prevalence of Spanish-language signage, advertisements, and media.

In addition, the business community is discovering the economic influence of the Hispanic population. Today, businesses are relying on and will increasingly look at Hispanics as entrepreneurs, employees, investors, and consumers. The bilingual and bicultural nature of today's and future Hispanic generations will also position Hispanics as a valuable resource as the U.S. business community continues to globalize consumer markets and expand business operations into Latin America.

The higher education system will increasingly find demand for higher level education as Hispanics prepare to replace the labor force across major industries, and Hispanics will be among the ranks of educators. Political institutions will find that Hispanics will play a more powerful role in the outcome of elections, both as voters and as political candidates. In addition, the health care system will see Hispanics as health care recipients and providers. Religious institutions will find that more and more of their potential followers and leaders will be Hispanics.

These trends are well underway in the largest states and at the national level; the rising dispersion of Hispanics into parts of the country that traditionally have not had Hispanic populations suggests that all parts of the country will feel the impact of continuing growth.

The steps you take today to holistically assess this large and fast-growing segment and your organization's approach to align the needs and preferences of this marketplace with your corporate direction and business model will be critical if you are to position your organization for long-term profitable growth.

2

IS YOUR ORGANIZATION ALIGNED FOR THE HISPANIC MARKET OPPORTUNITY?

In general, when companies consider business growth strategies that will help them deliver value to key stakeholders—including customers (whether consumer or business-to-business segments), employees, and shareholders—they consider an array of external forces that represent opportunities or that threaten the company's ability to leverage its competitive advantages to deliver on its long-term vision.

In their book *Strategy: A View from the Top,* De Kluyver and Pearce point to several forces that are impacting corporate strategy across industries, including globalization, demographic shifts, the emergence of new growth industries, the state of the economy and random forces such as war, new technologies, and the collapse of foreign governments. They suggest that all of these macro forces introduce risk and uncertainty that are difficult to predict into the business environment, yet they will have a wide-ranging effect on how companies do business in the future.

They add, however, that changes in a company's industry environment often have more direct impact on a company's ability to exercise its strategic options than the broader environment. So whether these forces represent growth opportunities or threats often depends on an organization's ability to preempt market trends, carefully assess their relevance to the organization and its customers, and have the ability to respond quickly. In fact, aside from a company's competitive resources, De Kluyver and Pearce point to speed as a common advantage among companies that are ahead of the curve. More and more, companies are finding that the speed at which change is embraced has increasingly become a critical success factor in today's fast-changing environment.

According to De Kluyver and Pearce, successful companies find that embracing change quickly requires becoming a nimble organization; revisiting the company's mission and refocusing if necessary; creating a speed-attuned culture; streamlining the way the company communicates across the organization and to its customers; organizing to move in new directions quickly and effectively; and committing to new performance metrics, if necessary.

Sounds like common sense, right? It is. And it is this framework that I propose you consider as you embark on your assessment of and strategy development for the Hispanic market. Preparing to successfully do business with another customer or set of consumers requires a deep understanding of their needs—that's the trend in the 21st century. Reportedly, companies are moving from being product-centric to being customer-centric, and that means delivering more than a well-researched sales pitch through a salesperson or a commercial. It means organizing your company to meet those needs in a way that allows you to deliver value and satisfaction, which leads to profitable market share growth.

Too many companies become very excited about marketing to Hispanics and before taking steps to understand industry trends, the competition, the customer, and how the company's business model might allow it to compete for this consumer, they immediately think about turning all responsibility for knowledge building and strategy to a hired ad agency. Though you need culturally knowledgeable ad agencies to help you define communication and media strategy, produce commercials that resonate with your target, place them where Hispanics are likeliest to hear and see them, and help with the research to track and fine-tune communication efforts for obvious reasons, this should never be your first line of attack.

Put simply, you need to walk the walk before you talk the talk. So before you spend a single dime on an agency, producing commercials, or conducting advertising research, you have some up-front work to do to align your organization with Hispanic consumer needs and the environment in which you will compete for them including your own organization.

Whether you are a seasoned multicultural expert or just beginning, consider that the process of aligning the organization to the market need is ever-changing. It never stops because the external forces that impact your company's competitive advantages keep changing. So, whether you are just out of the gate or into your tenth year of targeting Hispanic consumers, you want to be holistic and strategic in your approach. Go beyond marketing to cover all your operational bases so you can optimize your success.

How do you define success? Well, one of the most critical aspects of this up-front alignment is defining performance metrics. It will look different for every company, but whatever your company's goals, your Hispanic metrics must flow from and into them. What should your goals be? You won't know until you do the math. But how can you do the math if you haven't thought through the operational areas that may require alignment, defined the type of alignment required, and determined how much it will cost the company? Once you determine the price tag for the alignment, you need to know how that price tag compares to the size of the market for your industry, your category, and your brand.

Only then can you begin to establish business goals for how Hispanics will contribute to your company's top-line and bottom-line growth. Only then will you know what it will take to achieve your goals and how long it will take see a return. The good news is that if you and your management have this information at the start, then everyone will know what to expect and when to expect it, and you will know what you are measuring and how to measure it. As you know, the metrics around sales and market-share performance are arguably the most important. But just as the metrics across a company are many and varied, they are just two of many areas to monitor and analyze to determine the success of your initiative.

As a manager, being aware of and sensitive to the Hispanic strategy's impact on the metrics of the operational areas that will support it will allow you to create efficient and effective operational strategies for targeting this consumer market and, importantly, will encourage the necessary support from the start.

To date, some organizations have been moving down a path to seize the opportunities being created by Hispanic demographic growth, others are just starting to think about it, and others have yet to acknowledge the impact that the growing Hispanic market may have on their long-term growth strategies. One significant reason is that corporate cultures vary so much; consequently, the reasons why and the ways in which managers arrive at seeing Hispanics as a business opportunity seldom have to do with recognition of the potential impacts of the significant demographic and distribution of income shifts on the United States.

Companies are generally attuned to external forces and key economic indicators, such as consumer confidence, gross domestic product (GDP), auto and retail sales, unemployment, inflation, and industry-specific indicators to help guide corporate strategy. Yet the magnitude and full impact of U.S. Hispanic market growth, their increasing buying power in the face of retiring baby boomers with decreasing buying power, and increasing domestic and international competition for U.S. Hispanic consumers hasn't been recognized as an important environmental force that is set to revolutionize the business environment in the near future. For some reason, much of corporate America is either in denial or still has not fully made the connection between this market explosion and the impact on their business—not only on potential sales but, equally important, on how the entire value chain may need assessment to determine how and if a company can adapt efficiently to capture those sales in the long term. With few exceptions, corporate America's approach toward this consumer market has been reactive, tactical, and ad hoc rather than proactive, strategic, integrated, and aligned. I propose that if a company goes after this market segment opportunity with piecemeal efforts, it will generate piecemeal results.

Several scenarios describe how most companies decide to explore U.S. Hispanics:

- Top management has successfully led Hispanic efforts elsewhere. This is perhaps the strongest organizational catalyst to change.
- Mergers and acquisitions (M&A) activity often drives comprehensive review of a company's operational model and revenue sources. During these in-depth reviews, attention turns to the Hispanic market as a revenue growth source.
- Companies going through reengineering or organizational change often revisit the entire business strategy, which results in consideration of the Hispanic market, as with M&A activity.
- Companies repositioning themselves after difficult business periods recognize Hispanics as part of their repositioning targets.
- In retail, corporate management realizes that the demographics in areas around their locations have shifted and same-store sales

are declining. Hispanics are either not shopping in their stores or not staying because the stores are not operationally aligned to serve and satisfy these new customers.

- The local sales force or regional leadership requests corporate support because they are frustrated that they are not able to satisfy the localized needs of their Hispanic customers.

- Retail customers comment or complain to a manufacturer's sales force about what a manufacturer is or is not doing to support Hispanic-relevant offers.

- The emergence and proliferation of Hispanic-owned businesses directly competing with corporate counterparts leads to loss of customers, sales, and market share—in some cases raising thresholds to become acceptable options among Hispanics.

- Sales decline and market share is lost to competition in Hispanic trading areas because competitors have adapted their business model to attract Hispanics to their products or stores.

- General market consumption trends that have not or do not impact Hispanics consumption patterns are seen as opportunities; for example, Hispanics' high consumption of carbohydrates in the face of the recent low-carb trend.

- After hearing more about Hispanics, curious managers start to attend Hispanic conferences as a way to familiarize themselves with the basics. Companies come away with powerful insights that sometimes motivate action back at headquarters.

- Multinational organizations with foreign parents (e.g., Nestlé, Royal Ahold, Kraft Foods) are inherently open to segmentation and adaptation to new markets and tend to be leaders in multicultural target marketing, setting examples others want to follow.

- The company decides that creating new offerings that are consistent with Hispanic preferences may be a good way of entering the market. Sometimes this means creating products from the ground up or adapting existing products to match characteristics of those marketed successfully to Hispanics in Latin America. Sometimes this means an acquisition or partnerships.

- The company started as a Hispanic-focused organization that has crossed over into mainstream, but doesn't want to lose its Hispanic core.

Obviously, interest in exploring and targeting U.S. Hispanics can come about in a number of ways, as it has for dozens of companies targeting Hispanics today. However, there are many more who have not found success. A quick diagnostic based on observations of how those companies go to market points to an overreliance on marketing communications to do the entire job, faulty or nonexistent operational alignment and implementation, a disregard for the complete landscape of competitive offerings, and absence of a comprehensive market strategy. Notice that I say market, not marketing strategy, because it requires the entire organization, not just marketing, and should be run by a business unit manager who has the ear of his peers and upper management support.

Still, you may ask, what's there to assess? Why would any company decide to overlook or pass on this huge marketplace? When it comes to creating a Hispanic business strategy, the question is not whether you should target Hispanics. It is whether you understand the market and your organization well enough; it's about your organization's readiness to deliver seamlessly today. In addition—and it can't be emphasized enough—it's about your ability to set realistic expectations based on well-analyzed market and organizational realities that are attuned to the direction in which the entire company is headed. Finally, consider that if you have been charged with this responsibility or have appointed yourself to the task, the challenges ahead will be much more difficult to address when you're knee-deep in the implementation than if you had considered and planned for them up front and had been able to mitigate risks, uncertainties, and resistance early on.

There are a host of organizational realities that tend to rear their ugly heads just when you need cooperation, not resistance. Trust that they will try your patience and may even lead you to abandon the project altogether, but if you know your company well enough and can think through some likely scenarios, you can plan for addressing obstacles at the outset rather than be blind-sided once you're in the process. Some challenges that may occur include:

- *There is no senior management support.* This is challenging, but surmountable with a solid business case that aligns with corporate strategy and goals.
- *The company's corporate culture does not embrace change.* Point to verbiage in annual reports and SEC filings that speak to the contrary and engage top management support.

- *The company claims insufficient resources to provide cross-functional support.* Understand cross-functional managers' hot buttons and sell them on the potential payoff. Show them the impact of inaction and what is at stake.
- *Creating the necessary infrastructure and/or integrating Hispanic activity into existing processes are perceived as disruptive.* Ask the questions that will prepare you to address concerns within the context of operational strategies.
- *The in-going investment to align appropriately is greater than expected.* Be inquisitive about what led to referenced cost assumptions and have data to refute them. Demonstrate financial scenarios for similarly sized initiatives with a comprehensive cost-benefit analysis.
- *The company doesn't believe the business case and wants to see results before they commit to incremental spending.* Point to other growth initiatives undertaken recently, respective investment, and results, and compare to the Hispanic scenario. Show them the impact of inaction and what is at stake.
- *The Hispanic market is perceived as risky.* Be inquisitive about what is feeding these perceptions, provide the analysis to refute the hypothesis, and/or talk about the type of output that will provide insight to mitigate risks.
- *The time frame to break even or reach profitability is longer than expected and inconsistent with the company's short-term orientation.* Point to other projects, leverage the company's vision and mission statement, and point to alignment with the Hispanic strategy; discredit "quarteritis" mentality in favor of long-term value building.
- *Other initiatives are taking precedence and are perceived to have greater ROI.* Suggest that the assessment will validate the viability of the initiative versus others. Ensure that market and financial analysis fully proves or disproves the case.
- *The market's characteristics and behavior are inconsistent with the company's operational model.* Point to environmental and industry trends toward customer-centric business models.

In light of these potential challenges, you can see that you will need more than ambition, passion, and perseverance to overcome these hurdles. You will need hard facts, relevant market analysis, and financials to remove these road blocks from your path.

Risk is the area of greatest concern for many companies considering the Hispanic market as a growth opportunity. In spite of the market's longtime presence in the United States, Hispanics still represent an uncertain marketplace for many companies, especially among those with no previous segment experience.

Because some companies do not perform up-front analysis, there is significant uncertainty about how the market's size and buying power translate into revenue for their industry and, more specifically, their company. Most companies are unclear about investment requirements because they don't understand where they stand operationally in their ability to serve the market or what they are up against in the competitive environment; nor do they know what their brand represents to this consumer, if anything. Consequently, with little to no market knowledge in hand, the risks associated with targeting this market often appear greater than the potential return.

In some cases this uncertainty leads companies to tiptoe into the market with intentions to test before making significant organizational changes or investment. Unfortunately, without the up-front assessment work, it is often difficult for companies to know what they are truly testing. Further, the validity of these tests is questionable given that, in many cases, the company is not staffed, organized, or trained to implement and measure the tests, which are often based on no more than a translation of tactical communication and promotional efforts as opposed to strategic operational changes to reach, retain, and satisfy this marketplace.

So where do you start? At this juncture, the wisest thing to do is to stop and ask the same questions your company might ask when it considers any other growth opportunity. If you have been down this path before, this may sound familiar.

CORPORATE CULTURE

Corporate culture is really at the core of a company's likelihood to succeed with these types of efforts, and it can be the catalyst or the screeching brakes on any new business development or change management initiative. When management is visionary and open to innovation, it is typically open to exploring new opportunities and rallies the troops to support change in favor of the potential prize.

Clearly, if you have this type of culture and support, your job, while not easy, will be appreciated and potentially rewarded. If, on the other hand, the culture is more conservative and noncommittal, don't be discouraged. Careful planning and quantitative support often will carry you through.

Start by asking whether or not cultural sensitivity and diversity issues are supported openly and enthusiastically by upper management. Do departments and divisions function as one company, or is the organizational culture more independent? How much cultural sensitivity training will your organization require? Does the company have systems in place to keep itself accountable to diversity and cultural sensitivity efforts? Being receptive to and understanding of new cultures is challenging to even the most open of individuals, and people often resist change and differences they do not understand. Keep in mind that you may be affecting supply chain relationships with which the company is comfortable or even traditional Human Resources channels for sourcing employees. In any event, the culture may push back changes to the status quo.

STRATEGIC FOCUS

As you embark on this venture, ask yourself about the type of management you have. Then study your company's annual report and SEC filing for the last three years. Pay attention to the language in the CEO's letter to shareholders because it will serve you well when selling your assessment plan back to management. Make sure that you understand where your industry is going and where your company fits in because what you ultimately propose and the size of the opportunity must align with it; in short, you must frame your business case in that context.

To achieve high-level recognition and support for your Hispanic market initative, keep two things in mind:

1. Make sure that your business case ultimately aligns with the company's corporate strategy. Speak in the voice of top management.
2. Ensure that the business case considers shareholder interest and that financial scenarios deliver top-line revenue and bottom-line profits consistent with industry and company expectations—even if it's longer term than expected.

These two conditions typically make the business case irrefutable. Remember, this is not about getting a budget to create a Spanish-language ad campaign; this is about adapting the company for growth and increased shareholder value.

The first step is to develop an assessment action plan that includes a list of your hypotheses and questions about the Hispanic market, the competitive environment, and your organization's infrastructure and operations. This process will help you think critically and identify information gaps and potential internal and external sources you'll need to tap for support throughout your process.

In order for this exercise to be most useful, you must be as honest and objective as possible as you go through the following sections.

Market Size

First, consider that, of the 40 million Hispanics estimated by the U.S. Census in 2004, all are no more likely to be users of your products and services than the remaining 246 million non-Hispanics in the United States. Only a segment of this population will be your primary target.

Do you know how to define your Hispanic segment? Do you know how large this segment is? Is the size of that Hispanic segment large enough to create a demand for your services or products? Is it large enough to satisfy sales and profitability goals? Do you know where they are concentrated? Do you know what projected growth rates for your specific Hispanic segments are for the next five years? How will it differ between segments?

Category Usage

Culture drives much of your own consumer behavior, and as we discussed in Chapter 1, the same applies to Hispanics, so you will want to understand the cultural context for your target's involvement with your category or industry. Consider that your U.S. Hispanic segment's experience with your product category may differ from Hispanics in Latin America based on their level of exposure and acculturation levels in the United States. Consider that Hispanics may prefer different flavor profiles, colors, and sizes. Hispanics may have different service needs, have less experience using the category, and may use the category in an entirely different manner. Do you have a sense for the category user profile? What are their attitudes toward your products, your brand, and your competitor's products? How well do your products and services align with these needs, preferences, and usage behavior? Are there needs that aren't being met that could help you differentiate and deliver higher customer value?

Competitive Environment

You may be in a first-mover position, or there may be several competitors in your industry already targeting Hispanics as part of their growth strategy. Do you know which competitors are targeting Hispanics? Do you have a sense for their Hispanic business strategy? Do you know if they are successful? Do you know why or why not? If they are successful, how are they positioned? Is this position sustainable or can it be copied or leapfrogged? What is their market share? What brand awareness levels do they have? What are the unsuccessful ones doing wrong? Do you know where they are located in relation to your own locations? What are their strengths and weaknesses? Are there any threats or opportunities that may impact them in the short term and may help you?

Infrastructure

Organizational support is critical to integrated implementation, so it will be important to understand consumer touch points across your organization that will impact your ability to conduct the assessment and, ultimately, the company's ability to implement against the strategy. On which divisions, business lines, or departments will you depend for the assessment process and implementation? How well, if at all, are they structured to implement a Hispanic strategy? How adaptable is your organization? Might the required adaptation impact the company's business model? Would building distinctive capabilities give you a sustainable competitive advantage? What are the trade-offs? Do you have the ear of these department managers, or will you need to sell them on cooperating with you? What will be company leadership's role in facilitating access and cooperation during the assessment and implementation?

The Value Proposition

How well do your offerings and benefits align with Hispanics' needs and preferences? How does your offering compare with that of the competition? What does being competitive require? Are there any unmet needs in the marketplace? How is the Hispanic market evolving within your industry? How are priorities changing and how does your brand deliver on these changing priorities?

R&D and Manufacturing

Is your organization capable of ground-up product development, reformulating, recreating, repackaging, branding, or repositioning Hispanic relevant offerings, if necessary? Are there any co-packing or manufacturing partnerships that can help provide the desired product in a manner that minimizes capital investment, resource allocation, and learning curve impact? Alternatively, do you have the internal resources to develop products and new brands with speed? Does licensing a Hispanic brand make sense for your product?

Distribution

We all have evolving preferences for how and where we like to shop. Do you know how and where this consumer shops? Is your offering accessible to this consumer in a relevant way? Do they shop close to home or close to work? Do they shop on different days of the week or even at different hours of the day? Do they shop alone or with others? Do they enjoy shopping for your product category? Are your locations present in the areas where your target is concentrated? How do you compare to your competition on market presence? How might you segment your retail locations? Are your distribution channels set up to serve this consumer in their language of choice? If your company relies on technology to be efficient and profitable, how can this greater automation be adapted to address limited distribution needs? If you are a manufacturer, does your current sales force enable you to expand access to your products through other channels where this consumer shops for your type of product? How does your distribution need to adapt? Do you have the right distributor, wholesaler, or importer?

Staffing and Merchandising

Is your staffing model culturally relevant at all levels? Would Spanish speakers feel welcomed in your retail locations? Would they feel acknowledged as customers? Do you have a consistent presence of bilingual employees everywhere your operations require consumer contact? Can they understand and relate to your merchandising and point-of-sale (POS) material? Which in-store messages are critical for this consumer to understand? Can internal processes be adapted to integrate bilingual employee hiring? Does HR have the skills to assess Hispanic hire needs? What systems are in place that will inform HR of bilingual employee needs? What is the current process flow and how does it need to be adapted? Can the organization's merchandising function handle development of bilingual POS, circulars, letters, contracts, sales materials, and other company consumer communication in Spanish?

Pricing

How are you priced relative to perceived value of your brand? How does your pricing compare to that of your competition? How price sensitive is the Hispanic target in your category? Does it apply to all your products? Can you develop new products that strike a balance between added value and profit? Where along the value chain does your company generate its greatest profits, and does serving this consumer allow for similar or better returns? What needs to be adapted in order not to affect profitability or to minimize impact? How might changes impact your business model?

Advertising and Promotion

Your company worked hard to arrive at a compelling value proposition to communicate through its advertising and other communications channels. Do you know how it resonates among your Hispanic target? Do you have a sense for the cultural context that your messages must consider to communicate with this consumer? How might your strategy consider cultural and acculturation differences while staying true to your brand position?

Do you understand the multidimensional nature of your Hispanic consumer segment? What attitudes do Hispanics have toward life, family, children, parenting, spouses, culture, countries of origin, religion, financial position, future outlook, social issues, government and politics, corporate America, discrimination, and their communities? Do you know how Hispanics feel about technology, fashion, and entertainment? Do you know how satisfied they are with their life in the United States?

Language aside, there are nuances of Hispanics' values and attitudes that shape how they prefer to see themselves reflected in marketing messages. You know this to be true among other segments. This community is no different. Having these insights will help you adapt your offering and ensure that your communications strategy resonates while staying true to the company's brand positioning.

ORGANIZING FOR THE ASSESSMENT

The above questions are just a few considerations that organizations must take into account when preparing an assessment action plan. The ultimate output will provide valuable insight into what you know and what you do not know. Depending on which level in the organization is driving this initiative, you may or may not have carte blanche to conduct your assessment, and you may or may not have support for ready access to the entire organization.

Whatever your situation, an assessment proposal will help obtain buy-in on the scope, timing, and cost of the assessment. This document should start by describing the preliminary insights into why the market represents a potential growth opportunity and the impact of not validating this opportunity quickly. This impact could depend on your specific situation and industry and could include competitive share gains, declining sales, or other symptoms being felt by the organization as a result of macro environmental changes, which in this case would be the demographic shifts and the large and growing Hispanic market.

The document should also acknowledge the various assumptions currently held by stakeholders within the organization, as well as your own hypotheses regarding the situation. It should clearly outline the assessment methodology, including market studies and analyses you'll need to conduct.

Identify important company management and staff from which you will need support and in what manner. You should also identify the need for outside consultants, market research companies, and information resources. Finally, you should outline timing, costs, and outputs from the process. These outputs should be organized according to external and internal environments and their implications.

For example, you can propose that a clear understanding of your competitive position among Hispanics who currently have bank accounts will enable you to determine product focus or product gaps that will provide a competitive advantage. Or you will learn where your retail stores are located in comparison to those of its competition and how much of the Hispanic market you can expect to reach given your current presence. Or you will know where your retail gaps are in large Hispanic areas so you can determine how to expand your presence there. Or you will find out how well your category is developed among Hispanics and how you may need to adapt your employee training to service this customer. For instance, if your category is underdeveloped, you will need to emphasize category building; if your competitor is investing heavily on category development, you'll be able to leverage that to build your brand.

Your proposal and the action plan are critical to demonstrating the thoroughness of your assessment thought process and will indicate that individuals driving the process have a clear understanding of the objectives, of the expected outcomes, and most important, that the assessment approach is consistent with the company's approach on these types of projects. These elements will be critical to the credibility of the project.

Once you present the assessment proposal, one of three scenarios may occur: (1) the assessment will be approved and funded; (2) the assessment will be approved but not funded, or it will be partially funded and your team will be asked to fund the remainder from existing budgets; or (3) the assessment will not be approved and you will be asked to take steps toward implementation based on existing knowledge and resources. If this last scenario occurs, you should point out the caveats of proceeding under the status quo if for no other reason than to be on record when results fall short of expectations. I have never seen the last scenario occur, but I suppose it is possible and should be considered.

ORGANIZING THE ASSESSMENT TEAM

Assuming you have approval, start by reaching out to the various stakeholders and organize a team. Depending on your industry, this team should include a representative from key areas of the organization: strategic planning, new business development, R&D, manufacturing, marketing research, retail operations, merchandising, advertising, corporate finance, human resources, accounting, customer service, information technology, sales, and media relations. This would be the team that would work with a consultant if one is hired.

HIRING A CONSULTANT

The reasons for hiring a consultant range from recognition that the organization needs outside expertise for guidance to having an objective party driving the assessment process. They can also be helpful in structuring the assessment proposal. When considering hiring a consultant, you should look for the following competencies and consulting focus:

- Core competency should be business strategy planning, development, and implementation. You are hiring a strategic planning expert, not a marketing expert, although they are not necessarily mutually exclusive.
- Must have a complete understanding of the U.S. Hispanic market.
- Should have a reasonably strong understanding of your industry and where your organization fits within it relative to your competition.
- Must be able to clearly outline the process, method, timing, and cost for accomplishing the assessment project.
- Must be willing and able to align processes and business language with those used by your organization.

- Must have a track record for conducting full-scale assessment consulting projects and be able to provide references who can attest to successful completion.
- And importantly, the consultant's sole business focus should be business strategy consulting with an emphasis on feasibility, strategy development, and implementation. While Hispanic advertising agencies and market research companies are very knowledgeable about the Hispanic market and very skilled within their areas of expertise, they are not in the business strategy consulting business; they are in the advertising and marketing research business. It is absolutely critical that you engage a consultant who can be completely objective about the business viability of targeting Hispanics. The consultant must have no vested interest in whether or not you ultimately end up targeting and investing in the market.

Remember this process is not about defining your communication strategy; it is about gaining the necessary intelligence and insight to help your company assess profit potential given its current competencies, resources, limitations, and competitive threats. While advertising and promotions may eventually play a critical role in creating awareness and demand for your product, you must first understand the full impact of establishing a strategic foundation across the organization that is in sync with your company's business model.

THE KICKOFF MEETING

The first order of business is typically the kickoff meeting, during which your internal project team meets the consultant if one has been hired and, oftentimes, even each other. The project leader typically shares the assessment proposal, including overall objectives, specific areas to be addressed, expected deliverables, and timing. Note that a thorough assessment process that builds in time for internal work sessions and interim presentations to upper management can take between six and ten months.

Depending on the profile of the project, it isn't unusual to have the president, COO, and a few senior VPs sitting in on this meeting—evidence that you have positioned the project at a high level. When this happens, consider yourself lucky because it sends a clear message to the team that the project has leadership's blessing.

Once this part of the meeting is over, senior management typically will leave and you can continue to the second phase of the meeting, which focuses on the action plan.

The core team continues with a discussion of logistics—how the work will be carried out, lines and methods of communication, point people on the project, and how responsibilities will be shared or assigned. The team can then decide whether or not to spend the rest of the time conducting the first work session, during which the team reviews its current knowledge and hypotheses.

The basis for formulating preliminary hypotheses can be anything team members have heard, read, or assumed to date, including contradictory hypotheses held within the organization and even points of view that could pose potential barriers if not surfaced at this stage.

Next, the meeting might move to a discussion about pending questions that any member of the team may have and any concerns or doubts held about the assessment process, team members, organizational culture, or opportunity itself. It is critical that team members feel that it is safe to voice their opinions and concerns and that they feel acknowledged. As such, it is important to establish ground rules or values that the team can rely on for assurance that the process will be fair and open-minded. You can finish with a review of the timeline and next steps.

THE ASSESSMENT PROCESS

A typical assessment process can be divided into two main components—the external assessment and the internal assessment—which we will discuss in subsequent chapters.

Some teams share the outcome of these components with management throughout the process, while others wait until the two phases are completed and the business case is written. In either case, most companies find that progress updates to top management, with some insights as to the general direction of the results, are still necessary and can provide very valuable feedback to feed the project going forward.

Chapter

3

CASE STUDIES: PRODUCTS AND SERVICES MARKETED TO HISPANICS

As companies move toward targeting the Hispanic market, their experiences hold valuable lessons for those within and outside their specific industries. In this chapter, I present three case studies from three distinct industries: grocery retail, financial services, and health care services.

FOOD SHOPPING—GROCERY RETAIL

Food is one of the pillars of any culture, and it's no different for Hispanics. Moreover, the need to have culturally relevant food that conjures up images of home, family, gatherings, celebrations, and familiar tastes and aromas intensifies among Hispanics living in the United States because it provides connection, grounding, and comfort in their "home away from home."

Because of economic realities in countries of origin, Hispanics bring certain behaviors around food, food shopping, and food preparation that are very different and difficult to abandon. This, of course, changes as the acculturation process unfolds, but for reasons mentioned, along with language, it is one of the most tightly held culturally driven behaviors. In the acculturation process, adoption of other behavior around food and food shopping is typically in addition to, rather than a replacement for, traditional food behavior.

If you'll remember the example of hypergrowth Hispanic markets like Tennessee, supermarket retailers like the Kroger Company—the parent company of the highly successful Food 4 Less format in Los Angeles that enjoys high preference among Hispanics—and Piggly Wiggly are starting to recognize the marketplace and are active members of the Hispanic Chamber of Commerce there. This, along with fewer relevant neighborhood choices, will no doubt impact the market's quicker acculturation to adopt chain supermarkets as a shopping destination.

In Los Angeles and other hubs, Hispanics have little problem finding the foods they prefer, either at the grocery store or their favorite restaurant. In large part, such offerings are provided by independent retailers that have emerged in large numbers to cater specifically to the Hispanic market or by chain supermarkets that have created separate operating companies to serve this consumer. Hispanics can continue their food traditions with ease and convenience as their food choices acculturate and grow. As they are exposed to shopping choices, acculturation is evidenced by the increased fragmentation in the channels where they shop for food. And with an average of 26 shopping trips a month (*El Mercado* survey, 2004), their shopping choices cover the gamut of food retailers, from the Hispanic independent to the mass merchandiser and club store.

Why so many shopping trips? There are several reasons, among them the preference for fresh foods for scratch cooking, the inability to find what they need in chain supermarkets, the comfort they feel shopping in places where there are others like them in front of and behind the counter, and the economies of scale reflected in pricing of relevant food and nonfood staples in mass channels like Wal-Mart, Target, and Costco.

And why do they cling to cooking from scratch when packaged foods are so convenient? The answer depends on one's definition of convenience. Scratch cooking is culturally ingrained by the environment and upbringing in country of origin. From an emotional and psychological perspective, it plays into the facet of identity that feeds on pride in Hispanics' roles as mothers, wives, nurturers, and indulgers. From a convenience standpoint, familiarity and comfort with the foods they know how to prepare drive choices—if it isn't familiar in preparation and flavor, then it simply isn't convenient, nor is it if it doesn't allow for exact replication of authentic flavors and aromas and the need to avoid risk. Therefore, among a significant proportion of the less-acculturated Hispanic shopper base, mainstream's orientation to convenience among manufacturers and retailers simply doesn't resonate—at least not in the same way as it does in non-Hispanic homes.

CASE STUDY: CARNIVAL FOOD STORES

Carnival is Minyard Food Stores' Hispanic banner in Dallas, Texas, and has for many years been a leader in its approach to multicultural marketing and merchandising, with special emphasis on the Dallas/Ft. Worth Hispanic market. Having recently been acquired, the company seized the opportunity to revisit Minyard's strategies in its Texas footprint.

Minyard's CEO hired an executive team to define the company's future growth strategies. Among them was a vice president of Hispanic merchandising, who challenged the company to redefine its Hispanic offering in the face of the fierce market competition that had mushroomed since Carnival first started targeting Hispanics in the early 1990s.

Minyard went a step further by ensuring that its operational ties included the expertise required to drive these strategies forward.

The Assessment

With the goal of assessing the total organization, Minyard hired supermarket retail demographic consultants to analyze several aspects of its business situation, including its trading areas, its competitive environment, and the operating models. Using U.S. Census and Spectra data, the company studied its stores' trading areas to define how these had changed demographically and socioeconomically in order to determine if the store banners operating in each location were still relevant or needed to change. In addition, Minyard moved to understand the location of its competition relative to its own store locations and the types of customers being captured by each.

To better understand its own customers, the company conducted market research among their shoppers to better understand customer perceptions about the stores' strengths and weaknesses. Surveys were conducted in Spanish and English at the exit of each store and were followed with a market-wide shopper study to gauge how consumers perceived the positioning of the company's three banners (Minyard, Carnival, and Sack'n Save) relative to the competition.

Carnival-specific research results indicated that the banner was well positioned with consumers. Awareness levels and ratings of brand attributes were strong. However, there were signs that the company's image around its perishables (meats, deli, hot foods, bakery, *tortilleria,* and produce) relative to its competition had declined, which was cause for significant concern given the importance of perishables among Hispanic shoppers.

While overall results implied that the banner could continue to grow marginally with few modifications, management decided on a much more aggressive stance: reinventing its Hispanic format and taking back its leadership position in the marketplace. This decision was critical in view of overall assessment results that indicated that Hispanics were and would continue to be a driver of total company revenue and profitability.

Minyard then focused its efforts to understand what redefining its Hispanic offering would require in order to differentiate itself from the competition in the long term. Members of Minyard's executive team, including Minyard's CEO, traveled to Mexico and other Latin American countries, which was critical to understanding supermarket models for all sizes of food retailers in this marketplace.

These trips alone opened management's eyes. It quickly realized that the difference between learning about a culture and experiencing it firsthand was like night and day. The learning has gone beyond assortment and merchandising into the cultural context—why it is the way it is and how that gets translated in the United States. The management team also studied the best-in-class supermarkets in Los Angeles and Phoenix, areas with similar consumer segments, to identify possible store concepts that would work well in Texas. This market research gave Minyard a unique ability to visualize its new generation of Carnival stores.

Although much of the changing marketplace information Minyard's executives was seeing was not new to them, this methodical approach to understanding the marketplace, along with the cultural context, provided sufficient validation that Carnival represented a strong foundation for overall company growth.

The Implementation

As part of its assessment process, Minyard conducted a thorough geo-demographic and customer survey data study. "What netted out," says Minyard's senior VP of strategy and marketing, Poul Heilmann, "was the realization that a great majority of our stores are in heavily Hispanic areas." In fact, it found that many of its markets were already 30 to 70 percent Hispanic.

So in July 2005, the company announced plans to convert 11 of its Minyard and Sack'n Save stores to the Carnival banner. Converting these stores increased the total number of Carnival outlets to 35, compared to 24 for Minyard and 19 for Sack'n Save, effectively making Carnival, and its Hispanic-marketing orientation, the company's main focus.

Although Minyard felt as though it knew its customers well, it spent nearly six months understanding in detail its customer base, "to make sure the data . . . came up the same as what our feelings were," says Heilmann. "After our studies, we know for a fact." The company didn't stop at determining the Hispanic density of its markets, however. Many of the stores' shoppers were Mexican-American, but Minyard also discovered that many of its customers were of Central and South American, Asian, Eastern European, and Anglo origin—each store had a unique population mix. And even within specific Hispanic ethnic groups they found significant differences. For example, Southern Mexico has spicier cuisine.

Additional insights gleaned from its research are being put to use in its Carnival stores. For example, while low prices are important to Hispanic families, the stores' atmosphere is just as significant. For many Hispanics, who tend to cook at home more often than mainstream consumers, the cleanliness of the store and a high-quality fresh foods section are paramount.

Bilingual employees provide a significant customer-service advantage, and bilingual signage is a must. Many of Carnival's customers don't speak English, and without signage in Spanish, they may not stay in the store long enough to find a Spanish-speaking employee. The company plans to have bilingual signage in all of its Carnival stores by spring 2006.

Minyard is keenly aware of the impact of acculturation. However, it did find that some things—like Hispanics' taste for traditional items—don't change. But it also found that, as consumers became more acculturated, they became more open to trying new, mainstream foods. This cuts both ways; many of the Hispanic-focused items it has introduced have found a receptive audience among mainstream customers as well.

Capitalizing on the learning that occurred while visiting markets in Latin America, Minyard began testing a "bazaar" concept in summer 2004, leasing out vacant stores to a variety of vendors selling everything from shoes, clothing, and cosmetics to CDs and furniture. In 2005, the chain married the concept to several of its Carnival locations, with vendors both inside and outside the supermarket. With Carnival, Minyard has gone beyond offering a Hispanic aisle, making it a truly Hispanic store. By embracing the Hispanic market with such commitment and depth, it hopes to differentiate itself from the competition and retake its leadership position in the marketplace.

Minyard is still undergoing its implementation process, which has already resulted in significant changes across the organization. Carnival's executives are continuing to make changes based on learning, realizing that immediate improvement and speed to market are critical in winning back market share in the Hispanic marketplace.

BANKING AND FINANCIAL SERVICES

Money management is seldom a problem in Latin American countries, where the concept of capitalization among the average consumer is not truly known or leveraged. Money is made and money is spent—it's that simple. High inflation historically has led to exorbitant interest rates, making credit not only unaffordable but, more important, inaccessible. Credit in the form of credit cards is seldom attainable (nor desired, except among the upper class) because many people work in informal subeconomy businesses that operate in cash; therefore, income is hard to prove. Financial paper trails are not common when one works for a family-owned farm, store, or factory.

Mortgages are even more difficult to obtain, as collateral is sometimes difficult to provide. As Hernando De Soto points out in his book *The Mystery of Capital: Why Capitalism Triumphs in the West and Fails Everywhere Else,* if collateral exists, the owner may or may not hold title to the land or building. Many times people pass down property, but even though everyone knows who owns it, there is no legal ownership documentation that can be presented to a bank.

Further, racism and classism in these societies are rampant. Banks typically cater to the (light-skinned) middle to upper classes and often have disdain for lower-socioeconomic-level consumers. This makes many people self-conscious and apprehensive about approaching a bank when in need. Much financing tends to come from savings or from family members who pool money to attain property or buy high-ticket items.

Finally, political and economic instability in Latin American countries have led to several severe currency devaluations and economic crises causing those with significant deposits to lose a tremendous amount of wealth and the common consumer to lose a life's savings. As such, banks and financial markets in Latin America have not always been seen as the safest places for hard-earned savings.

It is not easy to meld the experiences, values, and beliefs formed in a cash economy into the U.S. financial services environment. The U.S. credit-based economy—operating largely on the belief that one is nothing without a bank account and a credit card, especially if one wants to build a future—makes it difficult to get by without dealing with a bank. In the face of language obstacles and fear of ridicule and rejection, many unacculturated Hispanics don't use banks, rationalizing that they simply do not need to or make enough money to. However, many of these same people save thousands every year, much of which is transferred out of the country to help support distant family members.

A whole money services industry mushroomed in the mid-1990s that facilitated money flows between the United States and Latin America, notably Mexico. In 2004, this flow amounted to almost $40 billion, according to the Inter-American Development Bank Multilateral Investment Fund. This industry caters to Hispanics who operate outside of the banking system by offering them check cashing, money orders, calling cards, bus passes, and a host of other nonbank services; some services are loss leaders to attract the high revenue-generating money-transfer customer. This industry exploded in the 1990s because, in many ways, it was similar to how Hispanics were used to managing money back home, but more importantly, because their alternatives within the banking world were limited, especially without required documentation. Then in late 2003, after documentation had been a major barrier to opening a bank account and applying for credit for so long, banks began accepting the Mexican Identification Card obtained from the Mexican consulate and a Tax ID number from the IRS, an industry shift led by Wells Fargo Bank.

Couple traditional Hispanic consumer mindset with a banking environment that only recently began to target Hispanics and you have a population that has been relatively disenfranchised from the banking community, and as a result has not acculturated as quickly in this area. However, since 2003, there has been a significant industry shift in the banking sector in the United States. With national bank institutions like Wells Fargo leading the industry, the banking community has opened its doors to Hispanics, who are opening accounts in droves. Surveys document changing attitudes and values and, notably, the market's increased hunger for financial services education and guidance.

CASE STUDY: WELLS FARGO BANK

Wells Fargo & Company is a diversified financial services company with $453 billion in assets, providing banking, insurance, investments, mortgage, and consumer finance to more than 23 million customers from more than 6,200 stores and the Internet (http://www.wellsfargo.com) across North America and elsewhere internationally. Wells Fargo Bank, N.A. is the only bank in the United States to receive the highest possible credit rating, "AAA," from Moody's Investors Service.

While Wells Fargo has targeted Hispanics for many years, in 1994 and 1995 the bank decided to develop a cross-border initiative to capitalize on the significant and growing electronic money-transfer market. It saw major Mexican banks, including Banamex and Bancomer, pursuing the market, and given the size of the U.S. population, it decided to jump into the business.

Given limited initial investment and focus on the initiative, business grew slowly, but trends and results were generally positive. However, increasing competition in the market caused management to consider more focus on the business. In 2002, Wells Fargo decided it was time to focus strong energy and investment in this business and hired a dedicated team to achieve this.

The Assessment

The team conducted three assessments to support development of a business case for upper management. The first was a market assessment, which was followed by a financial audit of the business, and, lastly, an infrastructure and organizational readiness assessment.

Market assessment. In approaching its market assessment, Wells Fargo started by looking at where the money-transfer business was relative to its product and where its own product had been since its launch. It also looked at new competitive entrants into the market and what the future might look like in this business.

Initially, the Wells Fargo team conducted lots of secondary research analysis. Then the bank reached out to market experts at the Inter-American Development Bank and ex-industry executives from large competitors, who were recruited to share their perceptions about the business and its dynamics. The bank also hired a few consultants with specific expertise in obtaining data, and people who had access to key market intelligence.

WFB also spent time with financial analyst firms to obtain their perceptions of what they were seeing in the industry, and it spent considerable time with credit card associations and banks from around the world to learn what they were doing in the area of money transfers. WFB also spent time talking to community leaders and think tanks seeking their views about the how companies were approaching the business and their perceptions of banks' business practices in the sector.

The assessment included a thorough look at the competition to understand their offerings and to identify the strategies that were driving their approaches in targeting this market opportunity.

Financial audit. WFB worked closely with its financial department to analyze historical performance with the product. Specifically, it focused on the cost behind growth patterns and growth dynamics. Then it focused on opportunities to improve financial performance.

In looking at the numbers, the team considered the time the business had operated as a group of businesses rather than as an independent business unit. As a result, focus on the product had been limited, and this had potentially undermined its ability to grow more rapidly. It also became clear that the bank had not invested aggressively in the product since its launch, and this had limited the pace at which the product had developed.

However, looking forward, the numbers were used as building blocks. WFB started with a pyramid approach. The assumptions were based on knowing that revenue consists of fees and foreign exchange.

The expense side was determined by the cost to acquire a new account based on track records from previous years. Then, growth assumptions were made based on expected increased distribution, product optimization and innovation, pricing, and expected press coverage.

With these factors in the model, the team concluded that this product would have a positive impact on the bottom line. The team also sought support from the planning and acquisitions group, which helped them model and estimate the new customer opportunity, and they worked closely to define a cross-selling strategy. The team then used its methodology to define incremental revenue to other businesses.

In addition, this analysis helped the team quickly realize that a multiplier effect would occur. Ultimately, the team built a ten-year financial model and used the results that would be realized over that period to rationalize an aggressive investment for the first three years, supporting investment in awareness-building advertising and publicity.

Internal assessment. The third area the bank looked at was the organization as a whole and its ability to support the product in the past and future. WFB had several conversations with its regional leadership and its operations, systems, and marketing groups. Essentially, the team approached every area that potentially could have anything to do with the product.

The goal was to ensure that the company was ready to take the next step in this business and that, if it were to invest more aggressively, that all facets could and would work together to support the product. The team's approach was to take the gathered information and meet with key stakeholders to obtain their reaction and involve them in the process. It organized focused, off-site discussions to review the SWOT analysis with key stakeholders.

The team participated in a driver analysis where it mapped itself and the competition in terms of marketing and promotions, innovation, distribution network, market share, and price, and generated some conclusions about the competition as well as a soft idea of where the project stood.

It then looked at all of the players in the business and tried to determine the level of influence it has today and the level of influence it might have in the future. The team worked to determine where the new entrants in this business would come from and jointly identified the business drivers, including profitability, technology change, cross-sell, innovation, and distribution network, and used two-variable mapping to define its position versus the competition on each driver.

For instance, it used drivers like future market condition with rapid change and gradual change on one axis and plotted that against the company's approach of either reactive (adapter) or proactive (shaper) on the other axis to determine where the company was and where it could be.

The group agreed that in 1995 it had been in a proactive leader position with gradual change in the marketplace, and that in 2003 it found itself in a space where the market had changed rapidly. This new environment had potential to impact its future leadership position. With this in mind, there was agreement on the need to reverse that situation and move back into the proactive leadership position within a rapid-change environment, which it ultimately achieved.

Once there was agreement on all of the drivers, the existing situation, and where the company wanted to be, the team revisited the SWOT analysis and considered what its strengths, weaknesses, opportunities, and threats were, line by line.

When it looked at the results of the SWOT analysis and the driver analysis, the conclusions and recommendations were pretty obvious and, because they had been developed jointly, there was no convincing to be done. And while at times challenging, the off-site SWOT analysis process resulted in objective assessment of key improvement opportunities and successful identification of the critical success factors.

Business case. Each assessment was presented to the line management and then, once the three phases were complete, they were used to create a strategic direction deck, which was presented to upper management.

The three assessments together yielded questions, conclusions, and a set of recommendations. First, the team determined that if WFB was going to stay in the business, it needed to identify target markets and make recommendations about priority countries. It discovered that somewhere between 80 and 90 percent of U.S. Mexicans who send $400 to Mexico six to eight times a year were in WFB's footprint with a total volume of $13.5 billion. The team determined that even a small share of this market represented a huge opportunity and defined Mexico as priority number one. (Other countries that would become priorities included India and the Philippines.)

The team needed a corporate rationale for pursuing the market, so it analyzed the bank's annual report to see how well this project aligned with its strategic position. It saw that the bank's mission included "being a payment processor to its customer base." Because sending money back home was considered payment processing, the team had confirmation that the project was a fit with corporate strategy. Diverse Growth Segment clients have been growing, and a key element of the WFB and remittances are a key element of everyday needs for both Hispanic and Asian customers. Finally, Wells Fargo's Vision and Values Statement clearly highlights the importance of providing the services that WFB customers require: "We want to satisfy all of our customers' financial needs, help them succeed financially, be the premier provider of financial services in every one of our markets, and be known as one of America's great companies."

To get a reality check on its assumption, the team ran the idea by members of its leadership, who confirmed that this initiative was in alignment with the corporate mission. The team knew that aligning with the corporate mission would make it easier to get people to support the project.

A third yet key part of the business case was using the financial analysis to support the point that the project required incremental funding. The team also pointed out that since 2001, a number of banks, including Bank of America, had entered the space. It projected that within less than three years most financial institutions would be competing in the space and emphasized that the bank was in danger of losing its "first mover" advantage unless it moved aggressively.

After the plan was completed, the team did a road show and went out to the top people in the company to show them what had been discovered. They shared the strategy and told them that this was something that was being presented to top management. The group was asked to share feedback on what worked and what didn't and was asked for support. By the time the plan made it to executive management, many had already heard about it, and the strategy sold itself.

One key characteristic about Wells Fargo is that it is highly diversified and decentralized, which means that business units have to earn the support of other divisions to help achieve their goals when they have no direct authority over the other divisions. The way to do that successfully is to prove that the strategy you are asking them to embrace will also help the other division's business. This review with management was critical because it allowed the consideration and incorporation of ideas that met those managers' needs and interests.

The Implementation

WFB decided to support this business by investing aggressively in technology, people, and marketing resources. It set out to create new-found awareness of the remittance opportunity and to regain the industry leadership that existed in the business since 1995.

The team conducted market research to measure customer satisfaction and feedback about its current offering and process. The research validated the approach and a budget was developed and approved.

The team believed that, with minor adjustments, its product had advantages over the competition, which was focusing on card-based products for which Wells Fargo felt the target market was not yet ready. The team felt it had the experience with a high-touch approach, which would not only serve customers well, but would also protect the organization from money laundering and help them meet compliance requirements.

To lock in remittance distribution leadership, WFB expanded its distribution in Mexico by creating alliances with several banks, including BBVA Bancomer, HSBC, and Banorte. This tripled WFB's distribution in Mexico from 1,800 to 4,700 branches, and from 3,000 to 10,000 ATMs.

The Wells Fargo team moved to expand its product line because it recognized that *InterCuenta Express,* its original money-transfer product, was an account-to-account transfer process with limited appeal among a significant cash-based segment. To address this, it created *Dinero al Instante* and made certain retail locations look and feel more like traditional money-transfer locations where people could walk into the bank with cash in hand to make transactions. Even though *Dinero al Instante* was priced higher than *Intercuenta Express,* the business grew gradually in key markets.

The added corporate benefit was that many cash-based customers walking into the branches to conduct money transfers were, by their third transaction, converted to bank customers. While the bank distributes this product through several channels, branches are still its primary channel. The bank feels that the brick-and-mortar locations are critical to its success with the money-transfer products, and the interaction between employees and customers in Spanish is what keeps customers coming back.

Once a relationship is established, employees are able to transition customers into other bank products.

"We are not just selling money transfers," said Daniel Ayala, WFB's senior vice president of Global Remittances Services. "We are helping Hispanics in the States become part of the financial services system. For a large percentage of our customers, when they first initiate a money transfer with us through *Intercuenta Express* or *Dinero al Instante*, they are likely going into a bank for the very first time in their life in the U.S."

WFB's bankers located in Hispanic branches are trained to assess customers' financial needs and can guide customers to sign up for the set of financial products right for them; typically this includes a checking account, a savings account, a check card, a remittance account, and a credit card if they are interested. The bank is effectively able to introduce more advanced financial products over time, helping remitters get out of their cash-based behavior, giving them access to more sophisticated financial services.

The Results

At the time funding for the expanded effort was approved, the team consisted of two people. Since then, the department has grown to a team of over 30 people, and its business has grown by triple digits. Between 2002 and 2004, the money-transfer business more than doubled year over year.

"When I look at the plan deck today," said Ayala, "80 percent of the tasks are either done or in process, but I must say that one can only do this in organizations that embrace this type of culture change and are willing to take what some might consider risk in untapped territory."

WFB is still investing in the business, especially in technology. It is also developing some unique products and working on a few patents. WFB is working on building a "better mousetrap" through an end-to-end remittance platform with front-end and back-end pieces.

It is also working on integrating the overall sales process—namely, automating how *Matricula* card users should be approached in-branch and how to cross-sell other services more effectively. Even if the banker is brand new, the system will trigger to them that something has to be done to offer additional products to that customer to meet their needs.

"The bottom line is that the company sees current results as a strong indicator of future potential and they are pleased with the results," said

Ayala. "I don't think that a technology investment that lasts more than two years in today's world gets a lot of enthusiastic corporate support, but at the same time, everything we have done to date has been validated by the marketplace."

Since original conversations with WFB, the Global Remittances Services unit has increased its distribution to El Salvador and Guatemala through bank partnerships in those countries, increasing money transfer capabilities to serve a broader Hispanic audience. With this and other planned country expansion, expectations for future growth and success are good.

HEALTH CARE AND HEALTH INSURANCE

The United States is one of the most biotechnologically advanced countries in the world, and although medical costs are still high for many, services are provided by and attainable through private as well as public medical entities. This is not often the case in Latin America, where access to doctors is difficult and medical costs are often prohibitive. This has two consequences: (1) it is not a culture where preventive medicine and care is thought of, let alone practiced; and (2) illnesses tend to become serious before medical attention is sought.

In addition to costs, faith and healing traditions play significant roles. Hispanics' religious beliefs lead to a fatalistic outlook on life, where a person's destiny is in God's hands rather than his own. So, when illness strikes, prayer and products from the kitchen, backyard, or nearby field often become the front-line approach to treatment, especially in rural areas. Much of these healing practices are passed down through generations, with many having either native Indian or African origin. Herbs, vegetables, spices, and plants are the basis for common cures in Hispanic households. According to the 2002 Yankelovich Hispanic MONITOR study, 69 percent of Hispanics agree that one should take primary responsibility for one's own health and not rely so much on doctors, and 69 percent admit to only seeking help from a doctor when they are very ill. In Latin America, the corner pharmacist, not a doctor, is often sought out to prescribe medication among those who can afford it. The consumer tells the pharmacy about the symptoms, and the pharmacist provides medication often without the need for a doctor's prescription. Even injections are given on site. Once in the United States, Hispanics living in close proximity to the U.S.-Mexico border often seek medical attention in Mexico for expensive treatment, such as surgeries and dental work. And they seek out prescription medication, often buying in large quantities not only for themselves but also for friends and family who may have requested them.

In these communities, healers are also well-respected figures. The effectiveness of their herbal recipes and knowledge contribute to a following by the community, and is a confidence that is not limited to remote areas, indigenous cultures, or individuals with limited education.

The absence of reliable and accessible public health care also adds to the ingrained culture of not seeking medical assistance proactively. Through constant rallies and demonstrations, activists in Latin America are challenging and even demanding that the governments of these countries provide health care to the masses. Although some governments have recently responded to demands, most have not. It is easy to see that when people in these countries witness the inability to access medical care for AIDS and other serious diseases, they are unlikely to believe that they have options in Latin America's medical system to treat their own ailments.

Historically, the medical health insurance market in Latin America has been largely dominated by the public sector and, for various reasons, the private sector has not been well organized nor is it highly efficient, making health insurance coverage difficult for marginalized societies. There has been a trend toward privatization in recent years, and multinational corporations have capitalized on the privatization trend, gaining a significant foothold in the region by purchasing established companies in Latin America that sell indemnity insurance and prepaid health plans, establishing joint ventures, and entering into agreements to manage social security and public sector institutions.

These cultural and societal influences play themselves out among Hispanics in the United States. Cost issues, language barriers, deficient knowledge about preventive health care, and lack of urgency when illness first strikes, coupled with fatalistic beliefs and preferred home solutions, can present a challenge for health care services companies trying to attract Hispanics and manage their health care practices.

Hispanics often arrive in the United States and work in agriculture, manufacturing, and service sectors where, because of documentation status, they are paid through informal means or work in low-wage jobs with few fringe benefits. Both situations prevent them from obtaining health insurance through their employers. Many of these workers are considered "working poor"—that is, they cannot afford private health insurance yet do not qualify for public programs such as Medicaid. As Hispanics learn English and position themselves to obtain better-paying employment where health care options are available, they are likelier to sign up for coverage, especially if they have a family.

Another factor that affects participation is the availability of culturally and linguistically competent health care providers. Overall, the 2002 Yankelovich Hispanic MONITOR study reports that 47 percent of Hispanics claim having health insurance coverage. And in terms of health insurance coverage by acculturation segments, Yankelovich reports that 65 percent of acculturated Hispanics have coverage, followed by 52 percent of bicultural and 38 percent of unacculturated, compared to 88 percent of non-Hispanic whites. Yet, according to the Department of Labor, there are about 15 million employed Hispanics in the United States who represent an evolving and increasingly viable target for the health care industry here.

CASE STUDY: PACIFICARE HEALTH SYSTEMS

PacifiCare Health Systems, based in Cypress, California, offers commercial HMO, PPO, and POS health insurance plans and Medicare Advantage HMOs, serving nearly 3.2 million members. Its Secure Horizons plan for seniors is one of the largest Medicare HMOs in the United States. PacifiCare's specialty health services, which include behavioral health, dental and vision coverage, and pharmacy benefit management (operating as Prescription Solutions), cover more than 11 million people nationwide.

For several years prior to 2002, PacifiCare had implemented isolated efforts to reach Hispanics. The company had focused on the senior market and set up a Spanish-language customer service line, but this was a very small effort in California. Simultaneously in the San Antonio and Phoenix regional customer service centers, bilingual customer service agents were also in place. PacifiCare's sales teams repeatedly asked the company to improve its effort in reaching out to the Hispanic market. They found that many Hispanic members in small and large employer groups preferred receiving health care information in Spanish and that employer groups wanted that support from their insurance carrier.

However, the idea of seriously assessing and targeting the Hispanic market did not gain traction until 2001 when PacifiCare's new CEO was appointed and charged with turning the company around. He quickly evaluated the markets where PacifiCare operated and, in late 2002, hired Russell A. Bennett as vice president of Latino health solutions to develop the Hispanic market opportunity. Bennett had lived and worked in Mexico for 30 years and was the first executive director of the U.S.-Mexico Border Health Commission.

The Assessment

Hispanic-membership statistics was the first area explored. The results of this study caused PacifiCare to realize it had not been aware of its Hispanic-membership numbers. At the time, no one was tracking ethnicity, race, or language preferences. PacifiCare worked with a variety of external organizations to develop a fairly sophisticated Hispanic surname algorithm to filter its database and identify its Hispanic members.

This process determined that 19 percent, or one in five, of PacifiCare's members were Hispanic. In fact, in the states where PacifiCare offered its core commercial HMO plans (Arizona, California, Colorado, Nevada, Oklahoma, Oregon, Texas, and Washington), there were an estimated 20 million Hispanics. There was clearly an opportunity.

These significant findings validated the CEO's belief that targeting Hispanics was a critical success factor in achieving the company's growth goals through three core corporate strategies: membership growth, retention, and medical management.

Bennett realized that a tremendous opportunity existed despite well-known statistics about Hispanics either being employed with no health insurance or having a lower incidence of signing up for health plans during open enrollment. PacifiCare believed that immigrant Hispanics' earning potential would continue to increase and that the new generation of Hispanic labor would be increasingly better educated and would have better jobs.

The company also believed that among unacculturated or Spanish-dependent employees, lower sign-up rates were a symptom of an industry environment that had not historically created access to insurance products in culturally relevant ways, including, but not limited to, Spanish-language sales, customer service, health care providers, and claims processes.

PacifiCare set out to change this. It started to assess how this new consumer segment could contribute to achieving corporate growth goals. The company also looked at whether success in this market would be product-development dependent or whether it was about how its existing portfolio of plans could be made accessible and relevant to Hispanics.

As a first step to answering these questions, the company analyzed both its membership base by product segment, which includes individual, small group, large group, or mid-market; national accounts (larger accounts with regional decision centers); and labor and trust. It also identified where, across products and geography, its Hispanic members were concentrated.

PacifiCare found a significant number of Hispanic members across all its product segments except individual. This validated the decision that the Hispanic initiative would not be about developing a new product to generate a specific number of members. Rather, PacifiCare decided that its growth platform would consist of retention and membership growth by ensuring that its existing products could add value to its existing Hispanic members.

The Implementation

Bennett generated internal support for this strategy by emphasizing the potential impact on company profitability of increasing membership in a rapidly growing, relatively young and healthy market segment. The company considered what could happen if Hispanic membership growth were to slow or decline, and as the company studied the competitive activity, it was clear that, although none of its competitors were supporting Hispanics across all product lines or in every market, they were focusing on specific business segments. PacifiCare wanted to ensure that these threats could be surmounted moving forward by not underestimating competitors' investments in the marketplace.

Bennett and his staff began to develop the business plan with the help of continued external analysis. He quickly realized that the health care industry was a virgin field in terms of intelligence, and that information about Hispanic market share was nonexistent—a situation that challenged the process of defining share and retention goals. As the company learned what was possible in terms of growth, expectations were calibrated. In addition, rather than set total business growth goals, the company learned that, similar to the varying Hispanic penetration proportions it originally saw across its business segments, PacifiCare had to approach goal-setting proportionately. It had to measure success and profitability based on each business line's dynamics and revenue contribution in terms of total market contribution. Certain businesses could experience declines in any given year, and Hispanic goals had to account for that.

The business plan was ultimately presented to the CEO and PacifiCare's board. The board unanimously supported the plan and sent a strong message that this had to be an integrated corporate strategy, not just a marketing effort, sending a powerful message that health management of Hispanic members had to become an important strategic pillar.

PacifiCare's Latino Health Solutions initiative was well received internally and news of the initiative received broad and very positive coverage in the media. The company drove employee motivation to support and integrate the Hispanic initiative across company operations based on its corporate theme, "Caring is good. Doing something is better."

With retention and membership growth in mind and the expectation that growth had to be generated quickly, PacifiCare worked rapidly to create a customer support infrastructure that supported its goals. In order to better understand the components that had to be addressed, PacifiCare conducted an internal gap analysis, looking at the various consumer and employer touch points along the sales and marketing process that had to be aligned with its Hispanic strategy, including enrollment, retention, plan usage, membership accounting, claims, grievances, and other operational aspects.

After two years of assessment and operational implementation, PacifiCare also modified its Legacy systems to identify customers who preferred receiving communication in Spanish. Each operational area was asked to define which pieces of communication, such as provider directories, needed to be created in Spanish. Modifications to systems, which ran to a budget of seven figures, could then track language preference and generate communications in Hispanics' language of preference.

PacifiCare set a high standard for quality implementation early on, with the goal that everything that is consumer-oriented—from enrollment videos and forms to brochures and educational materials—would be usable across all markets. This resulted in the creation of bilingual sales and marketing materials that are unequaled in the industry. Bilingual customer service representatives, once only dedicated to its senior product, were crossed-trained to answer questions across all commercial products and all customer service regions. Ultimately, PacifiCare established one toll-free number for all Spanish-speaking members, which routes calls to the various customer service regions regardless of call origin.

PacifiCare also surveyed its provider networks and currently publishes a Spanish-language provider directory in California that grades provider front offices, nurses, and doctors on their Spanish-language ability, based on three language-ability levels so consumers can select providers that can serve them in-language. PacifiCare stresses the importance of the provider network's language ability because it knows that, in the general market, one in four patients leaves a doctor's office without a full understanding of doctors' instructions. Among limited English proficiency (LEP) patients, this number is one in two. Further, one in five LEP patients do not go to the doctor because they feel that they won't be able to communicate with their English-speaking physician.

In addition, PacifiCare developed a CD-ROM-based health assessment tool that generates a health risk profile in English and Spanish that can be filled in electronically, printed out, and taken to the doctor on a first visit. PacifiCare believes that health education is a critical success factor for any health care service's Hispanic strategy.

The Results

Given the member support provided by PacifiCare, employers now feel increasingly attracted to PacifiCare as a health plan because it unburdens the Human Resources office from the responsibility of dealing with health insurance problems and questions from Spanish-speaking employees.

Since launching its Latino Health Solutions initiative, PacifiCare has grown Hispanic membership by an average of 3 percent across its products and markets, including geographies where total growth was flat or down. Hispanics are now over 22 percent of total members, and in California, they represent over 27 percent of members. PacifiCare credits its success to the value it creates not only to its Hispanic members but also to the support that it provides to employers who are no longer burdened with having to explain health care benefits, plan characteristics, and enrollment logistics, or even handling claims issues. Now, employers refer employees to PacifiCare and trust that they will be serviced in Spanish and with cultural sensitivity. PacifiCare is optimistic about its Hispanic sales forecasts and indicates that, while retention is still being studied, there are indications that Hispanic retention figures are better than the general market.

As 2005 came to a close, PacifiCare merged with United Health Group, which will make the Latino Health Solutions capabilities available to Hispanics nationwide.

• • • • •

In the following chapters, we'll take a closer look at the process for evaluating the opportunity and implementing a business strategy to target the growing Hispanic population. In addition, we will look at other examples of companies in these and other industries that have begun and followed through on their Hispanic strategies.

4

EXTERNAL ASSESSMENT I: MACRO AND INDUSTRY TRENDS

A thorough understanding of the macro, industry, competitive, and consumer environments in which a company competes for Hispanics' business and their relative implications is vital to laying the groundwork for a successful Hispanic market strategy. Knowing exactly how these areas evolve can have important repercussions and, if carefully considered, will inevitably point to potential business opportunities to be optimized and threats to be averted in targeting U.S. Hispanics.

Assessing the macro environment requires a broad understanding of demographics and the economic, political, cultural, social, and technological landscapes. Additionally, understanding how Hispanics are driving changes in these areas, how they are being impacted by them, and ultimately how that impact will affect doing business with them and society as a whole captures the purpose of a macro assessment. While this is not a book on economics or the social sciences, some of these areas are touched upon to provide a framework for further thought and necessary context. To truly understand the drivers and their impacts, you will want to focus on the environmental trends or forces that are more relevant to your industry.

Aside from sources you normally use to understand your business environment, there are three excellent sources for environmental macro insights related to the Hispanic market, including the HispanTelligence®

division of *Hispanic Business* magazine. HispanTelligence® provides stan-
dardized research products with insightful data and trend analysis, useful
for market planning and strategic decision making, including "The U.S.
Hispanic Economy in Transition: Facts, Figures, and Trends—2005 Edi-
tion." This report highlights how the U.S. Hispanic economy is continuing to solidify its growing influence in the 21st century. It provides a
"comprehensive examination of the quantitative measures of the Hispanic market and its qualitative characteristics, as well as an interpretation of the market's expanding impact and implications for the nation's
future."

Another useful source is the Selig Center for Economic Growth. This
organization is known for its extensive coverage of minority buying
power and spending patterns. It publishes a yearly report titled "The
Multicultural Economy: America's Minority Buying Power." Lastly, the
Pew Research Center, a nonpartisan "fact tank" that provides information on "the issues, attitudes, and trends shaping America and the
world," publishes several reports on its Pew Hispanic Center Web site.
The site addresses immigration, economic, labor, education, and political issues and insights related to the Hispanic market. These reports are
based on government data as well as surveys conducted by the center. You
will also note several other sources throughout that are helpful in understanding the macro environment within a Hispanic context.

Just as environmental forces often present challenges for corporate
America, they also, as you are well aware, provide immense opportunities
if recognized early on. And staying at the forefront of environmental
changes created by or as a result of the Hispanic market will impact the
way in which your company does business with Hispanics. In fact, many
of the Hispanic market opportunities captured by successful companies
today originate from an ability to recognize environmental forces and
their inevitable impact on U.S. Hispanic society, economics, and culture.

Be aware of legal and regulatory issues that impact the continuous
flow of new immigrants to this country. Stay attuned to laws affecting
Hispanics' ability to obtain an education, health care, and even a
driver's license, as they all have an impact on their respective and complementary industries.

When you think of globalization, also think about companies coming into the United States to do business with U.S. Hispanics or export-
ing products to meet their needs. They may compete with your own

offerings, so stay on top of trade agreements between the United States and Latin America because it may mean increased or decreased competition in the United States in your product category or perhaps even opportunities for strategic partnerships and alliances.

Understand educational, immigration-related documentation and labor issues impacting Hispanics because it is likely to eventually impact your industry as boomers retire and you face a tight labor market.

Follow purchasing power and spending patterns closely, and learn to determine what that means for your industry. According to the Bureau of Labor Statistics's Consumer Survey of 2003 (the most recent available), lower incomes currently keep Hispanic consumption in areas of real estate, personal insurance and pensions, health care, education, entertainment, and a few other miscellaneous categories lower than the national average. However, these can also represent significant opportunity categories where spending will continue to rise as Hispanics' incomes approach the national average. These may well be industries where companies with "industry-shaper" cultures and mindsets will flourish among U.S. Hispanics.

Opportunity categories can be found nearly everywhere, especially given the increasing presence of Hispanics in the United States. While the Hispanic population is more evident in certain parts of the United States than in others, its impact continues to intensify. As it changes, so will demand for products and services that align with what Hispanics *and* mainstream consumers enjoy and desire, thus creating business opportunities even among mainstream consumer segments.

For instance, nowhere is Hispanic influence more evident than in the food enjoyed by mainstream America. Mainstream awareness and attraction to ethnic foods has grown dramatically. According to the National Restaurant Association, the Hispanic restaurant market in 2005 was growing 3.5 times faster than the national average. And, according to PROMAR International and McKinsey Consulting, both ethnic food service and grocery sectors are expected to continue growing at rates of 4 to 6 percent, far outpacing the national average of 1.6 percent expected through 2010. Overall demand for ethnic foods is expected to grow by 50 percent over the next decade. More to the point of greater cultural diversity on America's dinner table, three-quarters of the ethnic food sector growth will be driven by mainstream consumers.

Wholesale distributor Nash Finch has witnessed the importance of culture firsthand. The company spent more than two years researching

Hispanic culture and merchandising preferences, and implemented this knowledge into a successful line of Denver-based AVANZA stores that cater to the area's Hispanic market. Nash Finch's management has supported the Hispanic strategy from its start, keeping an eye on how Hispanic culture shaped the company's plans. "Understand the importance of the culture and heritage and incorporate this in everything you do" is a mantra. (See Chapter 8 to learn more about the Nash Finch strategy.)

Pop culture is also being shaped by ethnic America and is driving mainstream's desires across the board. Hispanics have a significant and growing share of the spotlight in music, movies, fashion, and media, from crossover stars like Ricky Martin and Jennifer Lopez to designers like Carolina Herrera and Balenciaga to television stars like Eva Longoria and Jimmy Smits. Recognizing this trend, the ABC television network recently announced that it would offer its entire prime time entertainment lineup in Spanish as of September 2005, making it the first English-language broadcast network to do so on such a large scale through a combination of closed-captioning and dubbing. And, with programming such as Nickelodeon's *Dora the Explorer* and PBS's *Maya & Miguel,* significant breakthroughs have even been made in children's English-language programming with appeal among both Hispanic and non-Hispanic children.

Macro and industry trends related to the Hispanic market often have far-reaching effects. The challenge is to think through these trends and effects and to think about what they might mean to your industry, your organization, your competitors, and to these potential consumers—Hispanic and, oftentimes, non-Hispanic.

INDUSTRY TRENDS

The value of having assessed the macro environment is that it often explains industry trends you may have already noticed. Some of the sources mentioned above also provide industry trend information, but additionally, every industry has associations and/or regulatory bodies that are increasingly tracking the Hispanic market. A few examples of industry trends follow, with emphasis on the competitive environment. It is incumbent upon you to search for and find those trends that are specific to your industry and that provide insight into opportunities and threats for your initiative.

Secondary research should be sought and analyzed for consistency and contradictory marketplace views. Most of this research can be found on the Internet and, along with sources already mentioned, should include government statistics, manufacturer-sponsored industry reports, annual company reports, directories, and press articles. The latter typically can be gathered through publication databases. Lexis-Nexis and Factiva are excellent sources for articles, as are trade publication coverage and industry reports. Access to online databases will greatly facilitate and advance traditional desk research.

Data from recently published consultant reports from companies such as Mintel, Packaged Facts, marketresearch.com, and Promar International are all great sources for industry-specific Hispanic consumer trends. Although many of these reports can be pricey, consider that they are actually a very cost-efficient way to obtain forward-looking industry insights quickly and concisely.

ENTERING THE MARKETPLACE

In the past several years, more industries are adapting their products and services to meet the tastes and preferences of their Hispanic targets. And there are several business models for how this is being done. In some cases, internal resources allow for in-house development. Other times, when requirements fall outside of core competencies, development and manufacturing are outsourced. In other cases, companies expand their assortment by acquiring smaller specialist companies that have the assortment they need for their ethnic portfolios.

Entry through Acquisition

Some companies acquire Hispanic-oriented companies to compete for this marketplace. They opt for acquiring companies that are successfully meeting a need and, by doing so, bypass organizational restructuring and minimize impact to their business model and their learning curve. One example is Patrick Cudahy, a large meat-processing company that purchased a meat company that specialized in Hispanic processed meats to compete for a share of the Hispanic processed-meat marketplace.

It is more and more common to hear of investment companies acquiring and merging smaller, more specialized companies and then selling them to larger mainstream companies. There has been quite of bit of ethnic foods company acquisition activity in recent years driven by several capital management and investment companies:

- Señor Felix (fresh foods concept), a salsa marketer, is owned by Swander Pace Capital Management.
- Don Miguel Foods, a leading frozen food manufacturer, was acquired in November 2002 by Shansby Group.
- Shansby had earlier invested in salsa maker La Victoria Foods and combined it with Calidad Foods to form Authentic Specialty Products, which it then sold to Mexican food company DESC SA de CV.
- Fremont Partners acquired Specialty Brands, makers of José Olé frozen products from Tyson Foods.
- Excelline, a smaller producer of Mexican products, sold a share of the company to a Boston-based capital management firm.

The Threat of New Market Entrants

Some companies are creating Hispanic operating units to compete head to head with specialty Hispanic manufacturers and retailers. Several supermarkets have done this quite successfully, including Minyard Food Stores with its Carnival format in Dallas/Ft. Worth, Basha's with Food City in Phoenix, Nash Finch with AVANZA in Denver, Brookshire's with Olé in Dallas, and Albertsons with SuperSaver in Los Angeles.

No Need to Change

Whether or not your company needs to adapt its offering to meet Hispanics' tastes will depend on your category, the consumer, competitive actions, and a good understanding of your value proposition. It may be that customization is not necessary because what you offer is a concept unto itself, and Hispanics will relate to it on that basis. Denny's restaurants, as we'll see later, is an example of this. Theme parks are another good example. There are no Hispanic-oriented rides, for instance, though there may be some tailored opportunistic attractions, a selection of targeted food service offerings, and on-site language accommodations.

In these situations, it is important to have a clear position on the value you offer and define whether that value translates to Hispanics. It's more a matter of tapping into "why" the value proposition resonates well among Hispanics, then reflecting that in the marketing mix. In these cases, as in others, the value is delivered through the customer experience rather than the product assortment.

SPECIALIZED MARKET ENTRANTS

New market entrants may be other companies similar in size and core business to yours or they may be more specialized competitors whose sole purpose in entering your space is to serve the Hispanic market. Often, these entries are driven by recognition that Hispanics do not have access to products and services they want because larger businesses are not located where they shop, do not carry appropriate products, or the process for accessing a product or service is uncomfortable, confusing, intimidating, or difficult compared to what they are used to, can afford, or know how to access. Ethnic restaurants, supermarkets, bakeries, furniture stores, insurance and travel agents, and music stores are a few examples.

Industry Substitutes

Another form of competitor that has surfaced in different industries is one that serves as a substitute for what Hispanics need but for which they may be ineligible. Between 1990 and 2000, when the United States saw the most aggressive growth in the Hispanic marketplace, banks still required Social Security identification to open accounts. Much of the banking community saw the Hispanic market as a high-risk segment. Consequently, banks did not capitalize on the rising population for growth, and Hispanics could not access and become integrated in the U.S. financial services system. This led to the rebirth of what is now a $45 billion money transfers industry, a space originally dominated by Western Union and MoneyGram. By the late 1990s, over 50 money services companies with more than 30,000 locations existed nationwide to service the financial needs of Hispanics.

More Efficient Business Models

Smaller players with innovative business models that could pose a competitive threat in your industry are rapidly surfacing. These small companies are likely to operate on lower margins and may be equally capable of satisfying consumer needs and winning market share. These small but many times more nimble entrants can quickly change the dynamics of an industry.

Examples are specialized furniture, electronics, telecommunications, and appliance retailers that successfully cater to the Hispanic market because they have a presence in the heart of these communities, have limited and efficient assortments, and are willing to extend credit where large retailers are not. No matter what industry you are in, there are likely competitors that fill a product or service gap where the Hispanics cannot access a product or service through traditional channels or by traditional means. Do not assume that your competitive set is the same in the Hispanic market as it is in the mainstream market.

Foreign Competition

Most industries today are moving toward globalization at a rapid pace for a variety of reasons. For most U.S.-based companies, globalization means expanding their businesses into other parts of the world, or it represents outsourcing noncore activities that lead to more efficient manufacturing costs and lower consumer prices.

However, in the case of foreign companies, many are looking at the U.S. Hispanic market for expansion opportunities. The increasing rate of imported food products alone has been staggering in recent years, notwithstanding the already high volume that existed, especially in commodity products. Several Latin American trade associations have been embarking on sizable market feasibility studies across every imaginable export category to assess opportunities in the United States. The North American Free Trade Agreement (NAFTA) and more recently the Central American Free Trade Agreement (CAFTA) have been key drivers of trade and entry opportunities; additionally, Andean region countries are discussing the Andean Free Trade Agreement with the United States, which will surely continue to impact the competitive landscape as more Latin American imports become available to U.S. Hispanics.

Similarly, in the financial services sector, Latin American financial institutions are interested in the U.S. Hispanic marketplace and are exploring ways to enter this market to serve Hispanics not utilizing banking in a culturally relevant way. BBVA Bancomer entered the United States as a money transfer company in 1995 and currently pays more than $8 million in transfers through almost 2,000 branches in Mexico. And, according to the Federal Reserve Bank of New York, BBVA Bancomer's application to enter the banking sector to target U.S. Hispanics was approved in late 2004, and is now a viable contender to capture business from U.S. Hispanics who want to do business with the largest Mexican financial services brand. In the entertainment sector, Latin American production companies continue to sell an increasing volume of television programming, especially *novelas,* and movies that cater to Spanish-language entertainment preferences. Following in the footsteps of El Pollo Loco (originally from Mexico), food service companies like Pollo Campero (from Central America) have started to successfully enter the United States.

· · · · ·

The work involved in the assessment of macro and industry trends serves to bring forth the opportunity or threat implications for your Hispanic strategy. Identifying your strategic position relative to these different types of competitors will be important in assessing your ability to profitably win and retain Hispanic customers.

CASE STUDY: EL POLLO LOCO

In 1975, Juan Francisco "Pancho" Ochoa opened his first roadside chicken stand in the small town of Guasave on Mexico's Pacific Coast and named it El Pollo Loco ("The Crazy Chicken"). By 1979, Pancho's family and friends had opened 85 restaurants in 20 Northern Mexico cities. Shortly thereafter, the delicious marinated chicken traveled across the border into the United States. In 1980, people lined up around the block as the first American El Pollo Loco (EPL) opened on Alvarado Street in Los Angeles.

El Pollo Loco's famous chicken, served with warm tortillas, freshly prepared salsas, and a wide variety of side dishes, appealed to Hispanic families seeking wholesome, delicious, traditional food. In 1983, El Pollo Loco was purchased by Denny's; then in 1987, both Denny's and El Pollo

Loco were acquired by TW Services, Inc. (now Advantica Restaurant Group, Inc.). Most recently, in December 1999, American Securities Capital Partners, LLC, a private New York-based equity investment firm, acquired El Pollo Loco from Advantica. Today, El Pollo Loco leads the quick service segment of the restaurant industry specializing in flame-grilled chicken. The chain operates more than 300 restaurants in four states—California, Arizona, Nevada, and Texas. And in January 2004, El Pollo Loco signed an agreement to develop restaurants in Chicago.

The Assessment and Implementation

In planning its market expansion, El Pollo Loco used in-depth market demographic analysis to understand population trends and identify areas where Mexican consumers are concentrated. EPL looked for locations in areas that were primarily Mexican immigrant-based and expanded outward from there. It used demographic analysis to define and refine its Hispanic store set, which are stores in areas that are 60 percent or more Mexican.

Hispanic stores automatically receive bilingual point-of-sale (POS) merchandising, and bilingual merchandising kits are available to other stores if needed. All staff members and managers in Hispanic stores speak Spanish. EPL believes that its employees are crucial to creating and maintaining its relationship with customers, and while ensuring that the front-counter employees are bilingual, the back can speak Spanish but are not required to speak English.

Karen Eadon, Vice President of Marketing at El Pollo Loco, says she works closely with human resources to ensure that job interviews can be conducted in Spanish and has ensured that all training materials are available in Spanish. EPL also works to continually develop decor proto-types that will ensure an environment that is warm, fresh, fun, and contemporary, but not too far removed from its Mexican roots. It strives to create a communal feel—one of sitting around the family kitchen table—something to which all of its customers can relate.

As El Pollo Loco grew its U.S. presence, it successfully crossed over to achieve a customer base that is 50 percent Hispanic and 50 percent mainstream. As such, EPL has to continually work to understand food service dynamics and purchase drivers for two core customer groups: its Hispanic customer base with preferences for traditional grilled chicken on the bone served with traditional sides such as tortillas, beans, rice, and fresh salsas and garnishes, and its mainstream customer with varying preferences for "flavors from the kitchens of Mexico" driven by evolving fresh-Mex food trends.

And while EPL is committed to staying true to its heritage, its menu has expanded, mostly to include items that align with the mainstream palate. Even its promotional calendar is planned to deliver some value offerings appealing more to mainstream customers, while other promotions appeal more to its Hispanic customers.

In 2004, EPL was challenged to define how it would successfully transfer its "next generation" prototype for future franchises with broad demographic appeal and design flexibility to drive continued national growth of the 25-year-old proven concept. Its sights were set on Chicago, yet another highly Mexican marketplace.

The Results

When looking at results, promotional offers are evaluated based on how well they perform among their intended targets and the geographies in which these targets are concentrated. In others words, not all offers are expected to do well everywhere or among everyone. This presents a challenge among franchises that may not align with intended targets for every promotional offer, but EPL remains firm that as a company it must successfully cater to the product preferences of its two core targets.

El Pollo Loco has managed to successfully satisfy its growing mainstream customer while maintaining the integrity of its heritage and delivering on the authenticity that its Hispanic customers have come to know and love. And results couldn't be more positive. According to a D&B financials report by Hoovers, EPL experienced a 6.1 percent sales growth in 2004—an increase that is even more impressive given EPL's ability to outpace the industry's strong sales growth of 5 percent in 2004 and 5.4 percent in 2003 in the quick-service restaurant segment.

And, utilizing market analysis and consumer research tools to pinpoint the Mexican market opportunity, EPL opened its first new Chicago location in October 2005, which incorporates the new prototype elements. The opening of the Logan Square neighborhood restaurant marks the first of ten EPL locations planned to open in the greater Chicago area. The next is scheduled to open in Melrose Park in early 2006. In addition to Illinois, the company has a strong pipeline of franchise restaurant commitments in California, Colorado, New England, New Jersey, New York, Oregon, Texas, and Washington.

5

EXTERNAL ASSESSMENT II: THE COMPETITIVE ENVIRONMENT

The approach to assess your competition will depend on how many competitive sets exist for your industry or category—the competition's likelihood for growth based on the strategic resources they have in place that might give them a competitive advantage compared to your organization.

De Kluyver and Pearce define strategic resources as an organization's ability in two areas: (1) *knowledge management*—how effectively companies manage explicit and tacit Hispanic market knowledge, strategies, and implementation plans and disseminate them throughout the organization; and (2) *core competencies*—how companies define value for Hispanic customers, how easy it is to duplicate or copy an approach, and what resources and abilities companies have to help them adapt, innovate, and sustain a competitive edge.

Resources also include specific skill sets, perhaps in manufacturing or sourcing through specialty suppliers; having a corporate culture that lends itself to adaptation and alignment with different environments and consumer segments; and the competition's position among Hispanic consumers.

APPROACHES

Depending on the types of competitive sets that exist for your industry or category, different considerations must be taken into account to assess your competitive environment. For example, Chapter 4 indicated that the competitive environment across many industries has been impacted by different types of local competition that have entered the market to address Hispanics' unmet needs. It is essential not to underestimate the importance of local competition in your competitive set definition and assessment.

Because these companies are private, you will not find company overviews, financials, or insights into their operating models in any report. The best way to assess smaller specialty market entrants or industry substitute competitors is to go into the marketplace where you will be competing for Hispanic customers and see how these companies operate for yourself. Not only will you see what they are doing, but you will also see how their customers engage in doing business with them. Some distinctions should become immediately obvious. And while the intent for this observation and learning is not to replicate these business models, having insight into what drives their reason for being and how they generate their profit is useful in defining how and if your company can create relevant and competitive consumer alignment while maintaining consistency with your company's strategic market position and direction.

There are no shortcuts here. You must be willing to spend the time in the market to experience the services and products of competitors, talk to specialty distributors and brokers, meet with Hispanic trade associations like local chapters of the Hispanic Chamber of Commerce and the Latin Business Association, and talk to your competitors' customers while you are there.

In these instances, the best consumer interaction happens on site rather than in focus groups or through surveys. Truly understanding how these competitors create value that Hispanics are willing to pay for, at times even at a premium, and figuring out how they structure their operations to do so means blending in and jumping into the customers' shoes. It means living it.

When assessing large industry competitors—those that may resemble your own company—other methods are available. Keep in mind, though, that firsthand market experience is a critical component no matter the size of the competition. You want to read through at least 12 months of PR releases, which typically can be found on their Web sites or through the standard wire services. HispanicPRWire.com, Hispaniconline.com, Hispanictrends.com, and Hispanicmagazine.com are great sources for Hispanic-related industry news of the moment.

On the corporate side, you also want to go through recent annual reports and SEC filings, scanning for the competition's views on changing demographics and how the company is likely to address the change.

In addition, trade publications often have insights in this area, so having conversations with editors who cover ethnic market trends can yield competitive insights about existing and potential Hispanic market players in your industry.

Expert interviews can be extremely valuable in competitive assessment. They can provide multidimensional views on perceived strengths and weaknesses of competitors' Hispanic strategies, insights into new competitive developments and trends, and even a perspective on how your organization is viewed and positioned.

Through industry contacts, you can often obtain access to trade magazine archives or make requests for them to provide articles that discuss your competitors and their efforts in the Hispanic market. Secondly, many trade Web sites often survey visitors for views on different topics, including the Hispanic market, and results from these surveys can be obtained. These results often shed light on what specific companies are doing or how an industry is responding to a Hispanic market business issue. Make sure that you reach out to trade publications across the operational gamut, not just marketing, to obtain comprehensive input from the various operational perspectives.

In addition, finding and contacting competitors' ex-employees can be invaluable. Often these individuals can be retained as consultants for specific industry and competitive information. Other expert sources include think tanks, government organizations, market research companies that sell syndicated data, consultants, and the media.

You will run into confidentiality concerns, so exercising good judgment, discretion, integrity, and ethics is critical as these contacts can be ongoing, valuable information sources. Remember that as the macro environment changes, so will industry and consumer trends, and with these changes, competitive dynamics will also evolve.

THE ASSESSMENT

Competitive assessment can be broken down into three main sections: (1) identifying and defining your competitive set, (2) defining market presence, and (3) quantifying brand strength and market share.

Typically, you want to start by identifying the companies or groups with which you compete. Your competitive set can be comprised of small, medium, and large companies. Start by identifying companies in your industry that target Hispanics in some way. In packaged goods manufacturing, for example, competitors may include imports, small U.S.-based ethnic manufacturers, regional ethnic manufacturers, regional mainstream manufacturers, and national U.S. manufacturers. There will be opportunity to streamline your competitive set as you define your Hispanic target and understand your internal strengths and weaknesses. But for now, think of your competitive set in broad terms because understanding the broad spectrum of the competitive marketplace will enable you to identify clear distinctions between existing business models and your own. In so doing you will be better prepared to make decisions that minimize impact to your business model while maximizing profit potential.

Defining your competitive landscape in a broad manner also helps determine whether your industry is fragmented with many small, medium, and large players, whether it is dominated by a few large companies, or whether it falls somewhere in between. Knowing this will help you determine where you fit and identify your immediate competition. A company's immediate competitive space typically includes companies with similar competitive approaches and positions in the marketplace, though not necessarily in their approach to targeting Hispanics. This is where opportunities become clear.

Understanding the competition requires an understanding of their business model in relation to yours. Slywotzky and Morrison, authors of *The Profit Zone,* focus on three key business model dimensions that should be considered when assessing the competitive landscape and comparing to your own organization. They include strategic dimensions, operating dimensions, and organizational dimensions.

Strategic Dimensions

Strategic dimensions include defining which segment of Hispanic consumers are targeted by the competition, how the competition profits from those consumers, why certain Hispanic customers choose to do business with your competitors, and which products and services your competition delivers to those customers.

Secondary research studies make it fairly easy to define the consumer profile that shops your competition. Understanding the values held by target Hispanics around your category and comparing those to competitive offerings will help you determine why those consumers choose to do business with the competition. Studying your competitors' supply chain, go-to-market strategy, customer values, service and product offerings, and pricing will help you define their profit model. Studying the Hispanic relevance of their offerings can help you understand the extent to which they are customizing or creating new products and services to meet their Hispanic targets' needs and the relative cost of doing so.

Defining these dimensions and how they compare to your own strategies in these areas typically results in market entry insights and implications. It also can reveal requirements and thresholds that a company must meet to be considered a credible option among your intended Hispanic consumers. Conversely, these insights may lead you to make decisions about who your Hispanic target needs to be and how you want to go after it, given your existing market strategies. The key here is to understand where there is alignment between what Hispanic consumers value and your offering. But more to the point of competitiveness, it is a benchmark of value delivery that may evolve based on your strengths within operating and organizational dimensions of your business model.

In the grocery business, ACNielsen and IRI, two well-known and utilized sales tracking services in the industry, provide sales data based on stores located in trading areas with high Hispanic concentration. The store sample is comprised of $2-million-plus supermarkets in trading areas that have 50 percent or more Hispanic density. However, these tools only partially capture sales volume movement. In order to understand sales and volume activity for a product category or brand in smaller neighborhood stores, you will need to go into the marketplace and talk to specialty distributors, brokers, importers, and retailers. Neighborhood retailers are not well represented by either ACNielsen or IRI, so volume is best measured by case movement in the market. For a retailer, this is important because product assortment strategies will depend on being able to identify strong Hispanic products that may not be captured in scanner data reports. If you're a manufacturer, you may not have a representative size of competitive Hispanic and non-Hispanic product movement without case movement numbers.

ACNielsen also offers household panel data among Los Angeles Hispanic households of various acculturation levels. This panel data reports on the items that Hispanic households are bringing home every time they go to the grocery store. These items are scanned by household members, and grocery channel and shopper data are also recorded. These insights help determine competitive preferences among Hispanics of various acculturations profiles, which helps to better define your competitors' customers. (For more information on such panel data, see Chapter 6.) As well, Hispanic household-based companies like Simmons Market Research and Scarborough Research provide extensive detail on competitive brand awareness and purchasing behavior. A critical point is whether your competitors' offerings are relevant to this consumer and if not, whether you are capable of creating enough relevant differentiation and value in your offering to make Hispanics want to buy from you instead. Study those retailers or brands where Hispanic preference is high to define their advantages.

When looking at relevancy, focus on whether your competition has highly or weakly differentiated offerings. Further, researching whether competitors are working on future product or service customization is very important, as is determining whether different branding strategies or co-packing and licensing partnerships are planned or being employed.

Once you understand your competitors' value propositions, you'll want to know how they create awareness and generate trial and repeat purchase among target Hispanics. Talking to the media community will help determine how active competitors are and their relative spending in advertising and promotions. Several trade associations, including the Association of Hispanic Advertising Agencies and the American Association of Advertising Agencies, as well as marketing trade publications such as *Marketing y Medios* and *Advertising Age,* track Hispanic marketing activity and will facilitate this fact finding. Unfortunately, there is no comprehensive service that tracks Hispanic media spending across all outlets, so often it will require piecing together information from various sources.

Hispanic Business tracks corporate America's marketing efforts on a regular basis and also can be a source for historical spending data.

One of the key things you'll want to look for is whether competitors have a consistent and integrated approach as opposed to one that is intermittent and opportunistic. For example, there are several companies that only advertise to Hispanics during high seasonality periods, or only to align with or support mainstream promotional efforts.

Another important area to analyze is the consistency between the message that is being advertised in broadcast media and what is featured in other areas of the company, such as the store flyer, in-store point-of-sale display, inventory, product focus on the sales floor displays, employee knowledge of messages, and the company's Web site. For instance, companies spend millions aligning themselves with Hispanic sports and entertainment properties and advertise them on television and radio, but the consumer never sees continuity of execution at store levels, in printed marketing materials, or on the company's bilingual Web site. Worse, employees are unaware of the messages being delivered on Spanish-language media. This is a clear sign that the company's operational infrastructure is not aligned to support Hispanic efforts, that the marketing organization is not following through, or even that the company has not allocated sufficient dollars to achieve an integrated strategy.

Other times, corporate advertising departments create mailers that focus on specific products based on Hispanic appeal, but the stores fail to display the featured products. Store-level execution can tell quite a lot about how competitive Hispanic strategies are supported throughout the organization.

Operational Dimensions

Operational areas include sourcing methods and necessary relationships for delivering relevant products and services to Hispanic consumers, the ability to manufacture Hispanic products in-house or the need to outsource, the degree of capital intensiveness of Hispanic operations, how well new products and services are innovated and developed, and the approaches used to go to market such as direct sales people or specialty distributors.

Talking to people in your supply chain and that of your competitors—some of which you'll have in common—will help you define sourcing methods and the relationships that have been established. In addition, be sure that you also tap sources outside of your usual supply chain because, as you might imagine, there will be several specialty distributors, specialty manufacturers, importers, and retailers that will likely fall outside of your current set.

Learn whether your competitors are manufacturing customized products or whether they are outsourcing, then talk to your R&D function to determine how an outsourcing option might work within your organization. Several questions are typically considered in this area. Is stepping outside of your core competency realistic and cost efficient? Would it be less expensive and more manageable to outsource or to buy a company that already specializes in the Hispanic assortment you want to offer? Ultimately, it's about assessing how this decision will maximize or decrease profit margins. Anytime you attempt anything that is not a core competency, it has the potential to impact profitability unless a better internal or external model to do so is adopted.

Obtain a read on how often your competitors are launching new products and services. Not only will it provide thresholds for you to meet or exceed if you decide to compete for a share of the same target consumer, but it will also provide a sense of your competitors' level of resource allocations to their Hispanic strategy. Also, if your company's source of sustainable competitive advantage is innovation, you'll want to ask if that same level of innovation can be maintained in the Hispanic market.

Lastly, study the competition's distribution model for insight into how they might be adapting their own retail locations or if their retail customer set has been adjusted (i.e., expanded) to reach their Hispanic target, perhaps through local neighborhood stores in Hispanic neighborhoods. If the competitor has a retail presence or is sold through customer retail locations, you will want to know where those locations are relative to their target market and overlay your own presence to theirs on a map to determine where you coincide and where the gaps are in their favor and in yours. This will give you a sense of the share of market to which they have access versus your own and it will point to expansion opportunities or a calibration of market share expectations. If you're a manufacturer, it gives you insights into the challenges you might face in obtaining shelf space for a similar product. This is especially true in mass market or chain stores, where shelf costs are high and a more aggressive and research-supported sell-in strategy is implied.

You will also want to determine how competitive retail operations may have been adjusted to meet Hispanics' shopping patterns, including days and hours of operation. For instance, do they have extended weekend hours to align with how and when Hispanics shop? Are they open later in some locations? This is where going into market comes into play. Not only will you be able to assess much of what we've covered so far, but also you'll be able to see firsthand how competitive store environments or store merchandising may have been adjusted to create a more welcoming ambiance or appealing offer. This would include an assessment of bilingual staffing, signage, brochures, and, if applicable, general ambiance elements like music.

A large automotive manufacturer, for example, ensures that even finance managers are bilingual in dealerships where the majority of customers are Hispanic. They also provide Spanish-language versions of every piece of paper the customer receives during the sales process. They produce videos for salespersons that discuss cultural nuances of selling cars to Hispanics. And, knowing that many Hispanics do not have credit histories in the United States, they rely on paycheck stubs, consistent rent and utilities payment patterns, and good banking relationships to qualify them for credit.

Using the same in-market approach, you'll need to have a sense of customer service experience provided by competitors not only in-store, but also across all customer touch points, including the toll-free phone number and Web site.

Organizational Dimensions

Organizational dimensions include how your competition is organized internally to manage their Hispanic strategies. Expert interviews can yield valuable information about the various infrastructures competitors have in place. First, you'll want to know the organizational structure in the company. There are, as you well know, several infrastructure models employed in corporations today. Some of the more familiar ones are designed around product and service lines, functions, or customer segments, and some are multidimensional.

You'll want to research whether competitors organize their Hispanic strategy as a business unit with its own support functions and P&L or as a business line or segment with cross-functional support. Further, understanding reporting hierarchy is essential because you'll have a sense of the relative importance of the Hispanic strategy.

There are, as you might imagine, pros and cons to each structure, but what is most important is determining whether the unit structure is in line with the overall organizational structure and whether it is at the same level as other business lines or units with the same reporting structure. This insight will yield a great deal of information because you will be able to see cause and effect—strategic and operational dimensions can be heavily influenced by organizational structure. In some instances, companies have gone through great efforts to create and manage separate Hispanic units that do not align with the overall organizational structure and have met with disaster because the unit has to struggle to fit in.

CASE STUDY: STOP & SHOP

Stop & Shop is a supermarket in the Northeast that operates 200 stores in Connecticut, Massachusetts, Rhode Island, New Jersey, and New York. It is a part of Royal Ahold, the world's third largest grocery retailer after Wal-Mart and Carrefour. Two years ago the company started to take note of the changing demographics around its stores and made a strategic decision to assign ethnic products to a category manager along with specialty and natural/organic goods. In early 2005, with the ethnic business experiencing double-digit growth, an ethnic category portfolio was created, and it became one of two segments being managed through a category manager with the support of an ethnic buyer.

The Assessment

Stop & Shop has seen a progressive growth of ethnic groups shopping their stores, so the retailer decided to position itself to capitalize on this growth for the long term. Stop & Shop's management goal is to be at the forefront of ethnic growth in the United States, and its senior management has been supportive of its ethnic focus because, beyond the demographic shifts, it also sees growing competitive challenges within its trading areas. Consequently, support has been strong across sales and operating divisions. As part of a global company, Stop & Shop capitalizes on its international experience through managers who travel internationally and then share and apply that knowledge domestically.

Stop & Shop's category management stresses education about its ethnic consumers horizontally and vertically within the organization. Efforts are made to communicate insights at all levels of the organization with special emphasis on store level, but without ignoring the necessary dissemination to gain continuous support from its five divisions, each operating between 125 and 140 stores. In fact, a significant amount of time is spent educating sales and operations vice presidents, sales managers who focus on specific segments, and district managers who focus on driving sales in each division. Each store is provided a demographic profile that includes the ethnic makeup within its three-mile trading area, something that had not been provided before.

According to Gabriela de Oliveiras Castro, the chain's ethnic foods buyer, "This allows store managers to see that there might be 8,000 Spanish-speaking persons within their primary trading areas who comprise 35 percent of their total volume. This really quantifies it for them."

Beyond sheer population figures, each store is also educated on the differences in nationalities shopping in the stores and how shopping preferences vary according to these differences. Stop & Shop develops different "plan-o-grams" according to concentration of nationalities, and these differences are also conveyed through ad and display activity.

The Implementation

Stop & Shop runs 14-week ethnic programs to make it easy for the stores to execute—stores can build displays and avoid having to constantly cut items in and out. Before each 14-week program is rolled out, the category manager holds conference calls with grocery and store managers to discuss the new program, the items that are changing, and the items that are being pushed.

Stop & Shop works hard to align its assortment and merchandising with not only the needs and preferences of its ethnic shopper, but it also recognizes the significant appeal of its ethnic offering among its mainstream customers, who are increasingly eager to try international flavors.

In this sense, it has managed to strike a harmonious balance between ethnic merchandising and international merchandising, ensuring that its customers, regardless of nationality or ethnic background, feel comfortable shopping in its stores. Education on mainstream and ethnic international food preferences are constantly communicated at store level, so there is an incentive to merchandise accordingly. Currently, each store focuses one full aisle to ethnic offerings, with continuous progress also being made across its perishables departments.

Stop & Shop's category manager uses store level quantitative data from IRI, ACNielsen, and the U.S. Census to drive desired action internally and to measure performance. With the support of internal IRI and Spectra Marketing representatives, it has set up special filters and formats so the data can be sent to each store on a quarterly basis. The data is also presented to highlight opportunity gaps. One such data example might indicate that rice is up 15 percent, while the market is up by 25 percent. This is used to show that the respective division is actually lagging the market by 10 percent.

These types of reports are run for all ethnic products across ethnic stores to show individual store performance across ethnic products from one quarter to the next and from one year to the next. So far, the results show that sales at some stores are up significantly, with ethnic products driving the business. The ethnic category manager has successfully used this type of performance data to generate remarkable receptivity across the organization.

When volume for specific items is low, the data once again serves to explain the pattern. For instance, when certain nationalities are concentrated around a few stores, then the item is only merchandised in those stores. Competitive buying patterns are also used to support new product introductions. The retailer recognizes that, while scan data is helpful, it is only directional when looking at Hispanic numbers. This is why they watch their competitors closely, focusing on low-cost operators' assortments and price points. Then they use best-in-class operations as benchmarks.

This competitive research is coupled with insights from manufacturers and distributors and is used to gauge market movement for products. After a while, a feel for the market is developed, and competitor displays and shelf presence become good volume indicators for new products.

This knowledge is critical because many items that drive the ethnic business sit in different category desks (e.g., rice and beans are part of the main meals desk while oil is on the enhancers desk), so ethnic business managers work closely with respective category managers and buyers to get the items that drive their business authorized. For instance, based on the knowledge about these items, they are pitched to respective category managers by the ethnic buyer, and then the buyer negotiates the deals directly with brokers and distributors. The deals are then taken to each category manager for authorization.

Stop & Shop has a very strong private label brand, especially in New England. The retailer believes that its private label offers consumers quality at a value that is only available at their store. The same philosophy is being applied to the growth of its Hispanic private label, *Mi Casa*. Yet each division and operating company had to be sold on the opportunity in order to capitalize on the buying power.

Mi Casa has evolved steadily, with the first product introduced at the end of 2002. The company started by looking at its highest volume items in the ethnic area, which were mostly commodity items like rice, dry beans, oil, and canned beans. The assortment has been expanded to about 75 SKUs (stock-keeping units) in 2005.

Beyond relevance, Stop & Shop decides to add products only if the product can be obtained at a cost that is significantly lower than the national brand. Other considerations include decisions around critical mass to justify central warehouse distribution versus direct store delivery. While Stop & Shop still sees opportunities for improvement in its private label business, *Mi Casa* has outperformed anticipated sales performance goals by tripling sales since its introduction.

Assigning ethnic products to a category manager rather than having a stand-alone department indicates Stop & Shop's commitment to its ethnic business and it aligns with the way the company operates. At Stop & Shop, there are a lot of eyes on the ethnic category expecting it to perform, not only to build top-line sales but also to run many of the stores in economically depressed areas profitably.

The goal of the ethnic category management team is to attract the ethnic consumer who is not currently shopping at Stop & Shop into its stores through key ethnic categories and then encourage the customer to shop the rest of the store. In this sense, the team's objective—to market the total offering at store level—is not unlike the goal of other category managers. In perishables, this means increasing ethnic variety and quality while staying cost-competitive and relevant to its ethnic and core customers.

The Results

The results have been nothing short of astounding. In 2004, ethnic category sales and profitability saw significant growth over 2003, including double-digit same store sales growth while also increasing gross profit dollars—quite a sales trend, considering impressive 2003 over 2002 all-around sales and profitability growth results.

6

EXTERNAL ASSESSMENT III: THE CONSUMER

As Chapters 4 and 5 covered macro and industry trends and the competitive environment, this chapter will break down the various consumer dimensions of the external assessment.

As discussed in Chapter 1, the Hispanic market has undergone explosive growth, and projections for future growth are dramatic. But only those Hispanics who are category users or potential category users will matter to your organization. Understanding the demographics, category and brand development, attitudes and values, and psychographics of these Hispanics is critical to determining the answer to the most important question to you and your company: What is the size of the opportunity today, and what is its potential size one, three, and five years from now?

This chapter explores the first part of that question. The more difficult—though not impossible—question to answer is, how much of that opportunity can you expect to capture moving forward? The answer depends on the external environment and your company's ability to align itself to do business with this consumer by creating value that gives your organization a sustainable edge over others. Pretty straightforward, yes, but not always easy, which only heightens the importance of the up front assessment.

This chapter also provides useful data sources to address questions on demographics, category and brand development, attitudes and values, and psychographics of Hispanic consumers. An example of questions that should be considered a foundation for understanding this consumer is included in Table 6.1. Specific questions depend on your industry as well as category life cycle and development among Hispanics.

DEMOGRAPHICS

The U.S. Census Web site, http://www.census.gov, should be your first stop to obtain a full understanding of Hispanics' demographic profile. The U.S. Census Web site is a comprehensive source for basic characteristics of the U.S. Hispanic population. The site has powerful tools that allow you to run a variety of standard and custom tables and to generate maps based on demographic characteristics for trading areas anywhere in the United States and Puerto Rico (see the Appendix for samples of tables corresponding to key demographic questions).

Are There Any Hispanics in My Trading Area? Where and How Many?

The Census site will allow you to define the Hispanic population for any geography from the entire United States down to the block level and even around a specific address. As you begin, you'll want to run data for each state, market, ZIP code, and Census tract where you have retail locations or retail customers that sell your products. This is a first step in creating your umbrella segmentation scheme to define Hispanic store sets or clusters.

Also, looking at the data for an entire market will help identify geographic areas within the market that have high concentrations of Hispanics, but where you may have no presence; this is particularly important if your competition does have a presence in those areas.

Once you have defined the Hispanic concentration for the markets in which you operate and for your individual trading areas, add up the total. When you compare this number to your competitors, it will give you a relative sense for your market reach and how well you are positioned to compete for these consumers from a market presence standpoint.

TABLE 6.1

Understanding the Hispanic Consumer

Demographic	Category Development	Attitudes and Values	Psychographics
Are there any Hispanics in my trading area?	Are Hispanics involved with the category?	What values and attitudes do they hold that may impact category decisions?	What culturally relevant values and attitudes do they hold about life in the United States that may impact category decisions?
How many are there?	Who in the Hispanic household consumes it?		
Where are they exactly?	Do they have brand preferences?		What culturally relevant interests do they have that may impact category decisions?
What are their general characteristics? • Foreign-born vs. U.S.-born • Country of origin • Length of U.S. residence • Language ability and use • Media language • Household composition	• How do they use it? • How much do they use? • How often do they use it? • How often do they purchase it? • Where do they buy it? • How much do they spend? • Can consumption be increased?		
What are their category-specific characteristics? • Age • Children in the household • Income			

Source: 2002 Yankelovich Hispanic MONITOR.

For example, you may find that of Chicago's 754,000 Hispanics, who make up 26 percent of the city's total population, your locations only provide market access to only half of this population. So your total market reach becomes 377,000, or 13 percent of the market, rather than 754,000. You may find that your competitors have access to a greater or lesser proportion of the market's Hispanics.

Taking this one step further, each individual trading area should be assessed for Hispanic market density. Is your Hispanic reach comprised of a few locations in high-density areas or is it made up of many locations with low Hispanic concentrations? This is important because Hispanic density in a given geography is an acculturation driver, so the lower the Hispanic concentration in a trading area, the more acculturated Hispanics in those areas are likely to be, and vice versa. This same assessment should be done for your competition. You may find that although their market reach may be higher than yours, they may be in locations where Hispanic density is low and therefore not as well positioned to capture the market as you might be.

What constitutes high or low concentration? A good rule of thumb is to look at the total percentage of Hispanics in the market and that becomes your baseline—areas with higher Hispanic concentrations are considered high and those with concentrations below that percentage are considered low.

A second step to the segmentation process is to stratify the high-density locations even further. For instance, if you have 30 locations in areas that have Hispanic density of 44 percent or higher in a market that is 40 percent Hispanic, you may want to stratify them and create tiers (as shown in Table 6.2).

This framework allows you to plan for the type of operational alignment that will coincide with the stores' demographic and acculturation requirements.

What Are the Demographic Characteristics of Hispanics in My Trading Area?

Foreign-born versus U.S.-born. Demographic characteristics are critical to determining acculturation levels of Hispanics in your trading areas as well as those of your competitors. Defining what proportion of the Hispanic population was born outside of the United States is one of the most crucial factors because it is a valuable indicator of category experience. Hispanics who are foreign-born have a completely different view of life in the United States than those who are U.S.-born. But category involvement, attitudes, and values will vary dramatically, as will their cultural tendencies and degree of adoption of U.S. culture. This is especially true if they arrived in the United States in their teen years or older after values, attitudes, and behaviors are well-formed.

TABLE 6.2
Hispanic Store Segmentation

Tiers	Trading Area Hispanic Concentration	Store Base
Tier 1	70–95%	Stores #59, 24, 29, 69, 91, 61, 19
Tier 2	55–69%	Stores #89, 54, 87, 65, 96, 74, 97, 29, 39
Tier 3	44–54%	Stores #5, 7, 9, 56, 78, 23, 54, 58, 69, 63, 47, 12, 13, 95

On the other hand, U.S.-born Hispanics' view of life in the United States and their place in it is shaped by the location where they were born and raised, as well as historical, social, and political influences and their impact on individual experiences within U.S. society.

Generally speaking, once foreign-born Hispanics decide to stay in the United States, they want to fit into mainstream society while at the same time retain their cultural identity at home. U.S.-born Hispanics are Americans and want to be recognized as such. They believe it is their right to be unconditionally accepted into mainstream society and to enjoy all opportunities afforded to Americans—above all, respect.

This dynamic drives a wedge between the two groups. One outcome is that U.S.-born Hispanics often feel disdain for foreign-born Hispanics because they believe that their place in society is compromised by the stigma that Hispanic immigrants have in the United States. For example, many U.S.-born Hispanics of Mexican descent in the west and southwest—especially in California, Texas, Arizona, and New Mexico—have experienced racism and prejudice for decades, despite the fact that a good proportion are second-, third-, and even fourth-generation Mexican-Americans. Although their whole life and history have been experienced in the United States, they often have been confused with and treated like immigrants who, according to some, "have no right to be in the United States" or "are in the United States illegally."

A company needs to know the length and type of history experienced by Hispanic consumers in their trading areas or risk unintentionally offending them with efforts that are culturally and linguistically irrelevant. From an operational perspective, the alignment strategy necessary to target U.S.-born Hispanics will differ dramatically from one that is created to target foreign-born Hispanics.

Country of origin. Related to U.S.-born or foreign-born characteristics is country of origin. In Chapter 1, we covered in some depth how different U.S. Hispanics can be based on their nationality, and even nationality doesn't tell the whole story behind cultural heritage or race. So first ensure that you know the country of origin for your Hispanic target. Once you know nationality, make sure you understand the cultural context of country of origin and how that country's various ethnicities have influenced their culture. Recall the examples in Chapter 1 of Afro-Cubans and Chinese-Peruvians. You also want to know where in the country Hispanics are from. This tends to determine level of sophistication with product categories. After finding out the proportion of Hispanics from a given country (see the Appendix, U.S. Bureau of the Census), you'll want to contact the consulate for that country and determine its regional concentration in your market. Mexico, for instance, has 32 states with vastly different histories and cultures driven by geographic characteristics, climate, economic strength, proximity to the U.S. border, concentration of indigenous population, rural-versus-urban characteristics, and so forth. All of this impacts behavior and preferences.

Length of U.S. residence. Another key acculturation driver is the length of time Hispanics in your trading areas have lived in the United States. In general, the longer Hispanics have lived in the United States, the more acculturated they are, and vice versa—to varying degrees, of course (see Table 6.3). However, as discussed in Chapter 1, a market with a high Hispanic density tends to insulate Hispanics, and this slows acculturation across a variety of areas. The key thing to remember is that there is no template that can be applied to acculturation when it comes to drivers such as length of residence—only parameters that may overlap. In order to accurately assess your market's level of acculturation on your product category, you must look at a cross-reference of demographic and category data, which we'll discuss later in this chapter.

Language ability and use. Language usage is a third acculturation driver, but use caution with this one. English language abilities or usage in situations that require speaking English doesn't automatically imply that Hispanics are not still tied to their mother tongue or culture. When Hispanics learn to speak English, they do not necessarily abandon Spanish. Rather, English becomes a functional tool that is used to fit in with a non-

TABLE 6.3
Acculturation Segments by Length of Residence

	Unacculturated	**Bicultural**	**Acculturated**
Length of U.S. residence	10 years or less	10–20 years	20+ years

Hispanic social group, including qualifying for and carrying out a job, socializing with peer groups, or even attending school. It does not mean that Spanish stops being the language of comfort. In fact, even when Hispanics learn to speak English, Spanish is still spoken in the home at least some of the time. In many instances, Spanish becomes a ticket for reentry into the Hispanic world of family, friends, and culturally relevant social activities. It is a source of connection. This is true even among the young echo boomers, who are primarily U.S.-born and increasingly English-dominant. Although Spanish-language fluency may be poor among much of this group, culturally relevant social occasions still require speaking Spanish and many find comfort in doing so or at least in hearing Spanish spoken by friends and family. The Census provides data on various levels of English-speaking ability among the Spanish-speaking population by gender and age group. The Simmons National Hispanic Consumer study, which surveys English speaking and Spanish-speaking Hispanics in the contiguous 48 states, includes questions on language usage in the home, outside the home, and language preference that can then be cross-tabulated with media, category/brand, and attitudinal data from the same study. Simmons disproportionately samples Hispanics in eight DMAs (Designated Market Areas) to provide analysts with sufficient samples for drill-down capabilities in the top Hispanic markets. It is possible to even map areas in a market or markets based on language usage.

Media language. Media language is a sign and a driver of acculturation. On one hand, Hispanics who are more acculturated tend to consume more English-language media, though because a strong connection to Latin music remains, a high number of acculturated Hispanics regularly listen to Spanish-language radio. They listen to formats like contemporary ballads and *rock en español* (Spanish rock), while less acculturated Hispanics tend toward more traditional formats similar to country music for non-Hispanics. The drivers to format selection among Hispanics are similar to how non-Hispanics might segment across mainstream radio stations, with more progressive and alternative music being more appealing to upscale markets, while country, top 40, and classic rock appeal to the masses.

Young Hispanics in particular listen to both English-language and Spanish-language stations, but television is viewed primarily in English. Much of this viewing behavior is content-driven. They simply find more relevant content on English-language television; it is content that aligns with youth culture in the United States, so psychographic segmentation of your target plays an equally important role in media selection depending on your target segment.

Media as a driver of acculturation is also an important consideration because it exposes Hispanics to U.S. culture and will drive changes in attitudes, values, and, perhaps ultimately, behavior. Less-acculturated Hispanic males are typically more likely than Hispanic females to venture into English-language television viewing, while kids are an enormous force and influence on family English-media consumption. A variety of research tools measure media language and provide good insights relative to category and attitudinal and behavioral statements. The Simmons National Hispanic Study, the Yankelovich MONITOR Multicultural Marketing Study, Arbitron, and ACNielsen are all very useful tools for understanding Hispanic media consumption across a variety of measures and can be helpful in defining target market profiles and their size in a given trade area, set of areas, or markets.

Other Demographic Characteristics

Other measures that can be obtained on the U.S. Census Web site that are acculturation drivers and good discriminators of acculturation when segmenting Hispanics in your trading areas include household income, household composition, educational attainment, age, employment status, presence of kids, and vehicle access. All of these variables help to accelerate acculturation, with kids in the household and employment outside of the household being the most impactful drivers. Kids create a very powerful bridge between culturally traditional homes and behavior they see and experience outside the home. And as mentioned, media—especially as it impacts children in the household—becomes a huge influencer and is often the catalyst to new products and services entering a Hispanic household for the first time.

Employment status is often a significant accelerator, especially for women. Once Hispanic women enter a work environment for the first time in the United States, they are exposed to new behavior and thinking from coworkers and bosses. Eventually, they start to adopt similar behavior and attitudes, if for no other reason than to fit in and survive. The bottom line is that once kids and adults start to function outside of the home, the process of acculturation accelerates as they willingly adopt certain aspects of American culture, while fiercely resisting others that run counter to entrenched value systems.

CATEGORY DEVELOPMENT

Are Hispanics Involved with the Category?

The question of category development is the first to answer when assessing the size of the Hispanic opportunity. In addition, you want to understand whether category usage was developed in the United States, or if Hispanics in your trading area arrived to the United States as category users.

If category usage existed in countries of origin, then likely brand awareness and preferences are also at least somewhat developed. If category development occurred in the United States, there may be loyalties to the brand that took leadership in developing it.

If the category is underdeveloped, it implies that you are in a position to develop the category first and the brand second, and you will pave the way for those brands that may enter the market in reaction to your initiative.

When defining category incidence, one of the best sources for obtaining overall spending on a category is the Bureau of Labor Statistics (BLS), http://www.bls.gov, which publishes the *Consumer Expenditures Annual Report*. This survey will show you how well developed a category is among Hispanics versus other consumer groups, including the proportion of household income spent across all categories (see the Appendix).

The survey is published in report form and includes three types of tables: (1) actual spending, (2) share of spending and aggregate spending, and (3) share of aggregate spending by year. The site also allows easy creation of customized data tables going back several years, which facilitates analysis of yearly consumption patterns and can be looked at in absolute terms. It can be used to analyze consumption trends among Hispanics versus non-Hispanics. This trend data can also be used as a basis for three-year and five-year projections.

An example of trend data for Hispanics versus other consumer groups for food consumption is shown in Figure 6.1. The chart shows how, on average, Hispanic households have outspent all other households on food consumption at home between 1999 and 2003.

Like U.S. Census data, these tables can be copied into a spreadsheet for further analysis and charting. This trend data can also be used to project category growth. If the category is underdeveloped, a more aggressive growth factor might be assigned. If it's well developed or mature among Hispanics, the growth factor might reflect moderate to slow growth.

Once a sense for where a category fits within overall Hispanic spending patterns and how it has trended for at least the last three years, secondary consumer research should be sourced to define category usage by specific demographics and other variables.

Compared to just five years ago, today there are several syndicated market studies available that measure Hispanic consumer behavior across hundreds of product and service categories and thousands of brands. These studies have robust samples, and the topics and areas covered extend significantly beyond what one company might be able to cost-efficiently explore in a proprietary study. And, because these studies offer flexibility to run survey data based on customized demographic and behavioral characteristics, it is possible to gain a multidimensional understanding of a company's Hispanic target relative to the category, its brand, and competing brands. As such, it is far better to first mine and model the data provided by these studies before prematurely fielding proprietary studies. Fielding proprietary studies will be much more productive when used to explore or test a specific market, product, or branding scenario once these have been developed.

Beyond category, brand, and behavioral data, most of these studies also cover attitudes, values, psychographics, and lifestyle questions often related to specific categories. And a couple of the studies also provide

FIGURE 6.1
Average Annual Food at Home Household Expenditure, 1999–2003

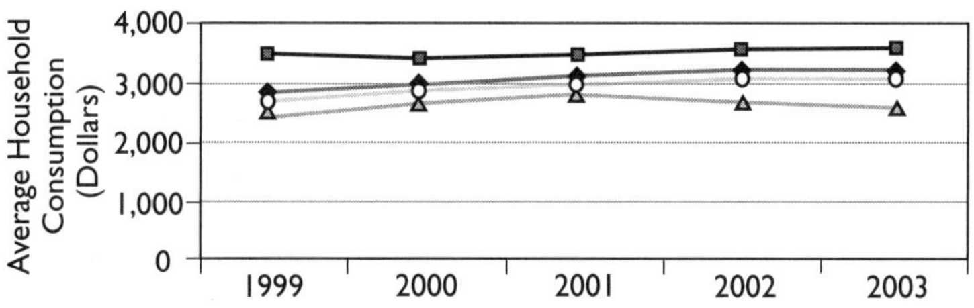

	1999	2000	2001	2002	2003
◆ total population	2915	3021	3086	3099	3129
■ Hispanic	3556	3498	3551	3643	3597
▲ black	2665	2691	2804	2669	2639
○ non-Hispanic	2854	2977	3039	3047	3056

very useful and detailed segmentation models. In general, these studies can be used quite successfully to obtain a solid understanding of how Hispanics are engaging with various product categories.

For instance, let's say that your bank hypothesizes that its target market for checking and savings accounts is foreign-born Hispanics. You might request financial category questions be run by foreign-born Hispanics or, more specifically, if targeting those who don't use banks, the profile might be Hispanics who have been in the United States ten years or less and who wire money outside of the country.

If you work for an automotive manufacturer and believe that Hispanics represent a growth opportunity, you could request data run by all Hispanic households and ask to see the data based on a variety of demographic and industry-specific variables. This will allow you to identify the proportion of Hispanics who own cars and their demographic profile, the percentage who purchased their last car new or used, and which profile is more likely to buy new or used. Lastly, you could run the percentage of Hispanics who intend to buy a new car within the next 12 months along with their demographic profile. You could also run the make of cars currently owned by Hispanics to obtain a sense for preference of imports versus domestics and the Hispanic profile that favors each.

Several studies provide the variety of data just described (see descriptions in the Appendix). Depending on the category, they include the Simmons National Hispanic Study, Spectra HispanIQ™, Yankelovich MONITOR Multicultural Marketing Study, Ciudad Hispana de Scarborough, and ACNielsen's Hispanic Homescan.

The Simmons National Hispanic Study is an excellent source of category development intelligence. The study measures usage incidence for 450 categories and more than 8,000 brands in the top eight Hispanic DMAs with a total sample size of more than 7,000 Hispanics. And the data can be compared to their total database of more than 24,000 respondents.

What Type of Hispanic Household Consumes the Category?

All the studies mentioned above include extensive demographic questions, so the profile of your category household user can easily be defined across several geographies. This enables you to identify which markets would represent category opportunities.

In addition, Spectra's HispanIQ™ study marries its census-based geo-demographic software with U.S. Census and Simmons demographic, category, and brand data, so you can easily define where your target profile exists at any geographic level—or analyze the profiles of Hispanics in your trading areas to determine which match the target profile. Spectra uses its Culture Point Model™ tool to measure similarities and differences in the behavior of Simmons study respondents and defines household profiles (based on acculturation) that buy a given category in a given trade area.

You could also profile a list of trading areas based on acculturation segments and category usage in order to define the penetration level of a category and how well the category indexes among Hispanics compared to total market.

Using the Simmons database, let's say you work for a dairy company and you want to know the market opportunity for yogurt. Based on a full year's worth of 2004 and 2005 data (see Table 6.4), Simmons indicates that, among foreign-born households with kids, yogurt penetration is 67 percent, or 4.53 million households, while penetration among the total study sample is 52 percent. You conclude that Hispanics of this demographic profile overindex the total market by 29 percent in yogurt consumption. You also now know the total number of Hispanic households of selected profile criteria that consume your category.

How often do they purchase/consume it? Using the same respondent profile, you can determine consumption frequency for the same yogurt example. The data indicates that 95 percent of foreign-born Hispanics with kids in the household ate some quantity of yogurt cups in the past 30 days. This compares to 89 percent for the total sample, or an index of 107.

Do they have brand preferences? Once you have established category penetration, you'll want to determine if brand preferences exist. Again, Simmons is a strong tool for defining brand usage incidence. You can easily get a read of yogurt brands in the categories "Used Most," "Used Also," "Any Brand Used," "Sole Brand Used," and "Primary Brand Used" among your target profile. Using the yogurt example and the same Hispanic profile of foreign-born Hispanics with kids, brand usage can be identified for the top yogurt brands in the country. For instance, the data indicates that 1.76 million households eat Yoplait, representing 99 percent of the target households.

However, you can also define the mean number of servings in the past 30 days for Yoplait (9.23 servings) to obtain the total volume of 16.28 million servings per month.

How much do they consume? Determining total consumption is critical to sizing up the total opportunity. We just saw an example of how to derive consumption volume for a single brand; now we'll calculate it for all projected households that use the category. So, of 4.53 million category user households, the average number of servings consumed in the past 30 days for all brands was determined to be 8.37, which comes to 37.87 million total servings per 30 days. Given that the database from which this average is taken is based on a full year's worth of data, it can be assumed that seasonality, if any, has been considered in the average. We could then estimate yearly consumption to be 454.49 million servings.

TABLE 6.4
Yogurt Volumetrics

Yogurt Volumetrics

Yogurt Volumetrics NCS/NHCS: SPRING 2005 ADULT FULL YEAR UNIFIED (MAY '04-MAY '05) Copyright SMRB 2005 Hispanic Foreign Born with Kids						
Yogurt Brands	**Elements**	**Weighted Sample**	**Mean Volume[2]** **Mean*Brand**	**Volume**	**Volume Share**	**Market Share**
Total Sample	(000)	4,525	8.37	37,874,250		
Suncrest	(000)	65	15	975,000	2.57%	1.5%
Stoneyfield Farm	(000)	71	14	994,000	2.62%	1.5%
Yo Crunch	(000)	158	14	2,212,000	5.84%	3.4%
Trix	(000)	353	13	4,589,000	12.12%	7.1%
Lucerne	(000)	105	13	1,365,000	3.60%	2.1%
Light'n Lively	(000)	146	13	1,898,000	5.01%	2.9%
Colombo	(000)	199	12	2,388,000	6.31%	3.7%
Tropicana	(000)	384	12	4,608,000	12.17%	7.1%
Breyers	(000)	282	12	3,384,000	8.93%	5.2%
Dannon	(000)	1,173	10	11,730,000	30.97%	18.2%
Other Brands	(000)	675	10	6,750,000	17.82%	10.5%
La Yogurt	(000)	779	9.5	7,400,500	19.54%	11.5%
Yoplait	(000)	1,764	9.23	16,281,720	42.99%	25.2%
					170.50%	100.00%

Simmons
An Experian Company

How much do they spend? Total spending can be derived by multiplying total consumption volume by an average unit price. In this case, let's assume that a conservative average retail price for a cup of yogurt is $0.50; the total estimated dollar volume could be estimated at $18.9 million monthly, for all category user households, or $4.19 average monthly spending per category user household.

While this represents a broad look at the size of the opportunity, this exercise can be replicated for any service or product category and by any geography; by a specific demographic profile such as, in this case, foreign-born Hispanics with kids at home; or even by retail channels shopped by Hispanic yogurt consumers. Note that these numbers are for illustration only.

Where do they buy? Both Scarborough and Simmons have extensive data on shopping channels. Using this data, you can determine how many times your Hispanic target shops certain retailers. It is also possible to find out which type of channel is preferred by Hispanics—

FIGURE 6.2

Victoria's Secret Shopper Attributes: Identifying the Hispanic Market

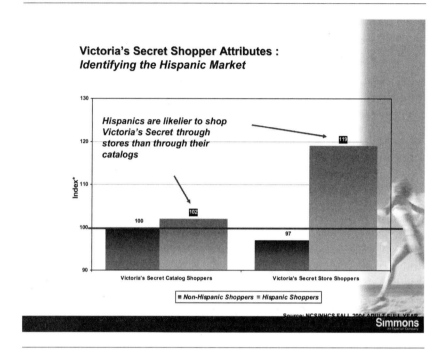

bricks-and-mortar locations, catalogs, online, and so on (see Figure 6.2) for different types or product categories. Knowing this will help you determine the areas within your distribution channels where focus should be placed to service this consumer.

Another excellent resource, especially for the grocery industry, is ACNielsen's Hispanic Homescan. This is the first household-based panel service that provides a complete view of Los Angeles Hispanic purchasing behavior and diagnostic information. It is a truly representative sample of the entire Los Angeles Hispanic market balanced on household demographics and acculturation variables, and is a continuous reporting of actual—*not claimed*—purchases from all outlets since February 1999. The tool includes measurement of consumption across channels and includes grocery shopping behavior among Hispanic households, including coupon usage.

Can consumption be increased? Several of the measures we've discussed will determine if consumption, shopping frequency, or purchasing can be increased. The first involves identifying distribution gaps. Comparing your product's distribution to distribution channels shopped by target Hispanics and whether or not you are in the locations Hispanics shop will identify how much access they have to your product; the second measure is offer relevancy; the third is the buying experience; and the fourth is category and brand development and behavior.

For instance, if you work for a restaurant, defining where Hispanics eat out most often should lead you to understand whether their behavior is driven by accessibility, customer service, eating occasion, or food offerings. Addressing improvement opportunities in any of these areas potentially aligns your business with Hispanics' needs, values, and behavior.

ATTITUDES AND VALUES

What Values and Attitudes Do Hispanics Hold That May Impact Category Behavior?

Aside from straight behavioral insights, understanding Hispanics' values and attitudes around a category will aid understanding of decision-making drivers for your products and services, and they can be the richest source for identifying how well a company's offering might align with what the market values.

For example, if a segment of the Hispanic population is fearful of incurring consumer debt, this will clearly impact how and if a financial services company targets them with credit products. One company may see an opportunity to educate and make inroads, while another may decide to de-emphasize credit product opportunities in their business case and financial model.

In addition, it is important to understand Hispanics' values and attitudes across a variety of dimensions and product categories. A broader understanding of how Hispanics think will help explain the reasons behind their attitudes and values around products, services, brand information sources, and shopping channels (see Figure 6.3). Though this is not new information, many managers have tunnel vision in analyzing His-

FIGURE 6.3

Attitudes and Opinions about the Internet

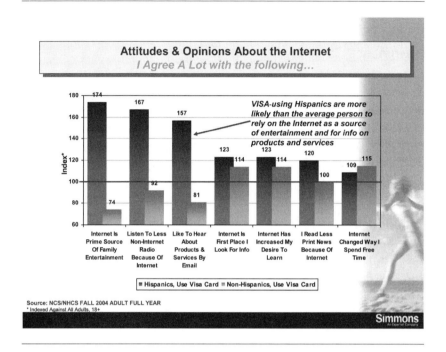

panic attitudes and values, seeing only their own business, and then end up asking "Why?" about every aspect of their behavior.

The Simmons National Hispanic Consumer Study and the Yankelovich MONITOR Multicultural Marketing Study are both very robust in terms of the battery of value and attitudinal statements measured among U.S. Hispanics—many of which are related to specific product and service categories. Again, the opportunity for understanding the relative importance of these values and attitudes can be seen across a variety of Hispanic profiles. For instance, you might find that users of a certain brand of pet food are more open to trying new products, which might signal to management that this type of consumer may be more open to the company's brands and products, and help the team frame the opportunity among this consumer in another way.

PSYCHOGRAPHICS

What Culturally Relevant Values and Attitudes Do Hispanics Hold about Life in the United States That May Impact Category Decisions?

Psychographic insights complete the picture for understanding Hispanics and their relationship with a company's category. An examination of social and lifestyle dynamics is critical because they drive changes in Hispanics' attitudes and values over time. For instance, understanding the importance among immigrant parents to give their kids a quality education has led to a significant increase in computer penetration in Hispanic households.

Also, the value placed on passing down culture and tradition to children inspires parents to maintain behavior around traditional food, music, and religion, and has led to an ever-growing ethnic food industry comprised of domestic Hispanic manufacturers, Latin American manufacturers, and mainstream manufacturers worth over $50 billion in 2004. These same cultural values, as mentioned earlier, have created a multi-million-dollar Hispanic entertainment industry in the United States that cuts across all aspects of entertainment—music, concerts, movies, and radio and television programming in Spanish.

What Interests Do Hispanics Have That May Impact Category Decisions?

How a company creates value for a consumer has as much to do with the intangible as it does the tangible benefits of its offering. If you understand the types of interests held by your Hispanic target and the activities in which they engage, you will begin to see how and why certain products and services become priorities in their lives. With the Simmons study, you can define all the activities in which a category or brand user engages (see Figure 6.4). This information can be leveraged to define what is important to this consumer in his or her daily life, as well as some aspects of behavior.

Another great source of this type of insight is the Yankelovich MONITOR Multicultural Marketing Study, which includes culturally relevant

FIGURE 6.4
A Day in the Life . . . of Category/Brand User X, Complete List of Activities

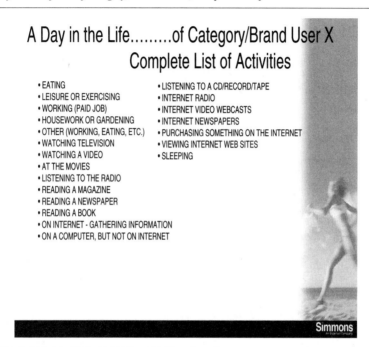

measures across key aspects of life, including self, ethnicity, trust, religion, leisure, consumer tendencies, and money. The Simmons National Hispanic Consumer Study also includes a significant battery of statements on leisure activities and hobbies, sports and fitness, life milestone events, gambling and lottery, as well as attitudes, opinions, and interests across a variety of subjects, including technical, personal finance, diet and health, media, political outlook, self-concepts, and shopping behavior.

Also useful is the 2002 Yankelovich Hispanic MONITOR Lifestage segmentation scheme. This segmentation scheme can be very helpful in understanding relevancy across the life stages of this consumer. The four life stage segments are "Young Progressives"—youth segment, "Home Builders"—young couples with and without children, "Home Hearted"—mature couples with and without children, and "Prime of Life"—seniors. The study provides very insightful profiles for each of these segments (see Figure 6.5).

FIGURE 6.5

Hispanic Dominant Young Progressives—2002 Yankelovich Hispanic Monitor

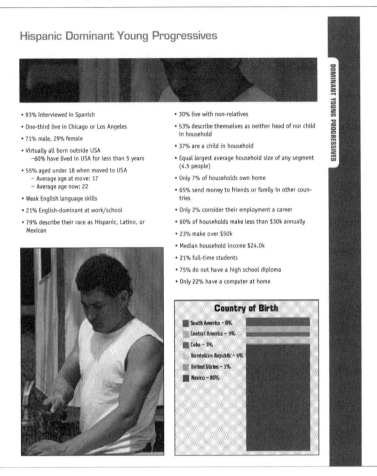

Hispanic Dominant Young Progressives

- 93% interviewed in Spanish
- One-third live in Chicago or Los Angeles
- 71% male, 29% female
- Virtually all born outside USA
  −60% have lived in USA for less than 5 years
- 55% aged under 18 when moved to USA
  − Average age at move: 17
  − Average age now: 22
- Weak English language skills
- 21% English-dominant at work/school
- 79% describe their race as Hispanic, Latino, or Mexican

- 30% live with non-relatives
- 53% describe themselves as neither head of nor child in household
- 37% are a child in household
- Equal largest average household size of any segment (4.5 people)
- Only 7% of households own home
- 65% send money to friends or family in other countries
- Only 2% consider their employment a career
- 60% of households make less than $30k annually
- 23% make over $50k
- Median household income $24.0k
- 21% full-time students
- 75% do not have a high school diploma
- Only 22% have a computer at home

Country of Birth

- South America – 0%
- Central America – 5%
- Cuba – 3%
- Dominican Republic – 5%
- United States – 1%
- Mexico – 80%

DOMINANT YOUNG PROGRESSIVES

The four life stages can be analyzed within the context of acculturation, with detailed profiles about each one, but again the beauty of this study is that you can run these segments by category-specific characteristics. For example, suppose a money services company wanted a deeper understanding of its money transfer customers. The company initially looked at the Hispanic-dominant segment, but when the data was run based on the proportion of Hispanic-dominant young progressives who wire money out of the country, instead of looking at it based on the total sample, a different, more specific profile emerged.

Having a multidimensional understanding of this consumer can aid your understanding of what your Hispanic targets value and how they will behave, so you can align your organization's offerings around what is important to your target Hispanic segment. This can help define the future potential of your product, which will lead to more confident projections of market potential.

CASE STUDY: WALGREENS

Walgreens operates nearly 5,000 stores in 45 states and Puerto Rico and has three mail-order facilities. While Walgreens has fewer stores than its closest rival, it is number one in the nation in sales. Prescription drugs account for more than 60 percent of sales; the rest comes from general merchandise, over-the-counter medications, cosmetics, and groceries. Walgreens builds rather than buys stores so it can pick prime locations. Approximately 80 percent of its stores offer drive-through pharmacies, and almost all offer one-hour photo processing.

Recognizing the size of the Hispanic market in the sun belt where its stores are concentrated, Walgreens decided to analyze the Hispanic market several years ago, but its Hispanic efforts are not grounded on having a Hispanic program, per se. Rather, understanding the Hispanic opportunity is and always has been about implementing its corporate strategy to achieve its objective of becoming the neighborhood store in any neighborhood, including Hispanic neighborhoods.

As such, Walgreens's assessment work to understand the Hispanic market stems from its need to understand all its customers' needs. Walgreens's major point of differentiation among nearby direct competitors—supermarket pharmacies and mass merchandisers—is not to be the type of store that is everything to everybody. Rather, the assortment is very selective and is based on the customer shopping patterns. This is how Walgreens leverages customization to attract all consumers, including Hispanics, to its stores.

Walgreens aligns with its corporate strategy by understanding Hispanics' buying patterns in Hispanic trading areas in order to merchandise the right items at the right levels to avoid stock outs, and minimizing items that don't sell well in Hispanic stores.

Importantly, upper management recognizes the need to understand this customer, and the U.S. Census helped to cement that among its management group. Knowing exactly what type of Hispanic neighborhoods exist and where they are located helps to drive upper management's customization strategy because it aligns with the company's commitment to become the neighborhood store.

The Assessment

Walgreens started its assessment work in 2001 using a tool called Basic Department Management (BDM). The goal was to use this tool to increase local customer loyalty by using customer insights to create stores according to the local customer buying patterns, regardless of culture or nationality.

The BDM system capabilities allowed Walgreens to create blueprints for merchandise allocation that helped it maximize sales and customer satisfaction by taking every category and doing a yearly review to make improvements. This analysis resulted in store groupings according to customer insights and sales patterns.

This new method of category management was a huge improvement over past methods. For instance, prior to BDM, hair-coloring products would be merchandised in exactly the same way in every store, with the lighter shades at eye level and the darker shades on the bottom shelves. BDM allowed the retailer to see that, in their Hispanic stores, darker shades outsold light shades, and this led to the creation of different merchandising plans for Hispanic stores that better met the demands and buying tendencies of this customer. Because of information BDM provided, Walgreens also increased emphasis on pediatric goods in Hispanic stores, where volume of such good is much higher and, consequently, assortment is much broader.

BDM also helps the retailer assess space allocations and assortment affinities, and this extends to Hispanic-oriented products. Walgreens has evolved category management from a single-minded approach to looking at the whole store by tailoring the merchandising of Hispanic and non-Hispanic items.

The Implementation

Every Walgreens store has a core assortment, especially the pharmacy, but management's goal for Phase I of its strategy implementation was to ensure that every department used the BDM system. This resulted in Hispanic store clusters for which specific assortment plans were created by category.

In Phase II, the retailer tested the Hispanic merchandising plan in a Corpus Christi, Texas, store, which was basically a Mexican market store layout. To fine-tune it, they conducted an even deeper study of the neighborhoods in the trading area. Its position was that the plan it had brought to the market was only a foundation, but that in order to truly deliver value, it had to go beyond that. So it customized the merchandising by closely observing the customers walking in the store. Its findings led them to seek and include more ethnic labels across the store as part of the market strategy, especially in an expanding consumables area.

It added several more Hispanic items, thereby building on the BDM model on a specific store basis. Walgreens also changed signage to include bilingual aisle markers, bilingual announcements, and bilingual music.

"Many of the Hispanic beauty products have been very successful for us," said Ysa Mayorca, manager of customer segmentation. "We're also seeing Hispanic beauty product lines that are crossing over to mainstream consumers—much like what we are seeing in food—and I think we'll continue to see that."

Phase III included an analysis and understanding of which departments needed to be upsized. This presented a space challenge, so it also had to find categories for downsizing. For instance, in the diaper category, training pants sales are virtually nonexistent because in the Hispanic culture, kids are potty-trained at a much younger age. This meant that Hispanic stores simply did not carry this item, thus freeing significant shelf space. Walgreens also analyzed profit per foot to confirm which departments could be downsized and to what extent.

Once Walgreens found an opportunity and tested it, the opportunity was turned over to a category manager. By doing this, the retailer has also been able to plan a total store package that includes Hispanic categories not typically carried by the retailer, such as party favors, baby clothing, piñatas, and strollers. Walgreens uses external research resources such as

IRI and ACNielsen and syndicated research to understand product movement.

Walgreens has also taken its pharmacy offering to another level of service. It has a consultation window staffed with bilingual pharmacists or pharmacist assistants, and there is a bilingual 800 number available for questions. Its prescription labels can be printed in 19 languages, including Spanish. Information about the various health conditions also can be printed in Spanish.

The company takes a team approach to its category management and is able to analyze store activity and understand the dynamics of a category on a general level, much like a brand manager.

However, in order for the group to understand the ins and outs of why Hispanic stores behave a certain way when it is conducting its analysis, the team relies on the multicultural group to help fill in the knowledge gap. This enables the category manager to understand the consumer perspective and the reasons behind purchase patterns.

"You really need to understand the 'why' behind the sales patterns," said Mayorca. "There is tremendous advantage in having a department that understands its customers regardless of cultural background with expertise in Hispanic, African-American, or Asian so we can really do this right. When you have brand managers or category managers looking at sales and wondering what is going on—it really is so hard for them to understand until they hear the soft side from someone who really understands the cultural drivers for these customers."

Walgreens has transported the Corpus Christi test to other markets with the support of district and regional managers. Some markets have always been ahead in targeting this consumer, but with corporate management encouraging it, achieving acceptance and implementation performance is much easier.

The Results

Walgreens is confident that its strategy works for its business. The company's key financial indicators reflect it. Walgreens is seeing the return on investment across all of its stores by making sure that it has the right items in the right stores at the right levels. The benefit has been strong, and customer satisfaction has increased dramatically.

At the store level, Walgreens has seen increases in every metric, including the number of shopping trips to its stores, market share, and same store sales increases.

Departments that were expanded have been growing across every item. Walgreens has also learned from mistakes and successes and continuously rolls out what it has learned to a broader store base and to other markets. The retailer feels that although what it has done has required a significant amount of effort, it's been focused on meeting the needs of each customer rather than on simply becoming an ethnic retailer.

CASE STUDY: DENNY'S RESTAURANTS

Denny's is the leading full-service, family-style restaurant chain in the United States, with about 1,600 locations nationwide. Its restaurants are typically open 24 hours a day, seven days a week, serving breakfast, lunch, and dinner.

Denny's has survived a very difficult decade that saw its image tarnished by a racial discrimination lawsuit, bankruptcy, and a challenging reorganization. Now Denny's is working to regain its strong positioning with a focus on excellent service and quality food, and Hispanics are seen as an integral segment of its target audience. The company is working on repositioning its brand among Hispanics who have been customers in the past, as well as Hispanics who may not be as familiar with the restaurants.

The Assessment

To do so, Denny's underwent a rigorous market research process to identify how users of family restaurants identify with the brand today. It was critical that Denny's reconnect with these consumers' dining-out dynamics and determine if and where Denny's fit in with consumers' recent and future restaurant choices.

Denny's discovered that its brand awareness was very strong, and that, especially among non-Hispanic consumers, the brand's concept as a family restaurant was clear. Most notably, it discovered that a strong sense of nostalgia was felt for Denny's, rooted in positive past consumer experiences. It was clear to Denny's management that the emotional connection was intact, and that with the right value proposition, consumers could be convinced to come back and give the brand another try.

This research process helped refocus the brand and create a positioning statement called "Abundant Value." Denny's found that this concept spoke to all the value drivers important to restaurant consumers in this segment, which includes expansive menus of reasonably priced, good quality American food served in a comfortable, clean, warm, and hospitable environment. And it found this value proposition cut across consumer nationalities and language ability.

Denny's learned that it was possible to deliver value to everyone through its core concept—that staying true to its concept of a sit-down restaurant that serves American food did not compromise the appeal of its offering among Hispanics. "Hispanics are looking for the same value drivers as general market consumers—a good, comfortable place where they can bring the family and enjoy tasty, quality food without spending a lot of money," said Margaret Jenkins, senior vice president of marketing and franchise development and chief marketing officer. And Denny's understood the common appreciation consumers have for a restaurant where kids are welcome and where it's "OK to spill food on the floor."

This was a significant finding for Denny's, not only because it has many restaurants in Hispanic, Asian, and African-American communities, but also because it allowed Denny's to stay true to its Abundant Value offering without having to create ethnic menu items. In fact, Denny's confirmed that its niche and point of differentiation was the ability to deliver predictable flavors that do not surprise or disappoint and that are considered "comfort food."

Of particular appeal to Hispanic consumers—as well as general consumers—was the family orientation of Denny's restaurants and their ability to cater to kids through an economical children's menu. This served as a catalyst for Denny's to immediately restructure its entire kids' presentation. Similar insights among other consumer segments led to a fine-tuning of its seniors', late-night, and its more traditional breakfast, lunch, and dinner menus—all of which cater to various consumer segments during different times of day.

With this learning in hand, and having done the groundwork of making people feel welcomed and accepted in the restaurants regardless of age, cultural background, or time of day, Denny's set out to reinforce its Abundant Value proposition through marketing.

The Implementation

Market research with Spanish-speaking Hispanics confirmed that Abundant Value resonated strongly in spite of little or no history with the restaurant. The challenge was therefore to address low familiarity with the brand and its positioning. Denny's Hispanic marketing focused more on brand-attribute education, with an emphasis on the sit-down, family orientation. Communication would reflect the family meal experience while simultaneously delivering Abundant Value through visuals of food preparation, finished plates, and price points.

A continuous tracking of consumer sentiment is in place now to ensure that expectations are met consistently across all customers. In addition, Denny's regularly conducts geodemographic analyses of its restaurants to ensure merchandising and staffing alignment with the customer groups it serves. Finally, Denny's regularly conducts in-store interviews as a basis for a yearly segmentation study, which feeds the company's understanding of consumer groups across the various times of day.

The Results

Denny's analyzes its sales activity on a total company basis and also breaks down its analysis by Hispanic and non-Hispanic store clusters to assess the relationship between sales, marketing efforts, and the results of consumer tracking studies. To date, Denny's has seen continuous improvement with its Abundant Value proposition across all consumer segments, including Hispanics. Denny's has managed to win over Hispanic consumers while staying true to its brand position and by identifying with and delivering on basic consumer needs rather than through tailored product delivery.

7

THE INTERNAL ASSESSMENT

GETTING STARTED

The internal assessment process addressed in this chapter is about looking internally at a company's resources, including its locations, human capital, knowledge base, capabilities, skill sets, technology, culture, and financials—essentially, the areas on which the business depends for its competitive advantages and profitability. This part of the assessment is critical to determine the readiness of not only front-end infrastructure and processes, but also to ensure that back-end operations can support servicing this segment. In the process of developing your assessment proposal and action plan, identify individuals within the organization who are involved in managing the company's resource pool to support the assessment process. Ideally, recruit managers who can provide input on their areas—how they function, as well as how their part of the organization contributes to the company's competitive edge and how it could adapt to cater to a new market segment while maintaining the integrity of its operation within the company's business model. Some of these areas may not be direct consumer touch points, but they are areas from which support is necessary in order to integrate the strategy into the company's operations. Ultimately, the goal is to work with individuals who can provide the internal perspective on how the company's business model plays out in their particular area. This understanding will serve as the foundation for assessing the viability of a Hispanic market strategy and will be what you build on to develop action plans that align with corporate, operational, and financial objectives.

Understanding your company's vision for where it wants to be in the future, its mission for the type of business it is in today, and its business objectives is a first step. The importance of reviewing annual reports and SEC filings from at least the last three years, suggested in Chapter 2, can't be stressed enough. This will help you understand how the company sees its various business units, regions, divisions, and departments, and how it represents their future state to its shareholders and employees. Pay special attention to the language used in the CEO's letter. This is useful because this language can be used to frame the meetings and interviews you will have with internal management as you start to look internally. As you go through your process, remember the importance of concentrating on the big picture. It will speak to your focus on total company growth and how Hispanics might contribute to it. This focus must be clearly articulated in every meeting you have with management and even within the assessment team. If the internal organization understands that linkage, they'll also understand the impact of not conscientiously pursuing at the very least an assessment of the opportunity.

A thorough review of marketing materials is also important. Here, I refer specifically to corporate marketing, especially materials related to investor relations. This information will give you insight into how the company sells itself externally. It will also tell you if, within your company's business model, Hispanics have access to what your company is selling.

An observation could be made that if they do not, the company is falling short on its customer promise and its values. Understand where your company stands on diversity issues and the programs, alliances, and commitments it has in place to ensure that diversity is part of the company's way of doing business. This assessment will also tell you whether the company has mechanisms in place or the potential to touch its Hispanic target through its diversity efforts, as well as how those efforts are communicated to community stakeholders, such as Hispanic community leaders, Hispanic media, and community-based organizations. This could be a source of considerable strength when developing a strategy that depends on supplier, distributor, and employee diversity. You will come away with a good sense of the company's espoused corporate values and whether the company's current implementation matches what it promotes internally and externally.

The internal assessment process holds a mirror to your company's values, promises, and objectives and assesses company practices and their relevance to U.S. Hispanics. If your company were expanding its business to Latin America, wouldn't the way the company does business in the United States need to adapt to the political, regulatory, cultural, and general business models and protocols observed by companies doing business in these countries? The answer would be yes, of course. So what your assessment needs to determine is how—not *if*—your company can leverage its strengths and minimize its weaknesses to align itself to serve diverse populations in the United States. The reality, however, is that most corporate cultures view external change as threatening while others view it as a challenge that requires immediate response.

What you should keep in mind during this process is the importance of maintaining a total business mindset by: (1) making sure you understand the business context in which you frame your assessment—corporate strategy; (2) aligning your assessment with the beliefs, values, and practices that your company upholds—in essence corporate culture; and (3) finding the nuggets within these areas that will help you ask the right questions and obtain answers from key stakeholders.

Ultimately, a large Hispanic population and significant Hispanic buying power is great, but if your assessment and business case don't align with the company's business—where it's been, where it's going, and how it plans to get there—obtaining full support from your leadership and internal organization will be difficult, if not impossible—people with bottom-line responsibility always want to know what's in it for them or how it will impact them because, ultimately, their rewards are tied to overall performance.

THE INTERNAL AUDIT

If your company culture is closed, reserved, or politically charged, internal audits are typically best handled by a third-party consultant. Even if not, you may be better off conducting the audit with a consultant who is experienced in the process, knows how to phrase questions, and is an objective party with no vested interest in any outcome or disclosure. Internal interviews are typically conducted in person, so developing familiarity and rapport between those involved early in the process will be advantageous. If using a consultant, it will be best if those who will be interviewed during this process have an opportunity to meet the consultant during the kickoff meeting or informally during one of the up-front project planning meetings.

Avoid telephone and Internet interviews. A high level of face-to-face contact increases trust, comfort, openness, and accountability between you and the consultant and the executives being interviewed. And, if people involved know the consultant is traveling to meet on site at a certain time, it is less likely that the interview will be rescheduled or canceled, which keeps the project moving forward.

Try to keep visits and interviews informal. Frame these meetings as work sessions during which you are seeking insight and understanding. Other people within respective departments should be allowed and encouraged to join if this adds educational value. Take advantage of being on site to tour facilities, plants, and store locations. Even if you have seen it a hundred times, those involved will find it helpful to look at the operation through the filter of servicing a new customer group. If you require specific data, product samples, ads, or a location tour, make the request in advance and in writing so all elements are prepared in time for the meeting.

Depending on the area, it is important to survey two or three people at different levels of a department because often management in a department has idealized views of the operation based on how it ought to be rather than how it really is. However, the people who work in these areas often have more realistic views—they are either more likely to hear about problems or challenges, or are on the front lines and experience the challenges and problems firsthand. As such, they are eager to share these issues and shed light on challenges of adding to or adapting a process or, conversely, to share specific strengths that can be leveraged to do so. They often also have insights into competitive comparisons that can be useful.

Take a banking organization and its branch network, for instance. Interviews should be conducted with the retail operations vice president, a regional manager, a bank manager, and a customer service representative.

Like any other important meeting, next steps, dates, and persons responsible should be clarified. If an interview has taken place in an area that does not have representation on the assessment team, this may be a good opportunity to ask for that manager's support by appointing him or a fairly senior person with ready access to his director and to relevant data to join.

Advise interviewees that follow-up data requests may be forthcoming, as it may be necessary to request additional fact finding and data crunching to help calibrate that area's alignment cost estimates for the financial analysis and implementation plan later in the process. And there will be questions resulting from insights gleaned as others in the organization are interviewed.

For instance, after several interviews across different operational areas at a bank, it became clear that hiring more bilingual employees and adapting operations would be necessary and would be a major cost component. So retail operations was asked to survey Hispanic branch employees on their Spanish-language abilities and then to calculate the number of new potential hires, the areas where the hires were needed, and salary levels. They were also asked to estimate additional costs for operating later on Saturdays and for opening on Sundays in certain branches. Human resources was asked to investigate whether competitors were compensating incrementally for bilingual abilities, to provide costs for producing additional training videos in Spanish, and to estimate the time and costs to add an additional training session for management on cultural sensitivity.

On the transaction side, retail operations was asked to define the number of Hispanic account holders and determine market share by level of acculturation versus the total market. It was also asked to calculate revenue contribution by Hispanic account holders based on the three levels of acculturation identified for its bank branches during the site analysis. Marketing was asked to investigate production costs for marketing materials based on recent spending on English-language versions and was asked to prepare for an alternative distribution concept and price elasticity test.

These are just a few examples of the internal fact finding that must occur to assess the company's readiness and alignment costs. The findings are ultimately summarized by the consultant. A high level of sensitivity must be exercised when sharing results. Firstly, insights obtained from interviews should not be attributed to specific individuals, and those who participate should be told this to increase their willingness to share more openly. Further, assessment insights must be framed within the context of strengths and weaknesses to help the company identify its critical issues and the critical success factors that will feed the Hispanic strategy development process. It is critical to avoid implying that current internal weaknesses that may impact exploiting the company's strengths in the Hispanic market are problems or that there is anything wrong with current operations.

THE APPROACH

The manner in which you assess your internal organization should mirror the approach in Chapter 5 when we looked at the competition, though you will obviously be able to go into much more depth in terms of your operations. Your focus should be on the company's strategic resources or those areas on which the business model depends—where they are today and where the gaps are. According to Slywotzky and Morrison, business model design depends on three pillars: strategic, operational, and organizational dimensions. These are the areas on which you want to focus to ensure that the required learning is achieved.

Product Assessment

When you think about your product line or the services you offer, first define how your company defines its value chain for its current customer set. What is your company's compelling proposition? Is it low cost, innovation, speed, customization, customer relationships or service, differentiation, niche/specialty, high quality, or something else? Then overlay what you have learned from the competitive and consumer assessment process to identify commonalities and differences in what the Hispanic consumer values and the value you deliver to current customers.

Use these insights to create possible product and service concepts and use these scenarios as talking points with R&D, manufacturing, distribution, sales, retail operations or customers, HR, IT, procurement, customer service, marketing, logistics, and finance. Emphasize assessing how your products compare and whether your value proposition is relevant. If there are gaps, discuss how the company can recreate relevant value while remaining within the scope of its value proposition. Do you have or can you obtain the in-house expertise and capabilities across your value chain to adapt and maintain a competitive edge with minimal disruption to the core business model? Keep in mind that if you disrupt the business model you inadvertently propose being in another business and impact your company's profit potential. Of course, it's entirely possible that a given market scenario may imply having to redefine a company's business model if Hispanics are expected to drive your company's future growth, as in the case of Minyard in the Dallas market (see Chapter 3). More often than not, however, this is not the case. A good ROI from your Hispanic strategy will depend on not upsetting your company's strong suit or those things that it does better than anybody else, which might be in supply chain, technology, strong distribution channel access, inventory control, manufacturing, sourcing, R&D, and so forth. This will lead you to two important questions: (1) do the differences in what Hispanics value impact your ability to deliver the same type of value under your current operating model? and (2) will the incremental business you expect to get or the business loss you expect to offset in the future compensate for the additional expenses and changes? The answers to these questions will help you define the scope of your offering and the scope of your consumer target—will it include Hispanics and if so, which segments align with your product scope? The interdependency between these two questions is clear and basically gets at what business you are in and which Hispanic customers will allow you to profit with your current business model. This is not to say that a company should not consider diversifying its offerings through an acquisition or another division or subsidiary, but doing so requires a long-term ROI outlook.

R&D and Manufacturing

Understand your organization's R&D and manufacturing capabilities, process, and technology. Does your company have the know-how and technology to adapt existing products or create new formulations relevant to Hispanics? Can your plant accommodate a potential new product line or an adaptation of an existing one without losing efficiency? What would it cost to produce additional products outside of the company's current scope? How long does it take to go from research and development to manufacturing? What resources does it require? Is outsourcing to a specialty manufacturer a better option? What might be some outsourcing options?

Identifying capabilities, skill sets, and costs scenarios in this area will impact strategic decisions about whether to buy or adjust equipment to meet new manufacturing needs or whether to outsource production or even whether the company should consider acquiring a small manufacturer already producing what you want to offer. In some cases, a decision to outsource manufacturing may be less disruptive, more cost-efficient, and will avoid the need to develop or hire in-house expertise. Obviously, an internal cost analysis should drive the best way to proceed if faced with new product development needs. In assessing internal capabilities here, you also want to take into account whether the company has the financial strength that would enable it to take advantage of outside partnership opportunities if required.

Distribution Channels

Operating dimensions consider relevant product access. By now, you are quite familiar with relevant distribution channels for your product category from your assessment of the channels competitors are using to make products accessible to their Hispanic targets. This may be one of your strong suits and you may have tremendous market access to distribution channels or your own distribution network.

Explore your existing go-to-market strategies and determine if distribution needs to be expanded to include other relevant channels, and the resources and costs related to doing so. What kind of a sales force will you require? How will it fit into the overall sales organization? What will it cost?

An assessment for a consumer packaged goods (CPG) company wanting to enter the tortilla manufacturing business came to a screeching halt after discovering that in high-demand markets, corn and flour tortillas require direct-to-store delivery (DSD) daily and even twice daily because Hispanics, unlike mainstream consumers, do not buy refrigerated tortillas. DSD-type distribution represented 40 percent of the cost of doing business, and because the company operates from a central warehouse, the type of distribution required for tortillas would have required realigning its distribution model. Such a change would have been fine except that the expected sales revenue would not have been enough to offset the costs, let alone be profitable.

In another situation, a bank trying to attract Hispanics was challenged to define a distribution model that would allow it to move with the industry toward greater automation while still being relevant to Hispanics' high-touch banking preferences. The bank decided that it would designate several of its branches in high Hispanic density areas as "high touch" branches, but emphasize education on the convenience and safety of using the Internet and ATMs to conduct transactions in their marketing. Industry trends indicated that competitive banks were moving toward debit cards for their basic checking and savings and those banks were taking a lot of one-on-one time to educate new Hispanic account holders by playing up the benefits of shopping and accessing their money in this manner. The bank expects that Hispanics will acculturate to greater ATM usage as this trend continues, but in the meantime, it adapted to align with current market behavior.

Sales

Share what you've learned about the distribution model with your sales force and discuss options for expanding distribution channels. Pose the possibility that expansion may mean targeting local Hispanic retailers or alternate channels. Ask about how current retail customers might react to a new product line; how retail customers might react to the company's expanded distribution plans; whether the sales organization has the capacity to handle the demands of selling-in a new product that is targeted to a new consumer segment to new and existing retailers; and whether the sales organization currently includes Spanish-fluent persons in target geographies. Nationality and language can become big obstacles to selling-in product to Hispanic retailers among whom relationships are important for doing business.

Take the case of a large CPG company with an extensive and sophisticated sales organization. During its assessment, it discovered that unacculturated Hispanics were more likely to shop in neighborhood supermarkets where the company had minimal distribution of its products.

It realized that in order to effectively reach that market, the company needed to extend its distribution to small independent grocery stores, which accounted for 40 percent of category sales. Upon surveying a sample of those retailers, it found that many spoke a good amount of English, but preferred to speak Spanish with most of their vendors because it provokes a greater sense comfort, trust, and openness—all critical aspects for relationship building.

It also learned that smaller retailers feel ignored by large CPG companies and because of language barriers, there is rarely open communication. Retailers added that even when the person calling on them is Hispanic, there is sometimes a non-Hispanic speaker as part of the sales call, which inhibits openness. Understanding these types of nuances requires companies to demonstrate a greater sense of cultural sensitivity when working with Hispanic businesses.

There also was another large CPG company with considerable knowledge of Hispanics' shopping, cooking, and eating habits. While its marketing organization has access to a wealth of analytical resources, its sales force lacked the necessary knowledge to gain credibility with mainstream retailers. This affected the company's credibility when trying to gain shelf space for a new line of Hispanic products.

Another CPG sales force tried to convince retailers that its brand and product portfolio has strong equity in Latin America and, as such, would do well among Hispanic consumers in the United States; however, retailer interviews revealed that the sales force had no knowledge of the company's Latin America successes or the products that would most likely appeal to U.S. Hispanics.

These examples illustrate the importance of assessing culturally relevant sales resources and distribution channels and the importance of Spanish-language communication and cultural relevance, even on a business-to-business level. But key to the point of the assessment is reconciling how you continue to excel in customer relationships and service, especially if it's one of your strengths. How do you maintain this standard as you expand to market-relevant channels while maintaining or increasing profitability?

Retail Locations

Site analysis, discussed in greater detail later in this chapter and again in Chapter 8, is a key consideration when assessing and analyzing your retail operations with respect to Hispanic consumer and market presence. Your competitive site analysis will reveal your current retail locations relative to those of your competition and your situation may or may not be optimal. If it is, it clearly gives you a competitive advantage.

If access to this market population is reduced based on the geographic locations of your stores, the reality is that even if you do everything right, your impact will be limited to Hispanics within those few trading areas of the store as a percentage of all Hispanics in the market.

If that represents 10 percent of the market's Hispanics, then those are all the Hispanics who have access to your locations. If your competition's share of market access is greater, it clearly puts you at a disadvantage, and in the absence of relevant retail presence, no amount of advertising will be effective in driving customers to your stores if they are far away unless your value proposition is so strong that Hispanics are willing to drive longer distances. This was the case for one financial services company in Los Angeles whose customers drove an average of 10 to 20 miles to do business with them because they are a trusted Mexican brand. In this case, this company had almost universal brand awareness and a strong image for which people were willing to travel. This is an example of a sustainable market advantage.

However, this is not a typical case. To compensate for low market presence with standard storefronts, you may need to explore alternate distribution channels, which we mentioned earlier in the context of market relevance. Here it is a matter of creating access. A bank in the Midwest faced with less than optimal market presence tested kiosks and store-within-a-store concepts in Hispanic retailers and successfully created a relevant presence in Hispanic communities through these channels. The costs of creating this type of retail presence would need to be carefully calculated by your real estate organization, and again, the question of impact on your strategic strengths would need to be assessed.

These are important considerations because physical locations are the preferred channel of distribution for most Hispanics. Keep in mind that while online shopping is growing rapidly, this is still from a relatively smaller base. Most commercial Internet activity among Hispanics is geared toward information gathering and price comparison. Acculturation-related factors contribute to this, including a lower rate of credit card ownership and a higher preference to use cash as a method of payment. As banks push debit cards instead of checks, this behavior will evolve.

Whether or not you have a significant presence in Hispanic communities, the issues of efficiencies and logistics to adapt a smaller set of stores must be addressed. Separately, the issue of sales expectations must be considered and tempered based on the reality of your total market reach. Your assessment in this area should also include aspects of retail operations such as which stores can be considered your Hispanic set. Do you stratify even further within that set, and if so, how? How relevant is the merchandise mix, signage, store circulars, collateral and POS, staffing, customer service, and store layouts?

Consider that Spanish-dominant Hispanics prefer to pay bills in person rather than through the mail and they also like to address customer service issues in person, so ask yourself if larger customer service or bill payment areas are necessary. A recent competitive analysis of wireless stores revealed that wireless market leaders understood this and reflect this understanding in their store layouts through large customer service areas that are almost half the size of the store. Hispanic-oriented supermarkets understand the importance of perishables among Hispanics and reflect that in store layouts that maximize the space allocated to produce, bakery, deli, and meat departments while minimizing the space allocated to center store.

An example of further stratification within Hispanic branches to drive operational strategies is a bank in the southwest that found its branches could be segmented into unacculturated, bicultural, and acculturated Hispanic branches. Its implementation around staffing, merchandising, hours and days of operation, and product focus was tailored to the needs of branches serving this segment.

Human Resources and Training

The human resources organization is a critical area for any assessment process. Once you go into the marketplace to assess the local competition, you will no doubt have an idea of the role bilingual staffing plays in the competition's operations. Before you approach HR, have a good idea of which organizational areas will require bilingual staffing. The questions for HR include sources and methods of identifying, interviewing, hiring, training, compensating, and retaining Hispanic employees at every level of the organization. Work with your HR organization to assess current recruiting, training, and retention processes to calibrate Hispanic strategy needs against organizational relevance. Ask what sources of staff are being used by competitors to find bilingual and experienced employees.

Discuss new ways of sourcing bilingual employees to fill the need. Define employee profiles and existing hiring criteria to see if there are gaps and challenges to address. In some industries, criteria may need to be modified in the interest of having Hispanics on staff. For instance, it may be preferable to have Spanish speakers even if their industry experience is less than what is typically required and even if their English skills aren't great. An assessment of where English skills are critical must be conducted as well as one of where the trade-off benefit of not hiring people with perfect English skills exists.

If HR doesn't have internal resources to assess the language proficiency of candidates, discuss outside consultants or organizations as a solution. Also, explore resources necessary to understanding immigration issues in case you need to import talent. For instance, Wal-Mart recently brought management from Mexico operations to the United States to help optimize U.S. operations, including Hispanic market strategies.

Discuss current training methods, including the need for creating and conducting job training in Spanish. Additionally, training to educate and sensitize non-Hispanic employees is always required when hiring and managing employees with different cultural backgrounds. Explore whether the company has the expertise in-house or whether outside consultants are required to create training modules. In "Working on Common Cross-Cultural Communication," DuPraw and Axner point to six fundamental patterns of cultural differences in communication: (1) differences in communication styles, (2) attitudes towards conflict, (3) approaches to completing tasks, (4) decision-making styles, (5) attitudes towards openness, and (6) disclosure and approaches to learning. Explore HR's and managers' awareness of and capabilities to recognize and address these differences in training and performance monitoring.

The organization's position as an equal opportunity employer also lands on the shoulders of HR, so assessing HR's ability to design a system to track minority hires at all levels and to track and promote their advancement within the organization may be necessary if it doesn't already exist. Requirements and costs for potential hiring, training, tracking, and retention practices for new and existing Hispanic employees will need to be developed very carefully with the help of various departments where those employees would be placed. If your company's value proposition depends on its human capital, ask the questions that will enable you to define the opportunities to align with this strength.

Information Technology

Metrics will be critical not only during the assessment and planning process, but also in implementation and periodic reporting of results. Work with your IT manager to determine if your systems can track and analyze Hispanic activity. Knowing whether Hispanic activity can be tracked will help determine if Hispanic transactions, sales, and other related measures can be mined. If not, and your ability to assess Hispanic customer base performance depends on it, this should become an area of considerable focus and brainstorming. Ensure an understanding of necessary metrics in areas that support the Hispanic strategy and ensure that systems are set up to deliver them.

You'll also want to pull in your Webmaster to discuss the possibility of a Spanish-language version of your site and what needs to be considered in terms of maintenance support. If you have a Spanish-language site, conduct a thorough review of your Web site content and discuss communication flow process for alignment between marketing and online services. Ask your Webmaster to provide a Web site traffic flow analysis to determine how Hispanic visitors enter the site, where they come from, how they navigate through the site, where they linger and for how long, and where they exit. Knowing this will be valuable in strengthening content, functionality, and intuitiveness of the site—and more important, it can help you measure traffic flow and site effectiveness.

If you do not already have a Spanish-language version, determine what pages ought to be in Spanish and the costs and timing for creating a Spanish-language version within the current site. Remember, while all Hispanics may not be purchasing online, many are, and others are shopping for information on products in which they are interested—it's about creating access. If technology is what gives you the service or efficiency edge that drives profitability among your current customers, make sure you understand how that might translate in the Hispanic strategy.

Procurement

Understand your supply chain and how it is managed. Is your supply chain a source of strength? Ask about how suppliers are sourced and authorized. If your product mix needs to be expanded to be relevant and competitive, ask questions about RFP processes. Are current vendor expectations realistic when considering minority vendors? Review requests for proposals—do they allow smaller companies to qualify? It may be that procurement is used to having vendors come to them. However, identifying, qualifying, and working with minority vendors may require going out into the marketplace and identifying them. Additionally, the company may need to partner with smaller suppliers and teach them how to do business with a large buyer. Minority suppliers may not have the capacity to supply the quantities required, so you may need to invest in growing your supplier so they are able to supply you at the required levels. One international food retailer on the east coast invested in a supplier's baking operations so that vendor could supply all of its Hispanic stores. The company knew that investing in their supplier would give them a valuable, costly way to imitate sustainable advantage. Explore the company's experience with importers, specialty distributors, and wholesalers. As specialty retailers and manufacturers seek international options to maintain a competitive advantage among Hispanics, the bar is continually raised and Hispanic consumers will expect those items on mainstream retailers' shelves and racks. If you're a manufacturer, understanding this competitive pressure should help you think about whether current product lines offer the desired customer value.

Customer Service

For many companies, customer service is the competitive advantage that sets them apart. Define Spanish-language capabilities among customer service representatives (CSRs). Determine whether or not the company's automated system is in Spanish and if there is a large enough pool of Spanish-speaking representatives to prevent calls from defaulting to English-language CSRs. Also explore whether CSRs are encouraged to use Spanish when handling calls from Spanish speakers.

When assessing the automated phone system, make note of how soon the Spanish-language prompt comes up. One health care organization complained that the drop rate on their Spanish-language automated customer service line was very high and averaged 150 dropped calls per day.

Once the Spanish-prompt was moved to within 15 seconds of the re-corded greeting, dropped calls fell to less than 100 per month.

Make sure that fluency, accent, and tone of the Spanish-language re-cording is appropriate and note the number of layers Spanish-speakers must navigate on the system before being given the option to speak to a CSR in Spanish. Ensure that the system doesn't reroute the caller to the English-language recording or an English-speaking representative.

During an assessment process of a financial services company in the southwest, it was discovered that it thought it could get around hiring bi-lingual customer service representatives, opting instead to hire the trans-lation services offered by phone companies. It found this option was far from optimal. In this scenario, the caller went through the recorded prompt until an English-speaking representative came on the line. The caller and representative spent the better part of a minute unsuccessfully trying to communicate until the representative left the line to connect the translator while the customer waited on the other end, wondering what was being done to provide assistance in Spanish. Once the transla-tor was on the call, there was the cumbersome and lengthy experience of having a translated three-way conversation. The company experienced many dropped calls and very frustrated customers.

When conducting an assessment in this area, consider that Spanish-language calls take longer—it takes about 20 percent more words to say something in Spanish than it does in English. Also, because Hispanic call-ers often require education as part of a sales process or problem resolu-tion situation, they tend to ask more detailed questions. Call length is a key metric in assessing call efficiency. Knowing that calls with this con-sumer can take longer will naturally require a different evaluation system so that bilingual representatives are rewarded rather than penalized for their language capabilities. In addition, these differences will impact costs, so this will need to be addressed up front.

For instance, one retailer finds that its customer service department receives calls from customers who do not understand the rebate process and call the store to complain after waiting several weeks for their rebate check to arrive. They are made aware that obtaining a rebate is not some-thing that happens automatically and requires action on their part. This illustrates the need for lengthy explanation and, beyond that, how more comprehensive store-level training during the sales process and a better understanding of the consumer experience with the category and product deliver across all dimensions.

Bilingual CSR compensation also needs to be considered. In some industries, being bilingual is considered a skill set and is a basis for higher compensation. One place this was discovered was in the banking industry where bilingual employees, and especially those in customer service, earn $1 to $2 per hour more because of their bilingual skills.

You'll also want to assess whether your representatives not only speak Spanish well, but are also fluent in industry terms. Many times, Spanish-speaking representatives explain a company's services using industry terms in English, which dilutes the explanation and confuses the customer.

Lastly, you'll want to assess schedules and Hispanic call volumes to determine how to staff customer service lines. One wireless telephone company's lack of understanding of Hispanic call traffic led it to omit weekend Spanish-language service on its toll-free number, the highest call volume period among Hispanics.

Marketing and Public Relations

Having assessed the competition's position, you'll want to discuss your company's value proposition and marketing strategy with an eye toward cultural relevance and how it is being communicated. In most cases, a company's value proposition should be consistent regardless of the segment being targeted—the key is to identify the similarities in how the company fulfills Hispanic consumers' needs and talks to their values.

In order to define this, the company will need to explore how its value proposition is perceived and how it comes to life among its Hispanic target. This was addressed in more detail in the external assessment, where the focus is on understanding Hispanics as consumers.

Once you understand how Hispanics relate to your company's products and services, the marketing focus can be more clearly defined, resulting in materials that are in Spanish or bilingual. They might have a creative execution with a culturally different context but that delivers on a single-minded communication strategy.

If your company already produces Spanish-language communications in any form, the content should be analyzed to ensure cultural and product relevancy. And of course, language quality and relevance is critical. Another place one should look is how marketing coordinates with other operational areas that use its marketing materials.

During a recent assessment in the wireless telephone industry, it was observed that while many of the leading companies are producing Spanish-language brochures, few actually made them available on the sales floor in the same way as English versions. In some cases, stores were out of brochures; in others, the brochures were provided only upon request; and in others, photocopies were provided.

The same was true of point-of-sales material, which was rarely seen on the sales floor, even in locations where Hispanic density was almost universal. This clearly demonstrates that these companies lack Hispanic merchandising strategies. Operationally, you want to explore whether it is the store or corporate that controls the on-site merchandising execution, and you want to have retail operation strategies that address how Hispanic communications are integrated. This is where you'll start to see how well the marketing and the retail organizations cooperate to ensure successful execution in Hispanic stores.

You should also look at your advertising strategies. Too often, companies interpret effective marketing communications as choosing Spanish-language media and having Spanish-language commercials, but that is only part of the equation. Media strategies that work in mainstream advertising may be completely wasteful when targeting Hispanics. For instance, if you do not have wide market presence or if access to your product is limited, then you're probably better off communicating through grass roots efforts versus mass media or using mass media selectively, such as directional billboards, radio spots tagged with locations, or cable television that target communities versus a total market. How a company reaches Hispanics should align with how Hispanics use its product category and the way they choose to access it. Because of this, product packaging is a key communication vehicle. Spanish speakers are likelier to find satisfaction with your product based on their ability to read your label and follow instructions in Spanish, but more importantly, it can drive trial. Companies often ask if it is necessary to have bilingual labels because the content of their packaging is obvious. Consider that the content of the package is also obvious to English speakers, but manufacturers still find it very important to design a label that contains a brand message, often highlighting product benefits, usage, preparation instructions, and nutritional information. So, it is just as important to leverage communication on packaging to sell your product to Hispanics at point of sale—the place where most consumers make last-minute brand decisions. A dairy manufacturer recently understood the importance of bilingual packaging when it learned that an overwhelming number of Spanish-dominant and even bilingual women mistake eggnog as a liquid egg formulation rather than the familiar *Rompope*, a Latin America favorite. Consequently, they never thought to buy it. A CPG company learned that repeat purchases of frozen pizza was low because Hispanics were defrosting before baking, ending up with longer preparation time and less than optimal end results due to inability to read preparation directions on the package.

As discussed in Chapter 3, PacifiCare has increased Hispanic membership by 3 percent across products and markets since launching its Latino Health Solutions initiative, including in geographies where total business growth was flat or down. This happened in large part because of their emphasis on a Spanish-language employer group and consumer marketing materials. A sales representative recently reported a case where 100 percent enrollment was experienced in a company with a high Hispanic employee base due to the Spanish-language sales tools, marketing materials, Spanish-language provider directory, and personalized services that the sales representative was able to leverage.

Marketing Research

Given the work thus far on your assessment, you no doubt already have a good idea about the resources and capabilities of your marketing research area.

Explore which existing tools can be used to measure and track Hispanic activities and which new tools need to be incorporated into the mix. Have a conversation about how similar, if not the same, research resources could be used not only to create efficiencies, but also to provide consistency and continuity in internal reporting. Discuss Hispanic studies that are comparable to those used by the company and that may be worth having internally. You'll also want to see the applications for the data that are used most often by the company based on past reports.

Lastly, you'll want to know how your internal sales tracking system can be adapted to capture Hispanic sales. At the very least, stores with a high proportion of Hispanic shoppers ought to be identified so that sales reports can be created, showing the differences between the two groups of stores and the proportion of sales and sales growth contributing to total sales and growth by the Hispanic store set.

In essence, you want to know what exists, whether you can obtain the sources for the measures that are important to your industry among Hispanics, and how much it will cost, not only to have the sources in-house but also to hire analysts who can study and disseminate the data internally in a manner consistent with what management is used to seeing, and, preferably, with a comparison between Hispanic and non-Hispanic results.

Logistics

Assessing logistics can become important in several areas. For instance, it can become important in the area of distribution when a product requires limited distribution in a select number of Hispanic locations. These are cases where it may not be efficient or even possible to distribute from a central warehouse. In these cases, hiring a distributor to handle a select group of locations may be optimal. You'll want to explore compatibility, options, and costs for this method of placing product.

Another example is distribution of marketing materials. It is important to know how Hispanic marketing materials can be integrated into a single system of distribution to facilitate access.

Corporate marketing at one large CPG company produced bilingual point-of-sale materials and stored it in local company warehouses because it thought that would make the materials more readily accessible to the sales force and drive its use. Instead, marketing found that the sales force never pulled the materials from the warehouse because it wasn't used to accessing point-of-sale materials this way. Once marketing consolidated the bilingual marketing materials with the rest and integrated them into its computer-based ordering system, the problem was solved.

Financial

Focus on revenue and profitability. Are sales declining for a specific business unit, region, or division? What's causing that? Sometimes sales decline is created by demographic shifts around a company's retail locations when the company response has been slow. Look at your own company's growth compared to the industry and compared to specific competitors. Then look at Hispanic versus mainstream consumption patterns and volume.

You may have a case for Hispanics representing a disproportionately faster growth opportunity than mainstream consumers and, therefore, a financially sound rationale for aligning the organization to target Hispanics. For instance, the recent low-carb trend led to declining sales across many food categories as companies hurried to formulate products that would meet consumer demand for low-carb or carb-free offerings. Meanwhile, Hispanic attitudes toward carbohydrates remained fairly intact—in Hispanic culture, carbohydrate-heavy foods tend to be dietary pillars—and research conducted among Hispanics during this time found that Hispanics were indifferent to the low-carb trend. This is a good example of a missed opportunity that could have offset sales declines in the food industry.

From a strategic resource standpoint, explore the financial standing for your company and determine things like its ability to make an acquisition or expand manufacturing facilities, the sales force, or its market presence. Financial resources can be a significant strength that few others can imitate, enabling you to take advantage of market opportunities and giving you a sustainable competitive advantage. Conversely, it may limit your ability to exploit market opportunities.

Finance can also provide details on average costs for sales staff, call center, customer acquisition, sales, and all other relevant costs. It is critical to capture all incremental costs of modifying the status quo to implement the Hispanic strategy. In time, the company will become more efficient as it adjusts to the changes, but for at least the first two to three years you must take into account how these incremental costs impact total Hispanic strategy expense in terms of sales and profitability.

WHAT IS THE HISPANIC EXPERIENCE WITH YOUR COMPANY?

After delving into the various facets of your organization, you'll want to find out what Hispanics actually experience when interacting with your organization. Mystery shopping is a valuable approach to learning how well your organization delivers on its intended value proposition across consumer touch points. This process involves selecting the stores or branches where the customer base is predominantly Hispanic. A team of Hispanic shoppers who match the profile of your Hispanic market are selected to visit these locations and interact with your organization in as many ways as possible. These shoppers pretend to be Spanish-dominant, with little English-language skills, and behave as if they are relatively unfamiliar with a category or how it works.

Only the task force members know that these locations will be shopped to ensure that what shoppers find is typical of "business as usual." This process is also a valuable tool used to identify where the competition's strengths and weaknesses lie. When you overlay the findings from your service over that of your competitors, you will see where greater alignment is necessary to be competitive or to seize an opportunity based on a competitive weakness.

This process includes visiting the company's stores and going through the sales and customer service experience with a detailed checklist of the areas to be observed. The shopper arrives at the location and takes note of the parking area and the types of people parking and entering the location. She enters the store and takes note of the number of customers and the mix of gender, age, and ethnicity. The shopper's goal is to experience as much of the sales and service process as possible by asking questions in Spanish that require responses in Spanish across varying service and product areas. In so doing, employees' language abilities are tested within the context of their ability to speak the company's language in Spanish, with ease and in a way that is easy for the shopper to understand.

The shopper will observe employees' tendencies to be helpful and their ability to answer complicated and basic questions and even questions that are out of the norm under the pretension that the shopper has basic or nonexistent experience with the product category. In some cases, the shopper will buy the product, apply for the loan, or sign up for the service for the sole purpose of obtaining an in-depth sense for the experience, procedures, and time requirements of going through a transaction. The shopper also notes the availability of in-language marketing materials and point-of-sale merchandising and will request help from employees to understand marketing materials that are not in Spanish. The shopper will take note of other customers in the store and of the experience they are having. She will note whether Hispanic customers are being serviced with the same quality and attention as non-Hispanic customers, and the mystery shopper will note if Hispanic customers' wait times are longer and if they are experiencing frustration and leaving the store before receiving assistance because of it. When waiting in line or for a customer service representative, the shopper will engage in conversation with other customers to obtain a sense of their experience and how long they have shopped the business. This type of customer intercepting can elicit some very valuable feedback because it integrates ethnographic market research and allows interaction with customers about their experience with the operation in real time and within a realistic context. After observing several stores, the inconsistencies and gaps begin to surface.

The Marketing Experience

The mystery shopper will pick up all brochures, flyers, handouts, circulars, and catalogs made available in store in both English and Spanish, and if none are displayed, she will ask about their availability.

For instance, some companies have Spanish-language marketing materials but only hand them out selectively to people who request them. Other instances include employees who provide black-and-white photocopies of brochures that were once available, but had been depleted; and in the worst of scenarios, shoppers are told that they can only look at a photocopy brochure while in the store because there are none available to give away. Sometimes, as a last resort, employees hand out Spanish-translated Microsoft Word documents with information pulled from the Web site.

The shopper will also note observations about point-of-sale merchandising, including the number of messages being communicated, which are emphasized more than others, the type of point-of-sale materials that are used—banners, counter cards, posters, displays, or decals—and their position both inside and outside of the locations. The ambiance is also noted. Is there music? Is the interaction between customers and employees friendly or curt and to the point? In essence, is the energy in the location one that would make Hispanics comfortable? Photographs are taken of location exteriors, with focus on exterior signage or lack thereof. When possible, interiors shots are taken, as well.

Some retailers go to great lengths to customize the ambience in their stores based on their Hispanic customer base and even based on the acculturation level of their Hispanic customers. This customization includes music, special learning centers in bank branches, children's play areas, large waiting areas, greeters, and other elements that reflect an understanding of the shopping behavior and lifestyle of this consumer.

The shopper also notes if Spanish-language-specific customer service numbers and Web site addresses are referenced or suggested and if there is awareness of their existence. It is often surprising to learn how retail-level employees are unaware of other company efforts to serve and inform this consumer, a clear signal that there are some procedural and marketing training breakdowns internally.

The material that is collected is reviewed for message focus, tonality, imagery—including if Hispanic themes or talent are used—and the quality of the creation of brochures from English to Spanish, specifically how well marketing materials have been conceptualized in Spanish versus literal translations of English versions. These materials are compared to messages on the Web site, messages seen on billboards, and other communications to determine if these various communications efforts are synergistic or fragmented.

In some instances, company press releases announce new products and services, promotions, or partnerships that never materialize at store level. While they are prominently featured on the Web site, the link to the promotional partner is not functional. Worse, a shopper walks into the store asking about these programs, products, or services, and store-level personnel have little to no awareness of them, often denying the availability of the products, services, or promotions, or conveying varying versions of them.

Having insight into how these programs are being implemented and carried out at store level will help you identify key operational areas to discuss and plan the logistics that will ensure full integration and alignment or realignment of your operational execution.

The Customer Service Experience

The customer service line also should be shopped to obtain a sense of the customer service experience over the phone. In order to do this, the shopper dials the customer service number provided on company and competitive marketing materials and Web site.

Shoppers make two to three calls to the company's customer service line and take note of the ease or complexity of navigating the automated system, if one exists. They note the various recorded options they must navigate to arrive at a Spanish-language option.

The shopper opts to go through the Spanish automated system until given the option of speaking to a Spanish-language representative, if any. If the option is given, the shopper will note the length of hold time before being connected to a live representative and the hold music or recording that is heard while on hold, especially whether it is directed at Spanish-speaking or English-speaking customers. Once connected to a live representative, the shopper will engage the representative in an information-gathering conversation under the guise of becoming a customer.

The shopper will note the representative's knowledge, level of helpfulness, and courtesy extended. If the option to speak to a Spanish-speaking representative is not given, the shopper will choose to speak to an English-speaking representative and test how the representative manages the language challenge and whether the representative maintains a pleasant attitude. The shopper will also take note of the time it takes for the English-speaking representative to resolve the language issue and how the call is ultimately handled and closed.

Often, companies who are not set up to handle calls in Spanish simply tell the customer they cannot provide help. Other times, they try to tell the customer in broken Spanish that a third, Spanish-speaking party is being contacted for help—usually this is someone internal but it can be someone in another location.

Other areas to observe are how calls are handled during nonoperational hours. In some instances, no Spanish-language options are provided, and English-language messages regarding operating hours are given, along with instructions to visit the Web site. In other places, the recording is the same as during operational hours, but never leads to a CSR; instead, shoppers are left in a repeating loop until they get frustrated and hang up.

Less-than-optimal, toll-free-number scenarios perpetuate an overreliance on face time with store personnel, they will be challenged to provide more than the typical question-and-answer support to retail customers. Ultimately, you will be able to transition customers, but you are better off not doing so until you have the support of a well-structured customer service line.

The Web Site Experience

The primary reason for visiting the company's Web site is to assess its intuitiveness for Hispanic visitors. The shopper notes the ease with which key information of services can be found and the language that is used, starting with how visibly the Spanish-language link appears on the English-language home page. The visitor also notes functionality of the site and if that functionality is made available in Spanish. It is common to walk through sites where transactions, applications, and even location finders take the visitor back to the English site.

In addition, it is common to see sidebars, navigation bars, and sky boxes left in English, or to see a combination of both English and Spanish—sometimes sky boxes are in Spanish, yet they link to details in English. This only negates their directional intent because the messages being highlighted fail to have the intended impact when the visitor cannot understand them.

As mentioned earlier, an eye is kept for consistency of communication efforts between store, advertising, promotions, and community outreach. Sometimes, when some of this marketing activity is found, it is buried so deep in the site that the likelihood of the consumer seeing it is minimal. If it's there, shoppers find it because they are searching for it, but the consumer is not going to search for your promotional messages.

Also, the shopper will note the quality and tone of the Spanish being used. Often, tonality and quality varies dramatically because different companies or people have worked on the site over time, and no one has been ensuring consistency—this has a tendency to happen with company brochures, as well.

In summary, the following provides a short list of the minimum activity you should watch for when conducting mystery shopping to determine an organization's ability to service Spanish-speaking Hispanics. Some questions relate back to meeting with other areas of your organization and many are equally applicable to assessing the competition.

Retail Locations
- Number of Hispanic employees by branch
- Number of Spanish-speaking employees by branch

- An account of the types and quantities of Spanish-language merchandising and marketing that are produced and sent to stores or branches
- How are these marketing materials developed? What is the coordination that takes place? Who drives it?
- List of branches that receive Spanish-language materials with rationale
- Details of specific training that occurs on Spanish-language activity or the consumer

Customer Service Number
- Number of seconds before Spanish language is heard
- Call volume that opts into Spanish
- Number of calls that are dropped after opting for Spanish
- Number of layers that the caller has to go through before being able to opt for a Spanish-language representative
- Number of times Spanish-language representatives are requested
- Length of hold time on the Spanish-language queue while waiting for a live representative
- Number of times Spanish-language representatives are not available
- Busiest time for Spanish-language calls
- If no Spanish speakers, estimate of times requested for one
- How Spanish-language calls are handled

Web Site
- Traffic on Spanish-language pages, if any
- The manner in which the visitor arrived at the Spanish-language pages—through the English-language home page or an outside link
- The traffic pattern within the Spanish-language site
- How long people stay on each page
- Where they linger
- The length of an average visit
- Whether or not they attempt to make transactions and, when discovering English-only option, whether or not they leave or proceed

SITE ANALYSIS

If your business has retail locations that are your primary channels of distribution, a site analysis is another powerful tool for assessing your position in the marketplace. The analysis focuses on profiling each of your locations in all your markets based on demographics. The goal is to understand the percentage of Hispanics in your trading area within a one-mile, three-mile, or five-mile radius. These percentages are compared to the overall Hispanic density in the marketplace. For segmentation purposes, you can develop an index against the market total that will tell you which of your branch trading areas have Hispanic concentrations that are above the market average, which are comparable to the market average, and which are below it.

Based on these findings, tiers or clusters of stores can be created. You typically will find that Hispanics in trading areas with higher concentrations are less acculturated and, as the density drops, the level of acculturation increases. Because that's not always the case, however, a second step to this analysis is profiling the population around each branch in terms of the percentage of foreign-born versus U.S.-born, length of residency in the United States, and language use and preference. Having this information will allow you to group your branches by acculturation levels of the Hispanic customers who do business in each location.

You also want to know what the collective reach of your locations is in each market versus your competition so you can establish realistic objectives for how much of the market is available to your organization. For instance, the Hispanic population in the Dallas/Ft. Worth metropolitan area is 21.5 percent, or 1.12 million Hispanics.

Let's say that the average Hispanic density around your locations is 10 to 15 percent, and that across your locations you have about 400,000 Hispanics. This would tell you that your market reach is 35.7 percent. This means that 64.3 percent of the 1.12 million Hispanics in the Dallas/Ft. Worth area are outside of your reach and are therefore not potential customers. This finding could lead your company to create alternate distribution channels to increase your reach of the market. Or, at the very least, it will help you calibrate expectations because the Hispanic population universe is smaller that the total market based on the locations of your stores or branches.

When compared to the total market access for your competition, you'll see where the market-presence gaps are, and you'll also know if your competition is better positioned geographically than you are. This becomes yet again another consideration for making market potential projections.

From an alignment standpoint, the implications for customization are many. In the case of products that are distributed through retail channels other than your own, you will want to work with your retail partners to help them mine their data and guide them on the importance of this analysis. Your mutual ability to provide the right product assortment, store-level merchandising, and promotional support will make the difference. Stop & Shop has seen this work firsthand and believes that, according to its ethnic foods buyer, Gabriela de Oliveiras Castro, "[our Hispanic initiative's] biggest successes have been the amazing execution we now see at store level." When the store locations are properly stocked—with appropriate product, personnel, and promotional material—the targeted consumers will respond.

For instance, in the case of cosmetics, you'll want to have Spanish-speaking counter representatives and visitors who run makeup and facial clinics assigned to stores where you sell to primarily Hispanic women. In addition, the emphasis on colors featured in your displays may differ. If you're a CPG, you will want to make sure you have the right product assortment and that you are cross-merchandising with the complementary Hispanic products. You'll want to make sure that shelf talkers, clingers, floor decals, coupons, and demonstrators are culturally relevant and bilingual.

• • • • •

When you marry an analysis of your organization's strengths with a thorough analysis of the environment, industry, and competitive and consumer opportunities and threats, you'll have what you need to assess which organizational resources can be leveraged to capitalize on opportunities and which weaknesses must be minimized to avert the threats. All of this will feed into defining whether your company can achieve profitable growth through a Hispanic market strategy while remaining aligned to its corporate direction. Chapter 8 will address this analysis in more detail.

CASE STUDY: LEADING
MAINSTREAM RETAILER

With a sizable proportion of its stores located in large Hispanic markets, a leading mainstream retailer had over time recognized the size and growth of the U.S. Hispanic market, and while it had attempted to target it, the retailer had never managed to do so consistently. Given the location of its stores, targeting Hispanics should have been a priority, but previous efforts never achieved sufficient traction. In 2004, however, after hearing nonstop requests for Spanish-language marketing support from store directors, corporate finally listened.

The Assessment

At about the same time, corporate had already begun studying the marketplace and found that growth projections for Hispanics far exceeded previous assumptions. It very quickly became clear that the company's future growth depended in large part on developing the Hispanic marketplace. As such, a task force was assigned to develop a formal business case.

To support the business case, the team took several steps to understand its business situation. It conducted extensive analysis of census data and a thorough demographic analysis of the trading areas around its stores to confirm population. The site analysis indicated that certain regional areas included a significant number of stores where the demographics had shifted dramatically and were now heavily Hispanic.

Market analysis based on secondary studies such as Simmons, Yankelovich, Scarborough, and others was conducted to define category usage. The team reached out to industry colleagues and industry experts for insights on best practices for both analyzing and targeting this marketplace, searched out several related market and cultural insight resources, and conducted several rounds of focus groups to explore brand positioning.

Secondary research analysis indicated that overall, Hispanics' category involvement was lower than the national average, but that, as a group, Hispanics' purchase behavior and intent to purchase within the category far outpaced mainstream consumers.

Industry expert interviews were consistent in stressing the importance of understanding and being relevant to the Hispanic culture. To gain a deeper understanding of the culture and market-share potential, the retailer applied an internal model to its Hispanic data, which helped to analyze the data in context of its overall business. Of utmost importance was defining the size of the opportunity from a sales and volume perspective.

Focus groups indicated that brand imagery was very strong compared to the competition, especially among less acculturated, Spanish-speaking Hispanics. This validated the team's theory that it should support the market. It found that Hispanics consistently rated the retailer higher than the competition, which showed to management that because Hispanics intended to spend a significant amount of disposable income on the category, the company was positioned to benefit from this purchase intent.

Using these insights, a formal business case was presented to upper management. From a classic business-case scenario, the team identified the potential volume it thought was available to it and allocated the investment to achieve this goal. The team was committed to champion, fund, and deliver the results.

The Implementation

Several U.S. markets were selected, and stores in these markets were clustered into tiers according to Hispanic demographic thresholds. Census data, which revealed geographic Hispanic concentration, played a strong role in enabling an analysis of sales in Hispanic stores. This led to the development of various Hispanic merchandising packages—including signage, brochures, and other selling pieces—as well as adapting the employee mix to align with store demographics.

Insights about Hispanic culture and the role the company's product played in Hispanics' lives helped shape the retailer's communication strategy. The company learned the importance of making a more emotional connection with the family and how its products related to that.

Early focus was on merchandising implementation—making sure it put the right signage programs in the right stores with care not to overemphasize Spanish.

The team strives to achieve an appropriate language blend for the customers going into the stores and stresses that ensuring the right mix requires extra effort and continuous fine-tuning, with certain stores receiving more bilingual materials at different times. Market selection and material allocation among stores is based on store clusters developed through census ZIP code data analysis. Merchandising strategies vary somewhat based on thresholds, and this drives whether a store receives more or less Hispanic-oriented program elements.

The implementation team works hard to keep the strategy visible to the entire company. It spends a considerable amount of time ensuring that executive meetings include Hispanic strategy updates, including store-level results. In addition, the team makes huge efforts to be in the stores as much as possible, interviewing store managers to learn about what is working well and not so well. Because initial interest came from the retail level, the team works very closely with stores to ensure that the right tools are employed appropriately and that positive store operations feedback reaches corporate management. As such, it does everything possible to keep the stores happy.

Further, the team works well across operational areas such as the store group, which is in charge of the store environment. This group owns in-store signage and brochure development so the team works to ensure inclusion in the development of bilingual signage and brochures.

Coordination with merchandising is also continuously pursued as it selects the merchandise that is carried in store and featured in weekly ads. Adapting the product mix for Hispanics is supported with sales data and the business trends seen at store level. While this proves somewhat more laborious for all involved, focus remains on what the stores ask for.

The team also works with the human resources department to ensure that the stores and internal departments are appropriately staffed and trained. The team works with customer service to make sure it has established a bilingual toll-free number, hired bilingual representatives for Spanish-language customer service, and worked throughout the company to address necessary infrastructure adjustments.

One significant step for the retailer was hiring a dedicated Hispanic manager in charge of procuring constant support across operational areas. As the strategy was being and continues to be implemented, this manager spends a lot of time with internal groups, communicating the strategy and getting buy-in on necessary operational support while sharing upper management's vision for the program.

The team finds that sharing internally makes the strategy tangible and generates excitement about it, often to the point that people now ask about the Hispanic program.

The company also created internal mechanisms to integrate the creation of a bilingual circular into the process. This was a significant challenge, given the complexity of its weekly English-language piece. Now the process includes development of different relevant versions for the Hispanic market.

The team continuously monitors results and ROI goals to address internal performance questions and works to constantly help its internal colleagues see the Hispanic strategy as part of the company's core strategy.

The Results

The retailer has a rigorous mechanism for analyzing sales. It partners with its financial area to come up with relevant ways to measure the data and report the results. It looks at specific store scenarios based on internal models. Sales reporting methodology is consistent with what it does for its overall business. It is a continuous, necessary process to prove that the program is working, but it is the part that drives support from the various internal areas.

The company is still in its first full year of heavy investment, but it has been able to validate the strategy through its financial reporting and, as one manager put it, "good old-fashioned business intuition."

The retailer is pleased with results so far and indicates it is on track with its goals. Being in its first year, management is not surprised to continually be identifying opportunities for improvement—it sees things that are working well and others that need to change. Specifically, it has seen improvement in core objective areas, such as awareness, store traffic, and sales, and corporate management remains supportive and encourages the team's efforts.

CASE STUDY: HARRIS BANK

Harris Bancorp offers financial services through Harris Bank, Harris Trust and Savings Bank, and other subsidiaries. All told, the U.S. arm of Bank of Montreal has more than 170 banking locations in the Chicago area, as well as in Arizona, Florida, and other major American cities. In addition to deposit and lending services, other operations include a private bank and wealth management unit, The Harris; a middle-market investment bank, Harris Nesbitt; mutual fund management services; and real estate investment trust services through Harris Preferred Capital. Harris Bancorp expanded into Indiana with the 2004 purchase of Mercantile Bancorp and is looking to other parts of the Midwest for expansion.

In 1990, Harris Bank recognized the growing presence and influence of Hispanics in the Chicago area. Harris's board was convinced that working on a Hispanic strategy is working on the future of the bank and assigned responsibility of the Hispanic strategy to Alberto Azpe, president of Hispanic banking. At that time, Harris faced several challenges including lack of bilingual staff, marketing materials, a high turn-down rate for loan and deposit products, poor wire transfer capabilities, limited knowledge of banking services relevant to certain Hispanic segments, and low recognition of the Harris bank brand.

The Assessment

A task force was created, including members of various departments in the bank as well as members of its Bank of Montreal parent company. An external analysis was conducted to understand its brand position among Chicago Hispanics relative to its competition, and a segmentation study was commissioned to learn about Hispanic financial behavior. In addition, Harris analyzed its branch locations relative to Hispanic concentration and competitive presence and identified those locations that would be considered Hispanic branches. Harris identified the upside opportunity by identifying the percentage of Hispanics in each ZIP code where it had a branch and compared it to the percentage of Hispanics that branch had as customers. It looked at account holders with Hispanic surnames to understand account behavior and profiles across its branches.

Harris was able to note the challenges right away, knowing that the lack of bilingual staff and Spanish-language marketing materials would have to be remedied. Feedback from its existing Hispanic account holders provided valuable insights, and it used account revenue contribution information to create a revenue model and the business case.

The Implementation

The Banking Unit was originally structured as a separate business line with its own support staff and budget. It was originally thought that this business model would ensure the greatest control and would maximize the Hispanic strategy's impact in the marketplace.

In fact, this silo structure resulted in creating a separation between Hispanic banking and the other business lines. It basically alienated the unit from the rest of the business because it was not visible across the various functions and businesses in the bank. As a result, what set out to be an integrated effort actually became an isolated effort with little support from the rest of the bank.

Recognizing the need for change, Azpe developed a revised business case for upper management to reposition and restructure the Hispanic Banking Unit as an integral part of the bank's business lines and support functions. Twenty-seven branches were redistributed under the direction of respective regional vice presidents. The restructuring also placed key Hispanic Banking Unit members in staff positions across marketing, R&D, and other departments, so that each member became an integral part of each business line, representing the interest of the Hispanic Banking Unit. The role of the Hispanic bank president evolved to working closely with region and business-line presidents on overall strategy, representing the Hispanic strategy in corporate strategy discussions.

Suddenly, the Hispanic unit had a voice across marketing, product development, human resources, customer service, information systems, finance, and retail branches. Initial reactions were mixed and revolved around the financial impact to each budget. However, these concerns were addressed with business-case support that showed greater efficiencies through integration. Not everyone was convinced, but learning that the Hispanic Banking Unit budget would help augment business-line budgets helped some. As it turns out, the lines of business that are most relevant to the Hispanic market are the ones that provide the greatest support, so goals and implementation have aligned successfully.

Azpe says that "having to sell the value of targeting Hispanics is a continuous process, but because projects are planned and coordinated at the executive level and implemented by a team that is strategically positioned across the organization, it is much easier to implement and manage."

Since 2000, when Harris launched its strategy, it has focused its implementation on supporting its 27 Hispanic bilingual branches, delivering a customer-friendly mix of alternative channel and traditional branch banking alternatives that helps Hispanics overcome a traditional fear of financial institutions, including a bilingual call center, a bilingual Web site, and bilingual ATMs.

In order to achieve its customer service goals of making the entire buying process comfortable for its Hispanic customers, Harris produces culturally relevant brochures and point-of-sale materials. Bilingual materials can be accessed by any branch and the need is determined locally by branch managers. The brochures are kept updated and branch management is made aware when there are new brochures. There also are established procedures in place to announce when new products and new bilingual support materials are available.

Further, Harris ensures that Spanish-language capabilities are present across channels and across business lines with bilingual bankers in key areas such as retail, mortgage, small business, and commercial banking. Harris's HR and training process is quite extensive. Any person that is hired must pass certain tests, including language tests. Requests for bilingual personnel come from the branch and HR follows a preestablished procedure that was jointly created by the Hispanic implementation team and HR. The procedure focuses on candidate selection criteria and training.

Bilingual position descriptions are created and everyone is aware of what is being sought for the position, such as language skills. Harris HR relies on its alliance with the Hispanic Alliance for Career Enhancement (HACE) for help with finding candidates. Applications are submitted to Harris online and candidates are then turned over to HACE for evaluation; if they pass the initial screening, they are referred back to HR for the interview process. A Spanish-language assessment is conducted during the interview.

Harris conducts its training through an integrated internal program called Institute for Learning, which includes classes to teach Spanish to bank employees. Employees choose from a catalog of courses and the program is continuously available. Classes focus on teaching financial terminology in Spanish.

Additionally, employee participation on a diversity council to provide training to everyone at the bank is encouraged. The bank found that it successfully generates affinity groups.

Harris also took steps to customize a series of products and incorporate new ones to make its offering relevant to this consumer. These products include a CD-secured loan product, a specialized wire transfer service, acceptance of the Mexican identification card, and a first-time borrowers program. Additionally, the bank worked with its community relations department to create community partnerships and financial literacy programs including bilingual seminars in money management, first-time home purchasing, checking account management, and investments.

Further, Harris learned that new Hispanic immigrants rely heavily on physical locations, so it has focused strong efforts in inner-city and minority neighborhood branches and addresses different traffic patterns through later hours during weekdays and weekends.

The Results

While Harris has taken an impressive integrated approach to its Hispanic strategy implementation, Azpe says, "We're still learning." The results have been nothing short of impressive. Between 2000 and 2002, the initiative's initial phase, it increased Hispanic accounts from 7,500 to 65,000—a 766 percent increase. Today its Hispanic accounts number about 150,000 and growing.

In part, Harris credits its draw of Hispanic customers to relevant product offerings, like its money-transfer product, and to acceptance of the Mexican identification card.

Offering the money-transfer product as part of its mix has resulted in a 45 percent conversion of originally nonbanking customers into profitable account holders of two to three of their bank products.

Harris also sees continuing improvement of its brand image. And in recognition that Hispanics are now all over Chicago, not just in pockets, Azpe aims to implement varying levels of the Hispanic strategy across all of Harris's almost 200 Chicago branches within the next two years.

8

ANALYZING THE DATA

Defining your company's Hispanic market opportunity is, of course, the ultimate output of the assessment process, but it must be done in context. Your analysis should consider the various components of the external and internal assessment covered in Chapters 4 through 7. While this may seem like a daunting task, consider that you will only use what is relevant to your business and industry. Having gone through the discovery process, by now you no doubt have an intuitive sense for internal strengths that can be leveraged to capitalize on opportunities discovered in the external assessment. But the final methodology in terms of how you frame it in a relevant manner is best defined by those in your organization who track corporate performance and whose job it typically is to identify and quantify new market opportunities.

This must be stressed because preference for analytical frameworks can be highly individual to different companies, so it is especially important to develop your analysis within the framework and models that are typically used in your organization. Quite simply, management is used to a certain approach, so adopting those tools will lend credibility to your process and your output.

You may already be working within this context, but if during the assessment process you did not involve one or two of your internal analysts in areas of finance, new business development, or strategic planning, make absolutely sure you do this now. Sit with these people and share what you have. Walk them through your team's preliminary discoveries and thinking. Then, ask them to help you set up and test your logic within the tools, frameworks, and models they typically use.

Your objective should be to get feedback and direction and to determine if there are any gaps to complete the analysis. Ultimately, you want to make sure that your inputs are complete for the financial analysis.

This chapter will focus on some preliminary analysis that you'll want to have ready when you meet with your internal analysts. The approaches and tools are almost certainly familiar. The intent of this chapter is not to demonstrate analytical methods, but rather to highlight examples of how findings might be framed. Please note that all the numbers and content in tables and figures are hypothetical.

OVERVIEW

Start with an overview of your company's mission, goals, objectives, and strategies. This is important because everything you analyze from this point on will be done within this context. Describe the business you are in today, the growth your company hopes to achieve, and how the Hispanic business case and your company's strategies align to further overall growth goals.

MACRO FORCES

Summarize the macro forces that have been or are likely to impact the business within the time frame discussed in your company's goal statements. Do these macro forces represent growth opportunities or threats? Do the opportunities point to the Hispanic market? For instance, in Chapter 1 we talked about three major demographic shifts in the United States. One was the aging of the U.S. population. A deeper study into the implications of this macro force would point to an analysis done by the Bureau of Labor Statistics in their 2002 Consumer Survey, which indicates that the total average annual expenditures for those aged 45 to 54 were $48,748, and that as people age, every category of expense except health care declines in each subsequent ten-year period, bottoming out at $23,759 by age 75. This amounts to a 49 percent drop in 30 years, at a compound annual decline of 2.37 percent a year. Specifically, key retail categories decline significantly, including a drop of 62 percent in apparel and services and a 42 percent decline in food and alcohol.

Almost immediately, you would think about what that means to your company's business in the next five to ten years, as significant proportions of the aging population start to exhibit this type of purchasing decline. If you're in retail categories, growth without an alternate source of revenue is threatened. You'd start to connect Hispanic market growth projections in the next five to ten years, high fertility rates, the coming of age of U.S.-born Hispanic children entering the work force, and the resulting acceleration of total Hispanic purchasing power. When you couple that with larger households, which, according to the same consumer survey, spend more on the same retail categories that are expected to decline, you can conclude that manufacturers and retailers may need to target Hispanics just to sustain business results, let alone increase them.

The impact of multiculturalism overlaid onto demographics is another macro force that is impacting business. As mentioned, the echo boomer generation is the most diverse and diversity-hungry of any other generation before it. Its views of corporate America as providing desirable places to work and products to buy will depend on companies' ability to mirror changing outlooks on diversity, not only in the people they hire, but in the types of products and services that are offered. This generation's wants and preferences will be increasingly related to multiculturalism, so you'll want to ask how your company is positioned to deliver and compete for a share of the $170 billion it spends annually, $40 billion of which is spent by Hispanic echo boomers.

According to *Times & Trends*, published by IRI, manufacturers in high-revenue echo categories may need to realign distribution strategies, and traditional retailers will need to invest now in building relationships with this segment given Hispanic echo boomers' preference for supercenter channels. But given that this is the most wired generation in history, it likely is the most reachable—and will likely shop—through Internet sites where content has a multicultural/Hispanic flare. You'll want to drill deep into the connection between macro forces and the implications on your future source of business.

INDUSTRY TRENDS

Considering the two examples we used above, you want to start to look at how macro forces may already be impacting industry trends. If you're a clothing retailer, you want to see what steps large retailers like Sears, JCPenney, Target, and Wal-Mart have taken to modify their apparel lines to meet the tastes of the growing population of Hispanic men and women. Target has refashioned its merchandise mix in heavily Hispanic markets in the United States. Wal-Mart's U.S. buyers team up with Mexico-based colleagues to bring more Latino-flavored women's apparel to U.S. stores, and select stores carry the elaborate *quinceañera* dresses Hispanic girls wear for their coming-of-age party. In early 2005, Sears launched Latina Life, an exclusive clothing line, one of biggest apparel launches for Sears in recent times. It is expected to hit 425 Hispanic stores, nearly half of Sears stores nationwide. JCPenney says customers ultimately drive the brand decisions regarding style, fit, and quality, and that, given the future dynamics of the American population, JCPenney offers diverse brands that relate to a cultural and/or lifestyle interpretation of fashion as a way to build customer loyalty. If you intend to compete for Hispanics' apparel dollars in the midst of existing retail activity, you must recognize that the bar is already high and a competitive strategy must surpass current activity.

In the case of Hispanic echo boomers, technology companies are springing up every day to deliver a Hispanic-relevant youth experience online and through wireless devices such as cell phone services. In spite of strong Hispanic targeting by Verizon, T-Mobile, and others, new wireless companies are emerging to meet Hispanics' unmet wireless service needs. In September 2005, Movida Communications Inc., a newly formed wireless service provider offering pay-as-you-go wireless voice and data communications services exclusively to the U.S. Hispanic population, using Sprint's all-digital, all-PCS nationwide wireless network, announced its expansion from Florida into 20 additional states. As the nation's first MVNO (mobile virtual network operator) targeted at Hispanics, Movida offers all standard custom-calling features plus a suite of international voice and data services including culturally and geographically focused content in Spanish.

In the same month, IDT Corporation, an IDT Telecom subsidiary and a major provider of telecommunications services to Hispanics in the

United States, launched TuYo Mobile, a new prepaid wireless service. The service provides many features and services that are important to Hispanic customers, including state-of-the-art handsets, fully bilingual customer experience, low rates for international calling and text messaging, and culturally relevant music, ring tones, games, and graphics. TuYo Mobile will leverage IDT's considerable expertise, experience, and infrastructure in the prepaid telecom market that includes an unmatched distribution channel in the urban market, an international long distance network, an innovative prepaid platform, and leading calling card brands.

These industry trend examples have significant impacts for the wireless communication industries. These are examples of competitive niche segments that are being created to fill in product and service offerings that miss the mark on providing cultural relevancy. If your company is in these industries or considering them, this activity must be acknowledged when developing a viable Hispanic strategy.

THE ANALYSIS

Chapter 5 cited strategic and operational areas as those that must be analyzed in order to understand an organization's strengths and weaknesses. There, we applied this framework to the competitive analysis. Now we'll use it more broadly to capture the internal as well as the external assessment, and within the context of the consumer and competitive environments.

Strategic Dimensions

Strategic dimensions include defining Hispanic consumer targets, how an organization profits from the chosen target, why those customers chose to do business with a particular company, and the products delivered to those customers. Depending on the industry, there are a variety of methods you can employ to analyze the data from the internal and external assessments of your strategic areas. For example, in the case of a financial services industry, you can use various data sources that track Hispanic banking trends to define the profile of consumers who have banking relationships and those who do not. Looking deeper, you would find that the incidence of Hispanics with bank accounts or any type of

TABLE 8.1
Acculturation-based Segmentation Model

Hispanic Dominant	Bicultural	Assimilated
57%	21%	22%
Persons in this category are closest to their original culture. This segment chooses to retain as much of its Hispanic culture, language, and family values as possible.	This category is composed of persons who desire to retain as much as possible of their Hispanic culture and values while also adopting aspects of the U.S. Anglo culture. These persons speak both Spanish and English and retain ties to both cultures through family, community, and leisure time.	This segment is composed of persons who have moved away from their Hispanic culture to adopt the U.S. Anglo culture, language, and family values.

Source: 2002 Yankelovich Hispanic MONITOR.

bank-related product and service usage is fairly underdeveloped when compared to the national average.

In Table 8.1, the 2002 Yankelovich Hispanic MONITOR study provides an in-depth acculturation-based segmentation model. (Note that the data and inputs used are for the sake of illustration. Please consult these sources and your own internal resources to obtain data that is up to date and reflective of your trading areas and specific needs.) Using the 2002 Yankelovich Hispanic MONITOR segmentation scheme can save the trouble of clustering demographic and psychographic elements and creating your own segments. To start, get to know the broad characteristics of each acculturation segment and then proceed to how Hispanics across the three acculturation levels behave and the values and attitudes they hold within the financial category.

Immediately, one can see that 78 percent of Hispanics feel ties to their Hispanic identity, in spite of the 21 percent that may be better integrated into the mainstream culture due to their language abilities. A closer look at the demographic profiles for each of these segments provides insights into the various demographic measures discussed in Chapter 6 (see Table 8.2). Significant demographic age, income, occupation, education, and length of residency differences are immediately apparent. Intuitively, you can start to imagine the level of resources and effort that will be required to service the Hispanic-dominant segment, not only

TABLE 8.2

Demographic Profiles by Segment

	Hispanic Dominant 57%	Bicultural 21%	Assimilated 22%
How many are there?	• 57% of U.S. Hispanic population • 5.26 million house-holds	• 21% of U.S. Hispanic population • 1.93 million house-holds	• 22% of U.S. Hispanic population • 2.03 million house-holds
How old are they?	• Average age: 34.8 • 38% 21–34 years old • 24 when moved to the United States	• Average age: 36.3 • 48% 21–34 years old • 20 when moved to the United States	• Average age: 33.3 • 39% 21–34 years old • 13 when moved to the United States
How much do they earn?	• $15,740K per capita • $28,760K mean household income	• $23,870K per capita • $34,790K mean household income	• $24,620K per capita • $34,200K mean household income
What type of occupation do they have?	• 85% blue collar • 50% unskilled laborer • 11% craftsman, fore-man, production, repair • 11% personal/domestic worker	• 56% blue collar • 28% unskilled laborer • 10% craftsman, fore-man, production, repair • 5% personal/domestic worker	• 38% blue collar • 16% unskilled laborer • 8% craftsman, fore-man, production, repair • 6% personal/domestic worker
Where were they born?	• 67% Mexico • 10% Central America	• 46% Mexico • 11% Central America	• 46% Mexico • 17% Central America
How long have they lived in the United States?	• 10 years • 39% 1–4 years • 22% 5–9 years	• 15 years • 11% 1–4 years • 23% 5–9 years	• 34 years • 58% 30 or more years
What is their level of education?	• 40% 8th grade or less • 41% less than high school	• 53% high school or more	• 53% high school or more
Do they own a home or rent?	• 11% own	• 22% own	• 31% own
Do they own a car?	• 75% own	• 85% own	• 75% own
Do they have a family?	• 53% married • 62% two heads of household • 19% one head of household • 74% are parent households • 68.5% children under 18	• 56% married • 62% two heads of household • 25% one head of household • 75% are parent households • 66% children under 18	• 32% married • 47% two heads of household • 42% one head of household • 58% are parent households • 58.9% children under 18

Source: 2002 Yankelovich Hispanic MONITOR.

TABLE 8.3
Financial Services Behavior by Segment

	Hispanic Dominant 57%	Bicultural 21%	Assimilated 22%
Which financial products do they use?	• 63% Money transfers • 40% Bank accounts • 29% Checking • 25% Savings • 26% Credit cards • 7% Loans • 11% Retirement plans	• 48% Money transfers • 74% Bank accounts • 61% Checking • 42% Savings • 58% Credit cards • 21% Loans • 26% Retirement plans	• 13% Money transfers • 59% Bank accounts • 48% Checking • 40% Savings • 47% Credit cards • 28% Loans • 33% Retirement plans
How do they manage their money?	61% saving money for: • 33% children's education • 40% emergencies • 22% major purchases (vehicle, home)	72% saving money for: • 31% children's education • 37% emergencies • 28% major purchases (vehicle, home)	63% saving money for: • 26% children's education • 36% emergencies • 26% major purchases (vehicle, home)
They are credit card revolvers:			
	• 58% pay more than the minimum amount • 15% pay required minimum amount due	• 59% pay more than the minimum amount • 7% pay required minimum amount due	• 44% pay more than the minimum amount • 10% pay required minimum amount due
	• 30% plan to purchase a vehicle or furniture • 26% plan to purchase a home in the next 12 months	• 32% plan to purchase a vehicle or furniture • 29% plan to purchase a home in the next 12 months	• 39% plan to purchase a vehicle or furniture • 21% plan to purchase a home in the next 12 months

Source: 2002 Yankelovich Hispanic MONITOR.

culturally but also in a socioeconomically relevant manner. From this data you could even deduce that the types of financial services targeted to each segment would differ.

When looking at the financial services behavior, analyze the various financial measures that relate to these segments. From Table 8.3, you can see that almost two-thirds of the Hispanic-dominant segment does not utilize banking and relies heavily on money transfers. You can see that usage behavior between these two products has an inverse relationship among more acculturated consumers. Of those with bank accounts, only one-quarter of the segment has any deposit account, and penetration of loans and retirement accounts is even lower. Interestingly, you can also see that almost two-thirds save money, so the gap between saving behavior and the penetration of savings accounts becomes clear. Understanding saving behavior drivers can provide insight into savings product characteristics that could deliver greater value to this consumer. Another interesting insight from a revenue standpoint is the fact that credit card holders revolve balances, which points to specific revenue streams, not only based on fees but also interest revenue. Loans are also an interesting insight because, as noted, only 7 percent of the Hispanic-dominant segment has loans, but more than three times as many of these consumers plan to buy a home or car in the next 12 months—yet another usage and product demand gap.

Based on this data, you can start to lay out some of the numbers that will be useful for the financial model. Table 8.4 presents a basic model for defining total market profit using the example of a bank, but it can be used to project total market revenue and total market expense for any industry based on which internal numbers are used as inputs. The columns on this table reflect the following inputs:

1. Column 1—The total number of Hispanic households in each segment based on the proportion in the market.
2. Column 2—The proportion each segment represents in the market.
3. Column 3—The number of current customer households in each segment.
4. Column 4—Calculate the bank's share of current customer households by segment.
5. Column 5—Calculate the bank's market share by dividing customer households in each segment by total number of households in each market.
6. Column 6—The projected incremental market share goal.
7. Column 7—Calculate incremental customer households by multiplying projected incremental market share goals by total number of households in the market.
8. Column 8—Calculate total market share by adding current and incremental market share.
9. Column 9—Calculate the total projected customer households by adding existing customer households to incremental customer households.

TABLE 8.4
Profit Model

	1	2	3	4
	Market Size (HHs)	Market Share of Segments	Current Hispanic Customer HHs	Bank Share of Segments
Assimilated	193,200	45%	39,600	20.5%
Bicultural	110,000	32%	36,520	33.2%
Hispanic-dominant	97,000	23%	5,600	5.77%
Total	400,200	100%	81,720	59.5%

	5	6	7	8
	Bank Share of Market	Target Incremental Bank Share of Market	Incremental Hispanic Customer HHs	New Bank Share of Market
Assimilated	9.9%	1%	1,932	10.9%
Bicultural	9.13%	1.5%	1,650	10.63%
Hispanic-dominant	5.77%	5%	4,850	10.77%
Total	24.8%	7.5%	8,432	32.3%

	9	10	11	12
	Total Hispanic Customer HHs	Monthly Hispanic Profit/HH	Annual Hispanic Profit/HH	Total Annual Hispanic Market Profit
Assimilated	41,532	$26.36	$316.32	$13,137,402
Bicultural	38,170	$23.20	$278.37	$10,625,385
Hispanic-dominant	10,450	$21.71	$260.54	$2,722,630
Total	90,152			$26,485,417

10. Column 10—The total monthly profit per Hispanic household based on internal records.

11. Column 11—Calculate total annual Hispanic profit contribution by multiplying monthly profit by 12.

12. Column 12—Calculate total market annual Hispanic profit by multiplying annual Hispanic profit contribution by total number of Hispanic households.

This model also can be applied on a product-by-product basis and then rolled into a total. The model assumes that you are able to use census demographic data to segment your branches by acculturation level or that you can use a tool, such as Spectra's HispanIQ™ model, to do so. You can do it manually or you can provide Spectra a list of your locations in each of your markets, and they can calculate it for you.

One other consideration is that not all segments end up being your target. For instance, if your organization focuses on specific products such as on investments and retirement plans, you may decide to only target bicultural and assimilated Hispanics. You can decide this based on competitive target profiles, expected acquisition costs, and profitability scenarios based on required investment to deliver your Hispanic market strategy to the various segments.

The finer you segment your market, your revenue, expenses, and profit by product, and branches, the better the estimates once you roll them into a total. Internally, work with your IT department to generate these dollar inputs and use the same model for revenue and expense scenarios to arrive at a total figure. Subtracting total Hispanic expenses from total Hispanic revenue will give you total Hispanic market profit. Or, as in this case, you can calculate profit per household first and use that as your input to arrive at total Hispanic profit.

To project incremental market share, you can take one of two approaches: (1) you can go back into your internal data base and calculate Hispanic account holder growth for the past three to five years and use an average, or (2) you can use an average of total market account holder growth based on historical Hispanic banking incidence for the past three to five years using a secondary data base. If your bank is large, it may be one of the brands included in the Simmons National Hispanic Study questionnaire, in which case you can go back in time and extract growth in this manner. If not, you may need to use an industry average. In either case, the incremental market share you calculate is only meant to serve as your base.

The incremental market share growth rate you ultimately create should consider macro forces, industry growth trends, competitive efforts to target Hispanics through advertising and community relations, and growth projections for your company's total business. The growth rate you calculate for incremental market share becomes the base for generating growth rates for a three-year or five-year pro forma, with adjustments for each year base, on the elements already mentioned.

So what will be your strategy and how will you align? The opportunities you uncovered during your external and internal analysis are the basis for how you create differentiation and value for this consumer.

In order to start thinking about a value model, it is important to review your findings around attitudes, values, and psychographics. Understanding these areas within and outside your business context, positions you to design your value proposition and to test it against that of your competition.

You can see from Table 8.5 that Hispanic consumers are somewhat credit adverse, they want products that better align with their needs, and they are hungry for information. On the other side, they feel financially challenged, which may be why a majority are value seekers and mitigate risk by turning to reliable support networks before making important decisions.

The implications are high sensitivity to balance requirements and account fees. The banking industry has so far responded with deposit accounts that have minimum requirements to open and maintain an account, including no minimum balance and free checking, although the profit models require paperless checking accounts, using debit cards, and a direct deposit requirement to avoid fees.

From Table 8.6, it is also clear that Spanish remains the language of comfort even among 46 percent of assimilated Hispanics. Internally, this has implications across staffing, point-of-sale merchandising, brochures, paper and electronic statements, application forms, contracts, Web sites, and customer service areas and numbers.

Having this insight allows you to compare the outcome of your internal assessment and the competitive assessment to see how these respective areas are aligned to meet market requirements. This comparison also will indicate why Hispanics may be doing business with certain financial institutions instead of your own. Your ability to improve upon current offerings to create differentiation will be a critical success factor. Also, consider that this comparison defines the various thresholds that you must meet or exceed to be competitive. These thresholds may differ between markets depending on competitive activity existing in each one.

TABLE 8.5
Financial Behavior by Segment

	Hispanic Dominant 57%	Bicultural 21%	Assimilated 22%
How do they think about money/finances?	• 37% "strongly agree" that credit cards are not really a good way to buy things; it's better to pay cash if you can • 37% "strongly agree" that they wish they had more information about saving and investing money	• 40% "strongly agree" that credit cards are not really a good way to buy things; it's better to pay cash if you can • 42% "strongly agree" that they wish they had more information about saving and investing money	• 39% "strongly agree" that credit cards are not really a good way to buy things; it's better to pay cash if you can • 25% "strongly agree" that they wish they had more information about saving and investing money
How do they feel about their current financial situation?	• 14% Comfortable financially • 54% Have just enough to get by • 28% Have financial difficulties	• 19% Comfortable financially • 56% Have just enough to get by • 22% Have financial difficulties	• 29% Comfortable financially • 53% Have just enough to get by • 15% Have financial difficulties
What are their consumer tendencies and expectations?	• 66% are price conscious • 50% are bargain shoppers • 56% distrust prices/look out for frequent sales • Driven by bargain prices, respectful treatment, cleanliness, selection, and location • Turn to family friends for advice before major shopping decisions	• 71% are price conscious • 48% are bargain shoppers • 55% distrust prices/look out for frequent sales • Driven by bargain prices, respectful treatment, cleanliness, selection, and location • Turn to people with experience for advice before major shopping decisions	• 66% are price conscious • 48% are bargain shoppers • 52% distrust prices/look out for frequent sales • Driven by convenience, equal treatment, and frequent sales • Turn to people with experience for advice before major shopping decisions

Source: 2002 Yankelovich Hispanic MONITOR.

TABLE 8.6
Media Preference by Segment

	Hispanic Dominant 57%	Bicultural 21%	Assimilated 22%
What language do they prefer for every situation?	• 73% Spanish • 12% Both English and Spanish	• 62% Spanish • 27% Both English and Spanish	• 173% Spanish • 33% Both English and Spanish
What media do they consume?	• Spanish-language media is preferred for every situation • 96% view Spanish-language television regularly • 92% listen to Spanish-language radio regularly • 59% read Spanish-language newspapers at least once per week	• Comfortable with media in both languages • 90% view Spanish-language television regularly • 82% listen to Spanish-language radio regularly • 55% read Spanish-language newspapers at least once per week	• Consume predominantly English, but use Spanish-language media selectively • 58% view Spanish-language television regularly • 63% listen to Spanish-language radio regularly • 17% read Spanish-language newspapers at least once per week
Do they use computers and the Internet?	• 17% have hands-on involvement with a computer • 17% check bank accounts online • 18% pay bills online • 31% shop online	• 50% have hands-on involvement with a computer • 40% check bank accounts online • 24% pay bills online • 43% shop online	• 61% have hands-on involvement with a computer • 39% check bank accounts online • 31% pay bills online • 39% shop online

Source: 2002 Yankelovich Hispanic MONITOR.

Operational Dimensions

Operational dimensions include sourcing methods and necessary relationships for delivering relevant products and services to Hispanic consumers, the ability to manufacture in-house or the need to outsource, the degree of capital intensiveness of Hispanic operations, how well a company innovates and develops new product and services to target this market and their methods, and the approaches employed to go to market. Analyzing operational capabilities of your organization versus the competition can be done in a number of ways depending on where a company falls in terms of its historical involvement targeting the Hispanic market. One useful approach used by companies that employ six sigma tools involves creating an assessment support matrix.

The assessment support matrix in Table 8.7 focuses on elements of retail delivery, with key operational characteristics listed in the first column. In the second column, an importance weight is assigned to each, with importance driven by consumer need and relevancy and by competitive activity, not by the company's internal need. The weights assigned to all characteristics should total 100. In the next column, rate your organization's performance on each characteristic on a scale of 1 to 10, where 1 is poor and 10 is excellent, then calculate the weighted score for each characteristic in the column next to it and total the weighted scores at the bottom of the column.

Repeat this in the columns that follow for each competitive organization assessed. Note that until now what you have is a collection of observations, pictures, competitive materials, and secondary research that must be synthesized into a score. This is as much an art as it is science, but, needless to say, you want to be as objective as possible.

The completed matrix will provide a clear picture of where you and your competitive set stands in terms of retail customer touch points. This type of matrix makes it very clear where your gaps are and which aspects of the business require the most attention in the alignment process. While this matrix relates to retail delivery performance, it is also clear that addressing areas where your company scores low will impact internally diverse areas such as human resources, training, customer service, marketing, merchandising, and various business lines.

Once you analyze how you and your competition are executing against these characteristics, these can be summarized into overviews that can then be compared on a market-by-market basis and which serve as top line overviews of the competitive landscape (see Figure 8.1).

Market access based on market presence is a key diagnostic measure for how and why the competition delivers the way it does. Understanding this can be tremendously helpful in defining a competitive strategy. And it is especially important in defining and calibrating growth rates and market share goals because market presence and, therefore, market access determines your ability to compete for one or all Hispanic segments.

TABLE 8.7
Assessment Support Matrix

Operational Characteristic—Retail Delivery	Importance Weight	Rating—Your Organization	Weighted Score
Bilingual Tellers	25	6	150
Bilingual In-branch Customer Service	20	6	120
Bilingual Loan Officers	8	5	40
Bilingual Point of Sale/Merchandising	8	5	40
Bilingual Forms, Applications, Guidelines	8	1	8
Bilingual Small Business Representative	9	5	45
Bilingual Educational Efforts	10	1	10
Total	100		461

In analyzing market presence, explore two questions:

1. How many of your branches in each market are located in areas that skew to one of the three acculturation segments?
2. What is the number and proportion of target Hispanic households that have access to your locations by trading areas versus those of your competition?

The first will be helpful in adjusting growth rate and market share expectations based on reaching a certain segment of Hispanics or all of them. If you recall the profit model earlier, most of the share growth was expected to come from the Hispanic-dominant segment. But if very few branches are located in Hispanic-dominant areas, growth goals within this segment may need to be adjusted down until presence in Hispanic-dominant areas can be expanded (see Figure 8.2).

Or the opposite may be true; a large proportion of your locations may be in Hispanic-dominant areas, in which case you might expect that an even higher incremental share might be achieved. The output of this analysis also helps to determine your Hispanic branch set, which can be divided into three segments, and strategy implementation adjusted accordingly.

The answer to the second question provides similar insight, but on a total market basis. This calculates household numbers and penetration for each trading area. The total number of Hispanic households in all your trading areas are then added and divided by the total households in the

Rating—Competition X	Weighted Score	Rating—Competition Y	Weighted Score	Rating—Competition Z	Weighted Score
9	225	9	225	5	125
7	140	10	200	5	100
5	40	5	40	3	24
6	48	8	64	2	16
5	40	6	48	1	8
6	54	8	72	1	9
6	60	8	80	1	10
	703		837		316

market to obtain total Hispanic reach for the market (see Figure 8.3). So again, it's a matter of knowing how you are physically positioned to compete for Hispanics in each of your markets. To have a better grasp of your market presence gaps, you should map your locations and your competitors' locations on a single map against a background that represents Hispanic population; then map each of your trading areas individually.

The first map (see Figure 8.4) will show areas where you are completely absent, while the individual map (see Figure 8.5) will show where your competition is within your trading areas. This approach also gives you the opportunity to look at the concentration of other consumer ethnic consumer segments within the trading area and the ZIP code.

Additionally, you can segment your locations based on acculturation by using census-based demographic variables covered in Chapter 6 or you can use a tool like Spectra HispanIQ™ to do this type of acculturation-based geosegmentation. If you provide a list of your locations and competitive locations, Spectra can provide you with a segmentation based on ZIP codes (see Figure 8.6).

Once you know where you stand with market presence, you may decide your bank is not poised to capture a large enough share of Hispanics in your market to meet growth and market share goals. This may be a factor that will lead you to recommend against moving forward with the initiative. Or, you may decide to move forward and recommend that in order to competitively position your organization to capture this market's business, it will need to invest to increase its market presence in neighborhoods where presence gaps exist.

FIGURE 8.1
Competitive Analysis

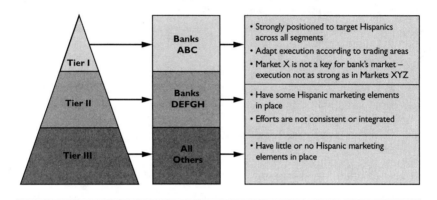

Banks in XYZ market fall into three groups with
regards to their Hispanic strategy execution

FIGURE 8.2
Market Presence Analysis

XYZ bank locations are
concentrated in bicultural
and acculturated trading areas

	Acculturated	Bicultural	Hispanic Dominant
	19	6	2

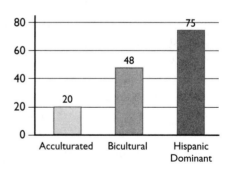

A trading area analysis around
XYZ bank locations indicates
that average Hispanic concentration
decreases with acculturation

Average Hispanic Concentration
by Trading Area

FIGURE 8.3

Market Presence Analysis

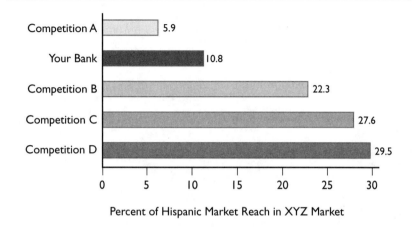

Percent of Hispanic Market Reach in XYZ Market

Your Bank reaches 10.8 percent of the Hispanic market in XYZ Market, which is 38 percent Hispanic.

FIGURE 8.4

Maps of Company and Competitive Locations Relative to Hispanic Density

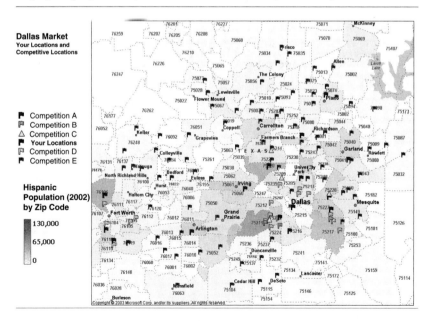

FIGURE 8.5

Maps of Company and Competitive Locations Relative to Hispanic Density

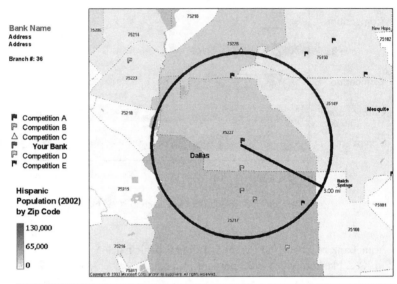

Geography	Hispanic Population	Percent Hispanic	AA Population	Percent AA	Asian Population	Percent Asian
3-mile trading area	47,160	42%	38,652	34%	1,617	1%
75227	23,269	44%	19,208	36%	694	1%

The latter option should lead to an analysis of viable distribution models that balance and minimize investment requirements while increasing presence. This is an analysis that will not be addressed in this book, but decisions about distribution models will depend greatly on the dynamics of the marketplace. For example, where does your Hispanic target shop? Do your target customers shop in large ethnic retail corridors or do they shop locally in their own neighborhoods? When do they shop and how often? How does mass transportation impact the market's ability to easily travel to your locations? What do competitive alternate channels currently look like?

FIGURE 8.6

Store Segmentation by Acculturation

Segmentation

- **Use behavior-based Acculturation to differentiate Hispanic stores**

  - Not all Stores with High Hispanic Populations <u>act</u> as Hispanic

Store Name	TOTAL POP	Total Hisp POP	% Hisp	% Least Acc	% Bi-Cultural	% Most Acc
Frys Food Store 109	2,572	738	28.69%	1.78%	38.34%	59.91%
Frys Marketplace 619	6,435	3013	46.82%	5.87%	54.10%	40.02%
Frys Food Store 43	6,844	2361	34.50%	8.93%	49.83%	41.25%
Frys Food Store 128	3,873	1027	26.52%	12.86%	49.48%	37.67%
Frys Food Store 135	3,996	1125	28.15%	12.96%	56.26%	30.76%

- Fry's 619 has a Hispanic population of 46%, but of those, only 6% are LEAST Acculturated (83 adults)

Store Name	TOTAL POP	Total Hisp POP	% Hisp	% Least Acc	% Bi-Cultural	% Most Acc
Frys Marketplace 618	5,040	891	17.68%	33.22%	47.25%	19.53%
Frys Food Store 41	4,583	1459	31.84%	24.95%	55.11%	19.95%
Frys Food Store 4	5,333	1593	29.87%	23.65%	55.49%	20.85%
Frys Food Store 69	5,686	1174	20.65%	22.66%	48.64%	28.71%
Frys Food Store 134	3,479	557	16.01%	22.44%	49.19%	28.37%

- Fry's 69 has only 20% Hispanic Population, but 23% of them are LEAST Acculturated (266 adults)

Acculturation is referenced to Hispanic Population

❖ Spectra
Intelligent targeting™

17

HYPOTHESES DEVELOPMENT AND VALIDATION

Once you have a good grasp of this up-front analysis, your team should gather to discuss findings and preliminary implications. This process is likely to produce as many questions as it does answers, but these questions typically lead to development of hypotheses to be validated with primary research.

The upside is that you will be defining the information gaps necessary to make key decisions, which will help validate the hypotheses inferred from the assessment analysis thus far. This internal work session should provide a great deal of clarity around what you know and what you don't know, leading to focused primary research objectives. This process is critical and should not be skipped. You will want to ensure that you have addressed these issues in the business case rather than run the risk of appearing unprepared if management unexpectedly brings up hypotheses during one of your updates that wasn't validated.

Create hypotheses across every aspect of your strategic, operational, and organizational dimensions. And then determine the best way to validate them. Some examples related to distribution, pricing elasticity, and product might include:

> **Hypothesis:** In order to adequately and profitably align with relevant product delivery for this new target, a new alternate distribution strategy needs to be created.
>
> **Research Implication:** The research should test receptivity to alternate distribution concepts.
>
> **Hypothesis:** In order to appeal to our price-sensitive Hispanic targets, our price structure needs to be adapted.
>
> **Research Implication:** The research should test several value propositions and product concepts with varying price structure scenarios to determine price elasticity among Hispanic targets.
>
> **Hypothesis:** Our product or service offering is more relevant to more acculturated Hispanics.
>
> **Research Implication:** The research should include consumers in all acculturation segments.

Depending on the nature of the hypotheses, the market research might be among consumers, industry experts, or members of your organization. You may choose to handle the research internally or hire a research supplier.

There are many qualified market research companies that focus on multicultural research. Resist the temptation to contract a supplier that claims multicultural experience, but whose focus is mainstream work. As good as it may be, it simply does not have the expertise or focus to help you craft a culturally relevant study design and provide meaningful in-depth analysis. Importantly, recommended methodologies that are used for mainstream projects and that include Hispanics as a subsegment are often inappropriate (see References for a list of several suppliers that are among the best in Hispanic market research).

SWOT: STRENGTHS, WEAKNESSES, OPPORTUNITIES, AND THREATS

After you have analyzed where you stand with regards to strategic, operational, and organizational dimensions, developed and validated your hypotheses, and looked at some financial scenarios, you can move on to developing a SWOT analysis.

As you know, the traditional SWOT analysis is used to develop strategies that align organizational strengths with external opportunities, identify internal weaknesses to be addressed, and acknowledge threats that could affect organizational success.

The process that got you to this point should provide clear insight into what your SWOT will consider—that's a pretty clear-cut process. Once you have this laid out, you'll see some key implications right away. But a more rigorous approach is to conduct a cross-impact analysis based on your SWOT where you test your resource-based strengths across strategic, operational, and organizational strong points with an analytical framework called VRIO, which is featured by Barney and Hesterly in *Strategic Management and Competitive Advantage*. The premise of VRIO is that if a company is strong or can develop strengths that can be considered **V**aluable, **R**are, costly to **I**mitate, and for which the company is **O**rganized to exploit, the company can reasonably expect a sustained competitive advantage that will allow it to maximize Hispanic market opportunities.

So review the strengths listed in your SWOT table and ask if each one is *valuable* enough to exploit an external opportunity or neutralize an external threat, if it is *rare* enough to prevent perfect competition, whether it is *too costly to allow imitations,* and whether the *organization's* structure, reporting hierarchies, relationships, compensation, and other control mechanisms are aligned or can be aligned to enable the company to exploit its strengths to target Hispanics.

Only those strengths that meet each one of these criteria provide a sustainable competitive advantage with high economic potential, while those that are valuable but are not rare nor costly to imitate and may be limited by organizational structure only succeed at positioning the company at parity with its competition and can create only average returns.

Once you have run your strengths through this analysis, place the strengths that provide a sustainable competitive advantage in the

TABLE 8.8
VRIO Analysis

Category	Resources	Valuable?	Rare?
Financial	Stable liquidity position	Yes	Yes
	Efficient asset management ratio	Yes	Yes
	Excellent debt ratio	Yes	Yes
	Solid retained earnings	Yes	Yes
	Positive cash flow position	Yes	Yes

Strengths column of a new SWOT table. Then identify those external opportunities that you can take advantage of because of those specific strengths and list those in the Opportunities column. Follow this with a review of weaknesses that need to be addressed and the external threats that need to be acknowledged in pursuit of your opportunities.

This process is most valuable with a core team because it will force everyone involved to come to terms with the idealized versions of organizational strengths and force a face-off with reality. It also typically helps to provide clarity on the critical issues the team will face as it attempts to develop its strategies and will highlight the areas on which success depends. To ensure focus and avoid distractions, hold an off-site meeting. Because team members have been working with you during various phases of this assessment, they should all have a good idea of the data by now, but it is beneficial to provide a preliminary SWOT that includes all strengths, weaknesses, opportunities, and threats in advance. To prevent setbacks, provide a list of required reference documentation to each member. Request that all participants come prepared to analyze, develop implications, and discuss critical issues and critical success factors. Then, as a group, run the company's strengths through a VRIO analysis (see Table 8.8).

It is typically difficult to objectively assess your internal organization because of the various people and sensitivities involved, especially at this point when resources, capabilities, and skills are being labeled as either

Costly to Imitate?	Exploited by Organization?	Competitive Implications	Economic Implications
No	No	Temporary Advantage	Above Normal
No	No	Temporary Advantage	Above Normal
Yes	No	Temporary Advantage	Above Normal
Yes	No	Temporary Advantage	Above Normal
Yes	No	Temporary Advantage	Above Normal

weaknesses or strengths. It is also easy to discount the strengths and over-emphasize the weaknesses of your competition, particularly if your organization typically leads the competition among non-Hispanic consumers. This is where analytical tools like VRIO can be most useful because they have built-in criteria.

You must take care to truly recognize your position and force yourself to look internally with a critical eye. Areas like core competencies, capabilities, skills, and any expertise in the marketplace must be put into context of requirements to compete for this new market segment. You must be realistic about the types of organizational resources available to you—they may represent strengths for non-Hispanic efforts, but are they appropriate for implementing a Hispanic strategy? If not, be willing to admit this. On the external side, it is equally important to be objective about your competitive environment and the potential threats they may represent. And, while you won't be privy to every detail of competitive operational strategies, trust that your assessment of the competitive execution, consumer awareness, usage, and future purchase intent are all clear clues about where the competition is succeeding or failing. Be willing to recognize that smaller competitors that don't pose a threat when targeting non-Hispanics may be a significant threat when targeting Hispanics. Separately, recognize the significant threat from competitors that have technology and models that are specifically created to target Hispanics.

The SWOT and VRIO analyses are critical steps in defining your strategic options; it should encourage further discussions and should raise serious questions about your company's competitiveness in the Hispanic market.

CRITICAL SUCCESS FACTORS

Once the SWOT process is complete, the team should move to summarize the critical issues facing the organization. These issues are directly related to the viability of moving forward and will drive the development of your company's critical success factors (CSFs)—specific actions necessary from identified areas on which the financial success of your initiative will depend.

These actions relate back to specific areas of your organization that must be aligned, created, or protected in order to be and remain competitive. They may involve developing certain core competencies internally, seeking them externally, or ensuring that (1) you have certain skill sets and knowledge; (2) your corporate culture is supportive; or (3) you are able to create the required reputation inside and outside the company.

CSFs relate to the successful creation and implementation of key operational strategies to which your organization must pay close attention and allocate strong resources.

In the banking industry, CSFs for targeting the Hispanic market are often retail operations and geographical presence, bilingual staffing and training, and relevant product offerings.

In the supermarket business, CSFs may include a strong supply chain including specialty suppliers of Hispanic products, bilingual staffing and training, relevant merchandising, and a customized category management system.

Critical success factors will vary from industry to industry and will even change as industries, competitors, and the Hispanic consumer evolves. For instance, the thresholds an organization may need to cross in order to be a preferred destination or supplier of a product or service among Hispanics will grow higher as more competitors move to meet these consumers' preferences in a given market, or if competitors innovate in terms of how they deliver their offerings.

This supports an ongoing need to maintain an updated understanding of how the competition is meeting or exceeding Hispanic customer needs relative to your organization. If you lose your position of strength, then you must examine how to regain it, something best done by revisiting the SWOT analysis and redefining your sustainable strengths and new critical success factors. You must know the industry, consumer, competitors, and your organization well enough to determine what is less important and what is more important to your success.

Importantly, an organization should focus on no more than three or four CSFs at any one time in strategy development. It is critical that you resist the temptation to develop more than these because it will dilute and detract focus from the most important ones critical to meeting financial goals.

Your ability to maintain focus on your critical success factors in light of prevailing and anticipated industry and competitive conditions should be a top analytical priority, enabling development of strategies grounded on your competitive advantages and opportunities.

CASE STUDY: PACKAGED FOODS COMPANY

In 2002, a leading packaged foods company attended a Hispanic marketing conference at which a session highlighted the size and growth of the Hispanic market in the United States and provided food consumption insights and trends, mentioning that Hispanics are heavy consumers of vegetables. This insight led the marketing director and VP of sales to wonder if Hispanics might be worth targeting with a Hispanic line of frozen vegetable products.

The team returned to the company excited about the opportunity and quickly reported back to the COO. The conference data was shared internally along with preliminary research insights that the competition had not yet moved to target Hispanics with frozen produce.

The Assessment

The COO was receptive, but as with any new venture, it would require building the business case to sell management on the opportunity. The team felt that, if they could be first to the market by developing a Hispanic line of good tasting, nutritious, affordable products that appealed to Hispanics' tastes, the opportunity could be significant.

The marketing and sales managers recruited the value-added product manager's support and assembled a core team that also included R&D, packaging, production, and legal to support eventual branding. The team developed an action plan for assessing the opportunity, presented it to management, and received approval to proceed.

The team conducted a substantial amount of Internet research to understand Hispanics and their food shopping and preparation trends. Because little secondary data exists on frozen produce, the company moved to understand the consumer through a series of focus groups and ethnographies. The information gained helped the company understand how Hispanics cook at home, if frozen vegetables are used in preparation, and if not, whether there is receptivity to using frozen produce. The company was concerned because it knew that frozen sales among Hispanics were limited, so it was important to explore receptiveness to frozen vegetables as an alternative to fresh for Hispanic meal preparation.

Surprisingly, the team found that frozen vegetable blends were used often to prepare meals in Hispanic households, and that vegetable blend products were quite popular. The big finding was that frozen vegetables were considered an acceptable way of facilitating the cooking process; however, there was a perception that frozen was not as good as fresh. Yet, these findings were enough to push the company to move forward with the initiative. The company developed a plan based on research that detailed how this initiative might be pursued. The team made some assumptions that helped it quantify the opportunity, including expected pricing, margins, and the scope of distribution. It developed case-specific projections on who could be the retail customers for this product in order to estimate the potential scope of its distribution and volume, all allowing it to more clearly define and size the market.

The team banked on the knowledge that some of its retail customers had started to focus on Hispanics and had been asking about Hispanic products.

With these projections and assumptions in hand, the company moved to conduct a quantitative consumer study to validate Hispanics' produce purchase habits. The study indicated that 70 percent of Hispanics use frozen vegetables at home, 50 percent buy frozen vegetables two to three times per month, and, in general, they liked the convenience offered by frozen produce. The research also provided some preparation ideas.

The frozen packaged foods company also found that Hispanics shop at Hispanic grocers often, so it would need to consider that in its distribution strategy. Having sold management on the potential, the team was able to allocate additional budgets to more product development research. Once again, the research confirmed the opportunity, and although the product usage index was 70 among Hispanics, it was considered strong enough to move forward because of the upside opportunity. Ideas were generated in brainstorming sessions and taken back to R&D for prototype development. Recipe ideas were gathered from a wide range of places, even local restaurants.

The Implementation

The products took six months to develop and were ready for testing in early 2004. In mid-2004, the prototypes were tested in focus groups where Hispanics tasted, touched, and discussed their reactions to several product concepts. Reactions were very positive, with participants consuming the products with enjoyment and enthusiasm. From this research, the Hispanic line was narrowed down to six products: two vegetable blends and four prepared foods.

The company then moved to develop the packaging and the branding. The brand name had to drive category and brand choice. This process involved not only the company's packaging manager, but also an agency that specialized in Hispanic packaging. The process was long and took several iterations before the right packaging was developed. Important considerations included food photography and the importance of depicting the food in an appealing and relevant manner. It was also determined that having a bilingual label, leading with English, would be critical, especially for the back panel, which communicates preparation instructions and directs consumers to the company's Spanish-language Web site. Even the imagery on the package had to be adapted between the vegetable blends and the prepared products. The packaging received strong marks in testing. At this point the product was ready to be rolled out.

In the meantime, the team was challenged to develop a brand name in a short period of time because the window for launching frozen products was fast approaching. Several names were developed and one of the favorites was owned by a company in South America. After much investment, the lawyers couldn't come to an agreement, so a different Hispanic brand name was created, tested, cleared by legal, and adopted.

The team then made a sales presentation to a Hispanic-oriented food retailer in the southwest with the idea to conduct a test market, which is currently in progress. It also hired an ad agency to develop a trade and consumer promotions program that emphasized demos and coupons, in-store merchandising including freezer door clingers, and floor decals in front of the product. In addition, the product is being supported on radio, lunch trucks, and by a nutritionist who is delivering the message that the products are like fresh versions because freezing retains nutrients.

Preliminary Results

To date, consumer pull efforts are moving product according to projections. The test is being evaluated based on case movement, volume thresholds, and other proprietary measures. The company is encouraged by results and is looking at the next phase of its rollout. It has hired a broker who specializes in selling Hispanic items to Hispanic channels. With the growing interest for ethnic products among mainstream consumers, the company also believes these products are poised for eventual expansion into mainstream channels.

CASE STUDY: NASH FINCH

Nash Finch is one of the largest U.S. wholesale distributors. The company supplies fresh produce, frozen foods, meat and dairy products, and nonfood goods such as health and beauty aids, tobacco, and paper products to more than 1,500 grocery stores and institutional customers in 28 states and about 300 foreign and domestic military bases and commissaries. Wholesale and military distribution accounts for an estimated 84 percent of sales, but it also owns and operates more than 80 primarily midwestern supermarkets, mostly under the Econofoods, Family Thrift Center, and Sun Mart names.

The Assessment

The decision to target Hispanics at Nash Finch was driven by Ron Marshall, its CEO, a strategic thinker who noticed there was tremendous opportunity to serve the Hispanic population in Denver, Colorado, a city that is more than 30 percent Hispanic, most of whom are Mexican.

To test the hypothesis, Nash Finch first tested appeal for a Hispanic assortment at a few stores in Omaha, Nebraska, and Greeley, Colorado, where Hispanics in the trading areas had shifted to represent almost 30 percent of each store's demographics.

This test went on for two years and allowed the company to learn about product assortment and merchandising that worked among this population. The test also consisted of bilingual signage and advertising. During this time, the company's market research team, led by Brian Numainville, also went into the market and conducted bilingual Hispanic consumer research to better understand the market. Telephone surveys and in-store interviews were also conducted. The test, research, and market analysis indicated that in Denver there were virtually no significant offerings of the kinds of products and services that Hispanics prefer.

The company continued its analysis, which included a detailed demographic analysis using national census data as well as a variety of syndicated studies and books on the subject. In-house studies and an internal geographic information system were used to understand current estimates and population projections. The company did an in-depth market analysis complete with sales projections based on Hispanic population numbers, but more specifically the Mexican population because that was its focus, especially the first generation. The research drilled deep even to the regions of Mexico from where the Mexican population originated.

Yet, as the company grew to understand some of the market's complexity, Numainville still felt it had a lot to learn. For several months, it conducted a significant amount of primary research and also set out to understand its competitive environment. Specifically, Nash Finch wanted to understand how the competition was addressing the market and the positioning they had achieved in the Hispanic consumer's mind. The company also wanted to understand the differences in market conditions between Denver and the test markets, with an emphasis on adjustment strategies rather than the actual operations of the stores. This was done through consumer market research and through store visits. Lastly, the marketing and operations team also surveyed best-in-class retailers in other Hispanic markets to help develop a framework for its offering.

Nash Finch decided to move forward with the creation of a Hispanic format for the Denver Hispanic market based on its assessment that potential for a meaningful return on investment existed. Yet, this was calibrated with an understanding that in order to do it right, the company would have to invest significantly, not only in research but also building and supporting the concept, making research and financial analysis a big part in the decision.

With the necessary intelligence in hand, it hired a Hispanic design firm and worked with them to develop the store concept. The concept was then tested with first-generation Hispanics in the Denver market. Consumers were shown concept boards of the store—the brand, the look, the colors, and even Paco, the store mascot.

The brand name, AVANZA, meaning "advance," was a spirit that was embodied in the store's interior design, which included murals showcasing the positive elements of Hispanic culture, such as work, family, and education. Community, pride, and culture were presented strongly in the concept. Spanish language was a key component across various aspects of the store's look and operations, including staffing, signage, and even employee name tags.

Today, Nash Finch looks at its Hispanic shoppers like any other shopper segment; first-generation Hispanics are the drivers for everything that is done in store. The company strives to continuously understand what this target customer desires and needs. As a cross-functional organization that is primarily a food distributor, it leverages the knowledge of the various people in the organization and brings them to the table together as needed. In fact, it is this cross-functional group that supported the groundwork for the development of the AVANZA concept and continues to support its implementation. The team is led by the company's CEO, so it was clear to everyone in the company that this was a top-down initiative.

The Results

When measuring results for its AVANZA stores, sales are top on the list of metrics, but Nash Finch also evaluates customer count, profitability, and other standard retail measures. Today, Nash Finch is pleased with AVANZA store performance in Denver.

"Obviously, we are pleased enough that we are still running them and we are using them as learning experiences," said Marshall. "[We are] using that knowledge for leverage with our independent customers who are operating in the independent markets. We are pleased with the performance there."

9

MOVING FROM ASSESSMENT TO IMPLEMENTATION

STRATEGY DEVELOPMENT

Chapter 8 briefly touched on defining your organization's critical issues, which is really a synthesized statement of your analysis—an assessment of the cross impact of your internal and external analysis. The critical issue statement is one that clearly brings to the forefront challenges and opportunities that will impact growth—business lines or operational areas that conflict with or support overall corporate strategy, culture, and values. Some aspects of critical issues might include:

- *The company's core competency is its supply-chain management and technology.* The Hispanic analysis points to a need to expand the supplier network to smaller, more specialized wholesalers that do not yet know how to operate within the supply-chain framework or with the company's technology. This endangers its rate of efficiency.
- *The company has been trending toward greater automation in its delivery of products and services.* Analysis points to requirements for high-touch delivery among Hispanics. This impacts efficiency and profitability.

TABLE 9.1
Decision-Support Matrix

Critical Success Factors	Importance Weight	Strategic Alternative #1	Weighted Score
Aligns with corporate ROI goals	20	3	60
Creates customized product assortment	15	9	135
Expands market presence	20	8	160
Expands supply chain to include specialty suppliers	15	4	60
Emphasizes diverse employee base and training	20	4	80
Enables speed to market	10	9	90
Total	**100**		**585**

- *The company doesn't have the products, services, price structures, or market presence to be competitive.* Creating the infrastructure, pricing model, and product assortment will require significant R&D investment or an acquisition.

If thoroughly thought out, your critical issues statement should highlight opportunities and challenges on which corporate success depends. It captures what the company should do in the face of what it can do. Remember, you are not only creating a strategy for Hispanic market success; you are creating a strategy for *total* market success. Hispanic is but one of the strategic pillars that will contribute to the company achieving its goals. This is why there must be full alignment. Think of it in terms of a business-unit or business-line strategy and how it aligns with overall strategy; this is no different.

In developing a Hispanic strategy, critical success factors (CSFs), which fall out of your critical issue(s), will be the cornerstones of your strategy. Any strategic alternatives that are generated must address CSFs to be in alignment with your company's direction. CSFs are where you want to focus your alignment and where the heaviest investment ought to be allocated initially. Your process for creating strategic alternatives is best developed in collaboration with your team of stakeholders. And the

Strategic Alternative #2	Weighted Score	Strategic Alternative #3	Weighted Score	Strategic Alternative #4	Weighted Score
5	100	8	160	8	160
8	120	7	105	7	105
6	120	9	180	9	180
8	120	7	105	5	75
7	140	8	160	5	100
7	70	6	60	4	40
	670		**770**		**660**

outcome of the session is to select the best strategy. You should have no more than one paragraph describing each strategic alternative.

Once alternative strategies have been developed, they can be tested for how well they support each CSF. A similar table to the assessment matrix used in Chapter 8 can be used here to identify the best strategy, except that, in this case, it is used as a decision-support matrix. This time, the CSFs and their inherent characteristics that must be considered are listed in the first column. Each CSF is assigned a number representing its importance weight; this number goes in the second column. The weights must total 100. Then, in the third column, you will list an abbreviated name of your strategic alternative at the top; you will use the fourth column to rate for the strategic alternative how well each CSF is addressed. (See Table 9.1.)

In this hypothetical case, the decision-support matrix indicates that the best strategic alternative would be #3 because, based on the strategy descriptions (the ones you created with your team), this alternative scored high on ROI that aligns with corporate goals, emphasizes diverse employee base and training, and expands market presence, which are the CSFs with the greatest importance weights and therefore drive strategy selection in this case.

Obviously, critical success factors and resulting strategic alternatives will be completely different and specific to your industry, company, and situation. As such, the importance and ratings you assign to each will also vary based on your specific critical issues. This process must flow directly from your cross-impact analysis based on your SWOT. It is very easy for teams to get sidetracked and develop strategic alternatives that do not flow from CSFs but rather on subjective criteria.

Once you select the best strategic alternative, it becomes the foundation from which operational strategies will flow. This chapter will address top-line considerations for implementation plan development (operational strategies and objectives) including performance, control, risk mitigation, and change management.

Your company may be realigning its Hispanic strategy, or it may be developing the business case for its Hispanic strategy. Either scenario requires that you develop a formal implementation plan that describes all aspects of running the Hispanic business.

THE BUSINESS MODEL

Keeping the CSFs in mind, define who will be involved in driving the Hispanic strategy forward. Think about your company's business model and overlay the Hispanic strategy over it. This means that you create a table in which you can reflect the alignment between your organizational business model and the Hispanic strategy business model.

The purpose of this table is to highlight how corporate and Hispanic strategy business models align and where adaptations are required to address Hispanic consumer orientations, different demographic profiles, the value proposition or positioning, how the proposition generates profit, and the product and service focus. It also details similarities and differences in how the company will deliver through its operational and organizational structure. (See Table 9.2.)

The strategy should identify the corporate leadership on whom implementation will depend and the required infrastructure and control mechanisms for the strategy being recommended. Control mechanisms are operational checks and balances, safeguards, policies and procedures, and organization structures that ensure that the implementation will be carried out as planned in the most efficient and effective way possible.

Remember that the Hispanic Business Unit's (HBU) organizational structure should align with the rest of the business units in your company.

TABLE 9.2
The Business Model

Business Model	Corporate Strategy	Hispanic Strategy
Fundamental Assumptions		
• Customer orientations		
• Profit drivers		
Strategic		
• Target customers		
• Profit model		
• Differentiation or value proposition		
• Scope of products and services		
Operations		
• Purchasing		
• Manufacturing		
• Capital		
• R&D/product development		
• Go-to-market mechanism		
Organization		
Structure		

Source: Adapted from Business Design Model, *The Profit Zone,* Slywotsky & Morrison, 2002.

One packaged goods manufacturer has a Hispanic business unit that supports Hispanic strategy needs for more than 40 brands in the United States and globally, with its leadership reporting to the same senior VP and C-level management as the brand and resource sectors.

The plan must describe cross-organizational interaction between the HBU and operational areas, including the way in which the HBU will be supported, with a description of activities, processes, and hierarchies. It must be very clear which functional areas will support the HBU and how it will be staffed to do so. In addition, the relationships between business units should be described, including how the HBU will be integrated into the activities of other business units, how often, and the desired output or support.

For example, HBUs often rely on functional areas such as marketing and advertising for development of Hispanic-specific mailers, circulars, and other promotional materials. They also work closely with R&D to develop products and services that match consumer needs. It should be understood that operational area budgets are inclusive of HBU-related

R&D costs. Sales must understand that its sales focus will include Hispanic-oriented products and promotions and add them to its sales calendars, including hiring bilingual sales representatives and extending its sales coverage to include Hispanic retailers.

The organization's supply chain, important in both product and service industries, must be managed carefully and may require collaboration with external companies to deliver Hispanic-relevant products and services or to distribute products into Hispanic channels. In some cases, distribution may need to be outsourced to provide direct delivery, as opposed to relying on central warehouse distribution systems, which may not be well suited to delivering to a smaller set of stores. So, companies hire specialty distributors to handle distribution of their Hispanic-targeted products to specialized retail channels.

The supermarket business is increasingly known for adapting its supply chain to create value for Hispanic customers through partnering and outsourcing. For example, one supermarket trained its Hispanic suppliers to do business with its category managers by coaching them on the buying process and sales presentations. This not only helps this retailer source relevant product, but helps create efficiencies in the procurement process. All supplier relationships, partnerships, and joint ventures, as well as how they deliver on the strategy, should be described in the plan.

Your plan should detail how technology and support system designs will be adapted to understand, manage, and track the Hispanic strategy across the operation. For instance, you'll want to describe the type of outputs required for analysis and reporting; how technology will support not only identification of Hispanic customers, but in building databases that track their buying and spending patterns, the expenses related to servicing them, and profitability. Technology must also be positioned in a support role to manage specialty inventory and its distribution and merchandising requirements across the company's Hispanic channels.

Some companies leverage their technology to facilitate automatic distribution of marketing materials to their retail locations. Others design their systems to identify Spanish-speaking customers so those customers receive company communication in Spanish.

THE OPERATIONAL PLAN

Operational plans that drive the strategy forward must be developed for the HBU and support functions. This is where you operationalize the HBU strategy across marketing, sales, R&D, manufacturing, procurement, human resources, business development, corporate affairs, technology, and other relevant areas.

The idea is to describe in detail how the HBU will implement its strategy and leverage each support function. This area falls right out of the internal assessment process and ties back to the SWOT and CSFs. In this section, you address the strengths and competencies that can be leveraged in each area, but, just as important, you work with the various task holders to determine how weaknesses related to each CSF will be addressed. For instance, if we refer back to the CSFs on the decision-support matrix, think about the various functional areas that impact the company's ability to address these CSFs, with special attention to the ones that were weighted highest.

For example, responsibility for creating a diverse employee base and training cuts across C-level management, human resources, corporate affairs, corporate diversity, procurement, and community relations. Strategies for each area can be developed that address corporate support for values and training around diversity, relationships, and inclusion. These might include goals and strategies around cultural sensitivity training, minority supplier procurement programs, and diversity hiring programs, including candidate sourcing, community outreach and relations, and Spanish-language classes for company employees. It would also be addressed through strategies that increase the comfort level among new Hispanic hires that may require bilingual training and even programs that teach English as a second language (ESL). These strategies all have costs related to them, and it will be incumbent upon the managers working on the development of the strategies to consider costs associated with them.

Responsibility for creating a customized product assortment cut across R&D, supply chain (procurement), HR, marketing, merchandising, retail, and finance. Operational strategies for this area can include innovation through R&D, supply-chain expansion strategies that allow sourcing from unique distributors and sources in Latin America, merchandising strategies that align with Hispanic buying behavior, strategies around staffing and customer service that out-services the competition,

TABLE 9.3
Defining Implementation Strategy Responsibility

Critical Success Factors	Management Team	Human Resources	R&D	Retail Operations
Aligns with corporate ROI goals	✔			
Creates customized product assortment	✔	✔	✔	✔
Expands market presence	✔	✔		✔
Expands supply chain to include specialty suppliers	✔	✔		
Emphasizes diverse employee base and training	✔	✔		
Enables speed to market	✔	✔	✔	

marketing strategies that truly resonate with the consumer, sales strategies to expand sales channels in unique alternate channels that align with shopping patterns, and store layouts that conform to how Hispanics shop in groups, especially with children.

One approach to defining strategic priorities and responsibilities across functions is to create a table that lists the CSFs in the first column and all of your operational functions across the top. Then take one CSF at a time and check the box for each operational area that would own some part of the responsibility for developing, implementing, and monitoring a strategy to support that CSF. The operational areas will differ by industry and company, but essentially you want to list the various areas on which each critical success factor depends. (See Table 9.3.)

Once you have selected the functions for each CSF, create one table for each function and copy the list of CSFs into the first column. Then copy one function column with the check marks for each relevant CSF. Create as many tables as there are functions. (See Table 9.4.)

Now you can start going down the rows, drafting strategies for each CSF that relates to that particular function in preparation for meeting with the team member from each area. Make sure you forward the outcome of the analysis from the internal assessment that relates to that area so everyone is reminded of the alignment gaps; then tie them back to the CSFs. Also, use this meeting to get a sense of the individuals, timing, and costs involved to implement the strategies.

Manufactur-ing	Procure-ment	Distribution	Marketing	Finance	Technology
				✔	
✔	✔	✔	✔	✔	✔
			✔	✔	✔
	✔			✔	
				✔	
✔	✔				✔

You'll also want to work with each area on the strategy implementation timeline. Lay out all the internal areas on a grid and define the implementation timeline by area. A typical Gantt chart is helpful for this exercise.

CHANGE MANAGEMENT

As you work on developing implementation strategies and the action plan, having a change management plan is significant. As sensible and as irrefutable as a business case for a Hispanic strategy might be, change is not welcomed by all in corporate America. Corporate culture has a lot to do with it, but in general, people tend to feel uneasy when the status quo with which they are comfortable changes. And change that impacts budgets—especially those that reallocate budgets from one area or several to meet the needs of a new priority—is immensely challenging, as is change that adds to people's workload and areas of responsibility. These are especially sensitive areas in today's corporate environment where flatter and leaner organizations are increasingly the norm.

Couple this with a sudden need to understand a new set of consumers who speak a different language and are fundamentally very different from most executives, middle managers, salespeople, and clerks found in corporate America today, and change can be paralyzing and politically—and even emotionally—charged. No matter how much people nod their

TABLE 9.4
Operational Strategy Development

HUMAN RESOURCES				
Critical Success Factors	Operational Strategies	Responsibility	Timing	Costs
Aligns with corporate ROI goals				
Creates customized product assortment				
Expands market presence				
Expands supply chain to include specialty suppliers				
Emphasizes diverse employee base and training				
Enables speed to market				

heads in agreement in a meeting where Hispanic strategies and implementation plans are being discussed, know that in private, there is confusion, skepticism, distrust, resentment, excitement, optimism, uncertainty, and fear. A medley of emotions must be recognized and managed in order to create the comfort level and confidence to participate in implementing a strategy that involves targeting a group of people few in corporate America understand today.

This is the area where most Hispanic strategy managers are truly tested. And if it feels as if you're trying to get an entire army to reframe the business and go against everything it knows and does, that's because you are. Teresa Mackey, vice president of marketing at BB&T, said, "Some days you will feel as though you have really climbed the mountain because you have seen so many good things come to pass. And then there will be days when you think, 'My God, nobody gets it . . .' but then you sit back and realize, 'You know what? We *have* made progress, and we will continue to evolve.'"

TABLE 9.5

Change Management Framework

Change Issue	Impact on Strategy Implementation	Change Management Strategy	Responsibility	Timing	Communication Method
Store managers resist Hispanic merchandising plans in a key market	Minimizes marketing and sales impact	Set up market test to demonstrate impact of integrated execution	Merchandising managers, implementation manager, retail operations manager, marketing manager	12 weeks	Daily reports, weekly meetings

The entire up-front assessment and strategy development process will provide tremendous insight into people's reactions and general disposition. Take notes of what you see and hear because this will be an excellent base for identifying potential change issues and for developing change management strategies to address them in advance.

Having worked with the individuals involved, you have a good idea of where the mental barriers exist, which will serve you well as you create strategies to manage the process of integrating the Hispanic strategy across the organization, but specifically when implementing the steps that are critical to the strategy's initial stages. Focus on these critical areas and accept that resistance is unavoidable, but manageable. Determine where resistance to change currently exists or where it is expected to be strongest (see Table 9.5). You must be highly aware and highly sensitive to implicit and explicit signals during the time you spend creating operational strategies and the action plan. It is so important to not have blinders on at this stage. Wherever you noted hesitation, skepticism, or lack of excitement, you can bet there will be resistance. So, consider that change strategies must not only be created with the change issue at hand, but also in consideration of what is important to the individuals responsible for making it happen. It is a fine line to walk and very particular to the situation and people involved. An implementation team at a national retailer faced temporary resistance from a merchandising director who worried that efforts allocated to the Hispanic strategy would adversely impact non-Hispanic business. The implementation team managed his concerns by keeping him informed of sales results on a daily basis. These results presented an analysis of Hispanic and non-Hispanic store performance that demonstrated incremental same store sales lifts that were higher during similar time periods pre-Hispanic strategy implementation. Then there is the category buyer who resists authorizing certain products because he "thinks" it won't drive enough volume, but who was shown that actual results were actually double than expected. People in numbers-oriented positions require quantitative proof, and if you can create the systems to provide the proof on a consistent basis and in a manner that is relevant, eventually the belief, trust, and acceptance will come. Many times it is perception and fear of the unknown, not reality, that gets in the way of accepting change.

As you prepare for implementation it is recommended to create a change management plan on a table similar to Table 9.5. State the change issue or challenge that is likely to be faced in as direct a manner as possible. Then state how this resistance is likely to impact implementation of the strategy. Next state the solution for addressing the resistance and how the change will be managed in this area, by whom, by when, and how will it be communicated. Then incorporate these actions into the control plan and risk mitigation plan that follow.

CONTROL PLAN

The implementation plan will be only as good as your ability to continuously move the company through the implementation process (and change process mentioned previously). This is critical because, when corporate leadership becomes excited about a promising strategy, the focus on speed is heightened. This can lead to losing control over certain operational processes on which successful execution depends.

To avoid unexpected surprises, make control planning an integral part of the implementation plan. No doubt the Hispanic strategy will compete for mind share and time with other corporate priorities, so building in mechanisms that ensure team accountability is crucial. Ensure that the Hispanic strategy and the resources to carry it out throughout the organization are built into each area's operational priorities. For instance, companies that are structured by function will assign an individual from each area to a strategy to ensure continuity and progress. Include this person in developing the control plan for their respective area. These individuals must buy in to the control plan, establish how it will be monitored, how

TABLE 9.6
Control Plan

	Daily	Weekly	Monthly	Quarterly
R&D				
Manufacturing				
Marketing				
Sales				
Finance				
HR				
Procurement				

often, methods, and communication channels. These are the people that will work with you to ensure not only that implementation is moving forward, but that it is being done to plan, strategize, and budget. And, where possible, these reviews determine if there is opportunity for improvement. The control plan should include progress milestones and reward systems that recognize and promote effective planning, implementation, and constant improvement, based on chosen operational metrics.

The framework must build in necessary review processes by operational area and establish specific time frames. The heart of a control plan is the type of communication that will occur, the channels to be used, the frequency, and the people involved. One way to set up a control plan is to blow up the implementation timeline with focus on CSF-based strategies and operational areas with responsibility for carrying them out. For each of these key areas, break down the timeline in terms of days, weeks, months, and quarters (see Table 9.6). Control timing will differ by operational area and the level of interdependency between them.

Risk Assessment

Implementation control plans should also include a plan for identifying and mitigating risk and should detail contingency plans and procedures for unexpected setbacks. Risks should be kept top of mind so that the team knows who is responsible for addressing issues as they arise. This goes hand in hand with the change management plan, but considers issues that seriously endanger Hispanic strategy implementation and results.

TABLE 9.7
Risk Assessment and Mitigation Plan

Risk Statement	Type	Impact (if occurs)	Probability (of occurrence)	Importance
Hispanic talent for required implementation is not found within required time frame	Human Resources	5	3	5 × 3 = 15 High
Cost overruns	Budget	4	2	4 × 2 = 8 Medium
Time frame for implementation and results do not meet expectations	Financial	5	2	5 × 2 = 10 Medium

A table that lays out the risk statements, the area that is prone to run the risk, the level of impact if it occurs, the probability of occurrence, the importance of the risk, the responsible individuals, how that risk can be mitigated, the time frame involved, and the status of completion for the area involved is a useful way to force the team to think through the potential problems and solutions before being faced with them (see Table 9.7).

The first column includes a statement of the risk, the second column lists the area(s) of the strategy that would be affected, the third column indicates the impact of the risk occurring and assigns a weight from 1 to 5 where 1 is low impact and 5 is high impact. The fourth column indicates the probability of the risk occurring and assigns a probability between 1 and 3. The fifth column indicates the importance of the risk to the strategy implementation and is calculated by multiplying impact by probability columns—the higher the number, the higher the risk is in importance. The remaining columns indicate the areas or people that are responsible or would be held accountable if the risk were to materialize, followed by the next column, which describes the actions that are or would be taken to mitigate this risk, by when, and the progress made on the action to date.

Responsible	Mitigation Action	Date	Status— % Complete
Executive Leadership, Corporate Affairs, Corporate Diversity, HR	Immediately identify minority executive databases such as the Minority Development Council and pay a premium for key positions	August 2006	30%
Finance, implementation team	Weekly budget reviews with finance and implementation teams; monthly review in overall program reviews with corporate leadership	August 2006	10%
Corporate strategic planning, finance, implementation team	Monthly assessment to leadership; weekly assessment with program implementation team	August 2006	20%

THE FINANCIALS

The implementation plan should include individual budget projections required to implement the Hispanic strategy across each operational area. Use these numbers to create a total budget and use these to project expenses for the next three to five years (see Table 9.8). This is an important input to the financials that will help define the ramp-up investment period and the point at which the company will start to realize a return on investment.

One way to look at the financial impact of a Hispanic strategy is to determine what revenues and profits might look like for the next five years if the company maintained the status quo. Status quo assumptions might be a growth rate equal to the average growth for the past three years for households in each Hispanic segment, and average revenue per household by segment, which is assumed to grow 1 percent each year over the next five years. This is then rolled into a Hispanic total. (See Table 9.9.)

Then look at revenue and profits for the next five years with projected growth rates based on the Hispanic strategy. Hispanic strategy might assume higher growth rates that vary by acculturation by segment, with the Hispanic-dominant growth rate being most aggressive—an average increase of 228 percent in the first year and 114 percent in year two. These hypothetical growth rates assume successful implementation of the Hispanic strategy,

TABLE 9.8
Hispanic Strategy Expenses

Operational Areas	Year 1	Year 2	Year 3	Year 4	Year 5
Human Resources					
Technology					
R&D					
Manufacturing					
Marketing					
Distribution					
Procurement					
Finance					
Alliances/Partnerships					

positive macro and industry trends, and comparable growth trends at competitive companies that have launched similar programs in the past three years. In this scenario, average revenue per household by segment is assumed to stay the same and is assumed to grow 1 percent each year over the next five years. (See Table 9.10.) Incremental revenue is then calculated to obtain a read between the two scenarios. (See Table 9.11.)

This can be depicted visually to demonstrate the revenue opportunity gap between status quo strategy and Hispanic strategy. (See Figure 9.1.)

Then you can calculate incremental profit by rolling up the projected expenses for five years from your operational budget and find the difference between incremental revenue and incremental expenses. (See Table 9.12.)

Based on this hypothetical example, this company will invest heavily in the first year of implementation, as a proportion of incremental revenue. But incremental expenses relative to incremental revenue are expected to decline after the first year, leading to a break-even point in year two and incremental profits in year three. (See Figure 9.2.)

Making revenue and expense scenarios transparent and allowing the team and management to see how and when the Hispanic strategy will add to the bottom line will be helpful because everyone will know what to expect going in—and expectations are then based on what was approved. The challenge moves from having to explain when the Hispanic strategy will produce a return on investment to actually managing the implementation plan to meet or exceed projections.

TABLE 9.9

Revenue Projections—Status Quo

		Revenue Projection - Market Strategy - Status Quo				
Segment	Current Year	Year 1	Year 2	Year 3	Year 4	Year 5
Total Hispanic HH	96,720	103,454	110,814	118,864	127,672	137,317
% Growth	7%	7%	7%	7%	7%	7%
Average Revenue/HH	$ 47.51	$ 52.26	$ 57.49	$ 63.24	$ 69.56	$ 76.52
Total Revenue	$ 4,676,692	$ 5,407,010	$ 6,370,846	$ 7,516,962	$ 8,881,415	$ 10,507,630
Assimilated	39,600	43,956	48,791	54,158	60,116	66,728
% Growth	11%	11%	11%	11%	11%	11%
Average Revenue/HH	$ 52.72	$ 57.99	$ 63.79	$ 70.17	$ 77.19	$ 84.91
Total Revenue	$ 2,087,712	$ 2,549,096	$ 3,112,447	$ 3,800,297	$ 4,640,163	$ 5,665,639
Bicultural	36,520	37,250	37,995	38,755	39,530	40,321
% Growth	2%	2%	2%	2%	2%	2%
Average Revenue/HH	$ 46.40	$ 51.04	$ 56.14	$ 61.76	$ 67.93	$ 74.73
Total Revenue	$ 1,694,528	$ 1,901,260	$ 2,133,214	$ 2,393,466	$ 2,685,469	$ 3,013,096
Hispanic-Dominant	20,600	22,248	24,028	25,950	28,026	30,268
% Growth	8%	8%	8%	8%	8%	8%
Average Revenue/HH	$ 43.42	$ 47.76	$ 52.54	$ 57.79	$ 63.57	$ 69.93
Total Revenue	$ 894,452	$ 1,062,608.98	$ 1,262,379.46	$ 1,499,706.80	$ 1,781,651.68	$ 2,116,602.20
Non-Hispanic	233,456	233,456	235,791	238,148	240,530	242,935
% Growth	1%	1%	1%	1%	1%	1%
Average Revenue/HH	$ 52.72	$ 57.99	$ 63.79	$ 70.17	$ 77.19	$ 84.91
Total Revenue	$ 12,307,800	$ 13,538,580	$ 15,041,363	$ 16,710,954	$ 18,565,870	$ 20,626,681

TABLE 9.10

Revenue Projections—Hispanic Strategy

		Revenue Projections - Market Strategy - Hispanic				
Segment	Current Year	Year 1	Year 2	Year 3	Year 4	Year 5
Total Hispanic HH	96,720	114,298	130,802	150,164	172,964	199,914
% Growth	7%	23%	15%	15%	15%	15%
Average Revenue/HH	$ 47.51	$ 52.26	$ 57.49	$ 63.24	$ 69.56	$ 76.52
Total Revenue	$ 4,676,692	$ 5,973,726	$ 7,519,951	$ 9,496,394	$ 12,032,109	$ 15,297,574
Assimilated	39,600	43,956	48,791	54,158	60,116	66,728
% Growth	11%	11%	11%	11%	11%	11%
Average Revenue/HH	$ 52.72	$ 57.99	$ 63.79	$ 70.17	$ 77.19	$ 84.91
Total Revenue	$ 2,087,712	$ 2,549,096	$ 3,112,447	$ 3,800,297	$ 4,640,163	$ 5,665,639
Bicultural	36,520	39,442	43,386	47,724	52,497	57,746
% Growth	2%	8%	10%	10%	10%	10%
Average Revenue/HH	$ 46.40	$ 51.04	$ 56.14	$ 61.76	$ 67.93	$ 74.73
Total Revenue	$ 1,694,528	$ 2,013,099	$ 2,435,850	$ 2,947,379	$ 3,566,328	$ 4,315,257
Hispanic-Dominant	20,600	30,900	38,625	48,281	60,352	75,439
% Growth	8%	50%	25%	25%	25%	25%
Average Revenue/HH	$ 43.42	$ 47.76	$ 52.54	$ 57.79	$ 63.57	$ 69.93
Total Revenue	$ 894,452	$ 1,475,845.80	$ 2,029,287.98	$ 2,790,270.97	$ 3,836,622.58	$ 5,275,356.04
Non-Hispanic	233,456	238,125	245,269	255,080	267,834	283,904
% Growth	1%	2%	3%	4%	5%	6%
Average Revenue/HH	$ 52.72	$ 57.99	$ 63.79	$ 70.17	$ 77.19	$ 84.91
Total Revenue	$ 12,307,800	$ 13,809,352	$ 15,645,996	$ 17,899,019	$ 20,673,367	$ 24,105,146

TABLE 9.11

Projected Revenue Increases

Projections	Year 1	Year 2	Year 3	Year 4	Year 5
Revenue Projections - Status Quo	$ 5,407,010	$ 6,370,846	$ 7,516,962	$ 8,881,415	$ 10,507,630
Revenue Projections - Hispanic Strategy	$ 5,973,726	$ 7,519,951	$ 9,496,394	$ 12,032,109	$ 15,297,574
Hipanic Strategy Incremental Revenue	$ 566,716	$ 1,149,105	$ 1,979,433	$ 3,150,694	$ 4,789,944

FIGURE 9.1
Hispanic Strategy—Incremental Revenue

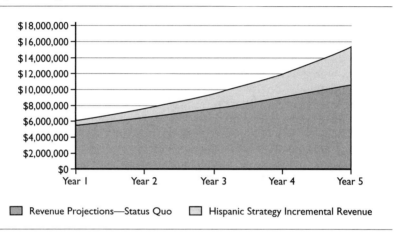

Revenue Projections—Status Quo   Hispanic Strategy Incremental Revenue

TABLE 9.12
Hispanic Strategy—Profit/Loss

Projection	Year 1	Year 2	Year 3	Year 4	Year 5
Incremental Revenue	$ 566,716	$ 1,149,105	$ 1,979,433	$ 3,150,694	$ 4,789,944
Incremental Expenses	$ 1,133,432	$ 1,149,105	$ 1,563,752	$ 1,575,347	$ 1,915,978
Total Impact	$ (566,716)	$ -	$ 415,681	$ 1,575,347	$ 2,873,966

The Budget

If approved, a budget for a Hispanic strategy that is aligned with the entire company is not just one budget, but rather distinct budgets across the areas where incremental costs will be incurred. While it might be tempting and seemingly logical to allocate a single budget to the Hispanic initiative, this approach is often counterproductive because it defeats the goal of integration and of implementing the strategy as one company.

How a company allocates budgets and resources ultimately depends on the company and the type of organizational structure that exists within it. But an integrated approach has worked for many. Some banking and retail companies with integrated budgets are operating such that, as marketing develops the next generation of brochures, it creates bilingual brochures as part of the same effort. If media is negotiating a media buy or promotion, then similar negotiations take place with Hispanic media. If

FIGURE 9.2
Hispanic Strategy—Total Impact

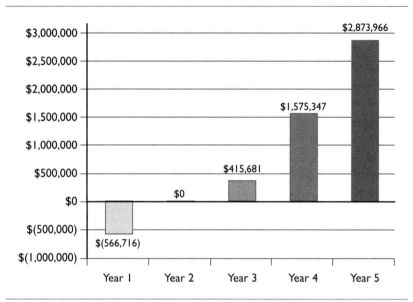

HR is redesigning the training module, it also plans for the creation of a Hispanic training module. If a new merchandising plan is being developed, Hispanic merchandising is considered for those stores where it is relevant, and so forth.

Having the Hispanic budget live in each operational area gives ownership and assigns accountability to those responsible for implementing. This can actually serve as one form of implementation control.

CASE STUDY: BB&T

BB&T Corporation, headquartered in Winston-Salem, North Carolina, is a fast-growing, highly profitable financial holding company with over $100 billion in assets.

Its bank subsidiaries operate more than 1,400 branch offices in the Carolinas, Virginia, West Virginia, Kentucky, Georgia, Maryland, Tennessee, Alabama, Indiana, Florida, and Washington, DC.

BB&T's operating strategy distinguishes it from other financial holding companies in that its banking subsidiaries are organized as a group of community banks, each with a regional president. This allows decisions to be made locally, close to the customer, which makes BB&T's customer service more responsive, reliable, and empathetic.

In 2001, BB&T decided to create a task force to learn about the Hispanic market, which was growing quickly in its footprint and increasingly visible in its communities and branches.

The Assessment

Its assessment approach included learning about the demographics of the marketplace to seize the opportunity in each of its regions. Population size, growth projections, income and buying power, and Hispanic attitudes toward and usage of financial services were used to create a revenue model based on Hispanic market share estimates and expected revenue by account types. It looked at the opportunity within its footprint and estimated that if it could garner just 5 percent of the existing Hispanic market, it would justify the investment.

In assessing the customer, BB&T gained surprising and valuable information. Among other things, it discovered a true entrepreneurial spirit: in its footprint, one in seven new small businesses is Hispanic-owned. This meant that if it could get the personal banking business of these business owners this year, next year it might be able to gain their business accounts. Looking internally, BB&T felt that it had a strong advantage with its customer service. Knowing that Hispanics in their markets valued service, it knew it would have a leg up on the competition and could build on this advantage.

With facts and figures in hand and with support from its executive management, the task force traveled to meet and educate regional management about this population's potential impact on BB&T's business. The task force encountered mixed reactions, driven mostly by fear of change and skepticism about whether Hispanic growth projections represented only a temporary phenomenon.

The task force realized that if it was going to get the ear of other regional vice presidents and make this a top priority, it would have to recruit one of its own to head the task force. With the permission of executive management, it recruited a regional vice president who was Hispanic. Soon, every regional vice president was on the task force, which now meets quarterly to discuss how to address the Hispanic opportunity in their regions. Now implementation of task force recommendations is rarely a problem.

The Implementation

BB&T went on to segment branches in every region and identified branches called Hispanic Banking Centers. This segmentation drives the language of its in-branch merchandising and product brochures; it drives how many bilingual employees can be found in each branch, with teller signs indicating that Spanish is spoken. It addressed cultural sensitivity within various forums: developing a video that talks about cultural sensitivity; training employees on diversity; and BB&T University, in which employees learn to speak Spanish.

As for its product mix, BB&T developed a totally different look and branding for the products and services marketed to Hispanics. It also developed the Six Laws of the Hispanic Universe, which addresses cultural issues such as language, emotion, family, and music, and fosters a customer-service environment that encourages its Hispanic customers not to limit their dreams.

BB&T's customer-service orientation has paid off. And the company realized that it's even more important than language. "We thought at first that if we didn't have everything translated we'd be in trouble," says Teresa Mackey, VP of marketing, "but we learned that we're going to be OK. Hispanics appreciate a smile and courteous service, and that makes a difference, regardless of the language we speak."

Its community outreach is based on videotapes that educate Hispanics on everyday life situations, including financial issues. The tapes play continuously in Hispanic Banking Center lobbies. Since the start of the program, more than 250,000 tapes have been distributed, with requests coming from all over the United States. There are more than 30 regions in the BB&T footprint, and each region has aligned itself with different spheres of Hispanic influence within its respective area. Corporately, BB&T has partnered with the North Carolina Governor's Office of Hispanic/Latino Affairs; the Mexican Consulate for North Carolina; and El Pueblo, which is a state advocacy organization. It repeatedly receives recognition from its partners.

The Results

Current account growth is well within expectations, and BB&T is looking for a majority of organic growth over the next five years to come from the designated Hispanic markets identified within its footprint. In addition, with the increase in Hispanic Banking Centers across its footprint, it expects to double new Hispanic household accounts and increase to at least double the current cross-sell of products and services to existing Hispanic households.

10

MEASUREMENT SYSTEM SETUP

A Hispanic strategy will generate continuous support only to the extent that you can continuously demonstrate it contributes to top-line and bottom-line growth. Do not wait until the first business review meeting to start figuring out what you can measure and how. You may find that necessary data or the format in which it is needed may not be available because the system was never set up to generate it. Managers often struggle with providing relevant and convincing metrics to top management because metrics and the systems to capture them were not defined during the planning phase.

Work through this process with each operational area as you develop operational objectives, strategies, and action plans. Jointly review performance reports generated by operational areas; not only will it make you sensitive to what drives those areas' priorities, but you'll have a sense for how the Hispanic strategy can be a part of each area's success story. Become familiar with top management reporting style preferences. If they like comparative data that looks at Hispanic versus other segments, provide it. If they like industry or competitive comparisons, provide it. If they need to see ratios, provide them. You want to be as relevant and meaningful as possible. Keep in mind that most managers are interested in results that demonstrate not only how the strategy may be capturing Hispanics as customers, but also how it is retaining them. Work with support functions responsible for generating the reports to determine which reports are generated by outside vendors and which are generated internally—those created by the company based on proprietary information and perhaps even using proprietary models.

STRATEGIC ALIGNMENT—WHERE THE RUBBER HITS THE ROAD . . .

If you think of a basic strategy map and Norton and Kaplan's Balanced Score Card model, there are four areas or perspectives that feed into the company's growth and productivity strategies and ultimately feed into the corporate vision. These are financial return, customer value proposition, internal management processes, and the company's ability to learn and grow.

Each area feeds into the next to achieve the company's goals and each area requires: (1) its own performance objectives, (2) defined measures, (3) targets that must be met to be considered successful and the learning, training, and management initiatives that will help achieve them, and (4) finally, they include the budgets required for implementation.

The Hispanic strategy must be measured in the same way. Depending on the strategy's critical success factors it must consider where in the organization growth and learning need to occur to enable the organization to be relevant to this consumer group. You should establish goals and metric around this. This could be related to creating and measuring success across culture, leadership, structural alignment, and teamwork. This is the foundation that allows the company to successfully implement operational strategies and action plans. This is the knowledge that enables the organization to address Hispanic recruiting and training and where cultural and diversity initiatives are created and measured. This is where communication systems are created and assessed and where initiatives for Hispanic market knowledge building are created and disseminated across the organization. These are critical areas because successful management of control and change plan is directly related to having these measurable foundations around people, information, and organizational structures in place.

Hispanic CSFs may require objectives, strategies, and action plans that relate to the following:

- *Operations*—sourcing new specialty suppliers, expanding or acquiring manufacturing capabilities, creating, adapting, or contracting more targeted distribution networks, and managing related risks
- *Customer management*—strategies for Hispanic segment target definition and acquisition, retention, and growth
- *Innovation*—the company's ability to identify Hispanic products and sales opportunities, develop a relevant Hispanic R&D portfolio, and to design, develop, and launch new products that specifically meet Hispanics preferences
- *Regulatory and social*—meeting diversity employment regulations, deploying community reinvestment initiatives, creating a diversity supplier program, or creating relevant health, safety, and environmental initiatives

Your company has metrics related to all of these areas to target its mainstream customers and to the extent that your CSFs are tied to these areas so will you need to develop related Hispanic metrics that align and are consistent with corporate goals.

Successful creation, implementation, and results from internal management processes and growth initiatives are the foundations that ultimately will enable you to deliver on a customer value proposition that aligns with the company's business model. Depending on industry and position within an industry, your company's value proposition may be related to price, quality, access, selection, functionality, service, relationships, or brand image, and depending on your current consumer value proposition, staying aligned to the current business model implies an ability to deliver the same value proposition, albeit in a relevant manner. Metrics are linked to sales growth that is driven by the corporate value proposition—when I say *corporate*, this may just relate to one business unit, but the point is that if the Hispanic strategy is based on the business unit's business model, the metrics must also align. Finally, your objectives, strategies, and results will be assessed in consideration of their compatibility to how the company measures financial performance based on its strategies to

- increase productivity by improving its cost structure and increasing its asset utilization; and/or
- grow through its ability to expand revenue opportunities and/or enhance customer value.

Again, developing a Hispanic strategy requires an ability to strike a balance between creating customer value for Hispanics while staying true to your company's reason for being and its strategies for gaining a sustainable competitive advantage. It's about ensuring external and internal alignment and relevance.

Once defined, these metrics and targets should become part of the control plan. If your company uses the Balanced Score Card, it can be useful to create one for the Hispanic strategy as an overlay to the ones created for total company performance. Many companies find that it is a very useful tool for controlling these four key strategy perspectives. Figure 10.1 is Norton and Kaplan's basic Balanced Scored Card framework, which can be used to address each operational area and the related Critical Success Factors.

As you can see, strategic context is tremendously important. Never get caught up in looking at Hispanic strategy results differently from those they see for the rest of the organization. Top managers do not want to see Hispanic results unless they are reported in the context of the total business, and by the same token you want to support thinking that Hispanic strategy success contributes to the company's overall results. Reference annual company reports and SEC filings, as these provide excellent direction on how the company and the industry define success. If you want to affect internal change in support of the Hispanic strategy, observing this context is critical. And while detailed reports from various operational areas may be necessary as you monitor and control implementation, your report to top management should focus only on the numbers that prove Hispanic strategy performance is contributing to corporate strategy success. One thing is for sure, top management only wants to hear about improved imagery among Hispanics if its corporate growth strategy is focused on enhancing customer value perceptions. It only wants to hear about new services and product gains if its growth strategy depends on expanding revenue opportunities. Your objectives strategies and metrics must link to corporate priorities if you want to be heard at the top. The closer your successes align with corporate goals, the higher in the organization your successes will be heard.

This proposition is not easy. It requires considerable coordination and collaboration across business lines and operational areas that impact or are impacted by the Hispanic strategy, but doing so will elevate the credibility of your reporting considerably. Once you've set up the systems to produce the reports you need, generating them on a regular basis should be fairly automatic.

FIGURE 10.1

The Balanced Score Card

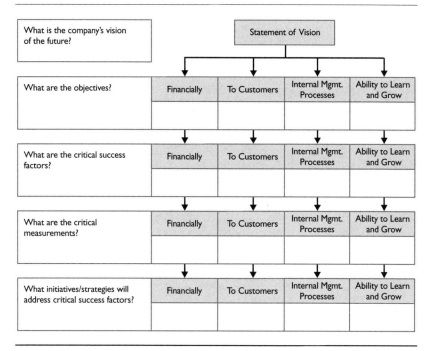

Source: Adapted from Norton and Kaplan's Balanced Score Card.

INTERNALLY GENERATED DATA

If reports are produced internally, find out how the necessary inputs related to Hispanic transaction activity can be generated so the system that tracks overall transaction activity can also track your Hispanic customers.

Take the time to meet with the people within your organization responsible for generating the data you need to obtain. Ask them to help you define how Hispanic measurement can be incorporated into the way the company measures overall activity. This is a conversation you should be having when jointly developing operational strategies with systems, technology, or logistics because it relates to implementing your strategies. It also fulfills one of your tactical goals—producing ideas for how the inputs that go into these reports can be obtained and used to generate the necessary reporting If you don't have buy-in for the metrics you intend to monitor, you do not have a viable strategy.

The internal department that will be most helpful in this area may vary, depending on your company, or it may be a combination of several departments, including outside vendors. In the case of one retailer, the marketing team partnered with its financial area to devise an objective way to measure and analyze the data that was being generated through various means. They then worked jointly to determine how to disseminate that information to key stakeholders.

In PacifiCare's case, systems were created from the ground up. PacifiCare had not tracked Hispanic membership before, and its system was not set up to identify its Hispanic members. The company worked with outside vendors to create a Hispanic surname algorithm that enabled IT to create and generate reports on Hispanic membership metrics, which were then compared to total membership.

Aligning report content to expected formats adds to its credibility and facilitates increased comprehension, though such alignment may require adaptation of hardware, software, and measurement models to capture relevant information across the system.

A leading retailer has a sales reporting methodology that is consistent with that which is generated for its overall business. It stresses that ensuring consistency and timeliness is a critical and continuous process as it is the only thing that truly proves that its Hispanic strategy is meeting its goals. It is the tool that drives continued support internally.

EXTERNALLY GENERATED DATA

Increasingly, companies augment their internal data reporting with industry reports purchased from outside vendors like IRI or ACNielsen in the grocery business. In some cases, representatives from those companies work in-house and collaborate with category and merchandising managers to generate reports that combine external and internal data.

If your organization uses companies such as these, you'll want to plan and budget for this in your implementation plan. These companies should be contacted through the proper channels to determine if they track Hispanic activity or if they can incorporate the software or databases to do so. The data these companies provide can be very helpful because these tools are critical for understanding Hispanic category and sales movement and trends—important not only in regular reporting, but especially helpful in measuring pre-impact and post-impact of retail level promotions, deal periods, or advertising. And importantly, this data is reported in an identical fashion to total market data. One word of caution on tools that are based on scanner data: their Hispanic store samples include only $2 million-plus stores, which don't accurately reflect total category movement because it omits much of the purchasing happening at neighborhood independents. Often, if you have done the segmentation, your internal data can be the most accurate sales tracking reporting resource, but outside resources can provide directional insight. Remember, though, finding opportunity categories requires in-market observation and conversations with specialty distributors.

For instance, Walgreens uses external research resources such as IRI, ACNielsen, and other syndicated research to track movement of Hispanic items in stores where Hispanic categories have been expanded. Coupled with its internal sales data, this works well because Walgreens is reflected in the store samples used by the other research resources and, therefore, Walgreens is able to see its Hispanic business in context of the total market.

Syndicated market research is typically part of any company's arsenal of resources. Aside from the companies mentioned throughout the book that have developed expertise in measuring the Hispanic market, several industry-specific research providers include Hispanics in their samples, which means that if you request it, you may be able to obtain a comparable reading that is based just on Hispanics. If you do this, however, make sure you have a solid understanding of the profile of the Hispanics included in the studies. You'll want to know how they differ from your Hispanic target segment so you can calibrate your findings based on these differences. For instance, a measure that is higher or lower than expected might be due to the acculturation level of the Hispanic sample included in the study. One sure way to readily determine this is to find out if the survey is administered only in English or in both English and Spanish and whether Hispanics are given a language choice.

If the sample allows, you may be able to request data based exclusively on Hispanics who are most like your target. Use the acculturation drivers from Chapter 6 to guide how you segment Hispanic survey respondents in secondary research surveys. For instance, one way of defining acculturation and language preference is to isolate Hispanics who chose to respond to the company's survey in Spanish or, if the respondent is part of a household panel, you might choose households that have been cate-gorized as unacculturated versus bicultural. Depending on your indus-try, you may want to look at results based on different levels of acculturation so you can determine which group is being most respon-sive to your marketing efforts or which group is most similar to your mainstream consumer.

In cases where sample sizes are small, you may need to ask the vendor to collapse several reporting periods to make the data more stable and rep-resentative. Your ability to do this will depend on whether your measure-ment is continuous or whether a specific effort such as a campaign or promotion is being measured. Also, keep in mind that if you are collapsing data, this implies that your reporting periods may be different, so make sure that this aligns with internal expectations such as planning periods.

In some cases, especially for large market studies conducted yearly or semiannually, research companies are willing to augment their Hispanic samples if a client commits to an extended contract. While this may re-quire a sizable up-front commitment, it is typically a fraction of the cost to field a proprietary study, and you'll have the advantage of "apples-to-apples" comparison. If your management trusts the reporting from a cer-tain company, it becomes critical to have the Hispanic numbers come from the same company; this will avoid questions and skepticism about the reliability of the data.

Using Hispanic IRI data, Stop & Shop has successfully been changing product assortment priorities among category managers so key Hispanic items are authorized by using data to show movement. Gabriela de Oliveiras Castro, ethnic food buyer for Stop & Shop, says she's been able to go back to category managers who said, "That stuff is not going to sell," and show that they doubled sales from $200,000 to $400,000 at every angle.

CHOOSING THE METRICS

As mentioned, focus on metrics that align with CSFs and corporate goals and strategies to stay relevant. It sounds simplistic, but companies often make the mistake of basing their metric only on market driven measures instead of thinking of the big picture. There is no quicker way to undermine the value of your results than to report metrics that do not align with your organization's interests and goals.

Sales

Sales are, of course, at the top of most companies' lists when looking at performance across all business units. Your Hispanic strategy is no different, though profitability must go hand in hand. There are many companies that boast revenue growth, but their operational strategies do not lead to bottom-line growth. However, if topline growth is emphasized in your company as it often is in companies that compete on a low-costs strategy, so must the tools to track Hispanic sales in the context of total company and even industry sales volume be in place. While absolute numbers will obviously be smaller, your growth compared to overall growth is important to show.

Stop & Shop demonstrates sales results through IRI, ACNielsen, and its internal data. Stop & Shop's internal data analysts work with in-house IRI and Spectra representatives to generate Hispanic performance reports. The systems and filters are set up in the databases so that, with minimal adjustments, the data can be run and sent out to each store monthly.

Stop & Shop also uses its data to highlight opportunity gaps. For example, if its internal sales data for Hispanic categories indicates that rice is up 15 percent, but the market is up by 25 percent, the implementation team uses this data to show the respective category manager that the division is actually lagging the market by 10 percent in this product.

These opportunity reports are run for ethnic products every eight weeks to show year-over-year individual store performance across ethnic products. Further, the team has been able to show double-digit same-store sale increases and prove that ethnic products are driving the business for many of its stores. The ethnic department has proven that quantifying this type of performance creates tremendous receptivity across the organization. This has been especially important because of the way categories are managed. Ethnic categories are spread across several category managers so the ethnic department delivers the numbers on a continuous basis to get key items authorized.

At Nash Finch's AVANZA stores, the team focuses first and foremost on sales, but it also looks at Hispanic customer count, profitability, and other standard retail measures, and it places a great deal of importance on understanding the impact of its marketing on brand position among Denver Hispanics. The company invests heavily on Hispanic market research to ensure that customer satisfaction is strong relative to its competition. Brian E. Numainville, director of research for Nash Finch, says, "A lot of people blow off the research part. To me, it means spending X thousand instead of losing X millions and later asking 'why didn't we do that?'"

The national retailer in the case study says the team validates the program to the rest of the organization through solid financial reporting and "good old-fashioned business intuition." It has rigorous mechanisms to look at sales. It looks at specific store scenarios and drills its analysis to a very fine level based on internal models. This allows it to report how Hispanic stores perform relative to non-Hispanic stores. This type of reporting ties to retail execution and advertising impact, and it is then able to validate whether merchandising decisions were appropriate and make the necessary adjustments.

They say more companies are being held accountable to deliver return on investment more so than a few years ago when marketing departments highlighted brand awareness and mind share. In essence, management is saying that just doesn't cut it anymore for any business strategy.

Denny's analyzes its sales activity on a total company basis and breaks down its sales analysis by Hispanic and non-Hispanic store clusters to assess the relationship between sales, its marketing efforts, and the results of its consumer tracking studies.

And when El Pollo Loco measures sales results of its promotional offers, the offers are evaluated on how well each performs among its intended targets in the geographies in which these targets are concentrated. Not all offers are expected to do well everywhere or among everybody. Sometimes promotions are targeted to Hispanics who prefer traditional recipe offerings, while other promotions emphasize new marinade flavors and new menu items targeted to the mainstream consumers. While this presents a challenge among franchisees that may not have stores that align with all targets for every promotional offer, Karen Eadon, vice president of marketing at El Pollo Loco, maintains that as a company, "El Pollo Loco must successfully deliver value to its two core targets, and [its] measurement and reporting focus aligns with this dual market strategy."

Customer Conversion

As discussed in previous chapters, the banking industry has increasingly turned its attention to the segment of Hispanics who do not bank. When Wells Fargo began to accept the Mexican identification card (in place of a Social Security card) along with a Tax ID number obtained from the Internal Revenue Service as identification to open accounts for Hispanics, the idea was to convert them into bank customers. Wells Fargo and Harris Bank successfully launched a money transfer option to capture these consumers. The intent, from the time that a customer opens the first account as a tool to transfer money home, is to eventually cross-sell other products. As such, conversion rate is an important metric for both banks, as is revenue contribution to bank products into which Hispanics are migrating.

Brand Awareness and Imagery

Because brand familiarity and trust are significant choice drivers among Hispanics, many companies that advertise heavily to this community do so to create or enhance their awareness and image position among this target market. As such, one of their key metrics becomes measuring brand awareness and imagery. Some companies conduct their own studies, others work with companies that augment their Hispanic sample to deliver more robust Hispanic data, and still others buy syndicated data as it becomes available.

El Pollo Loco subscribes to a restaurant-industry tracking study that measures total market restaurant trends, including Hispanics' restaurant consumption among various types of restaurants, and specifically measures brand awareness and imagery across an extensive battery of operational, food quality, and service issues. They are able to report Hispanic performance in the context of total market performance.

Customer Satisfaction

Companies in the service industry are naturally interested in how Hispanics rate their customer service. This allows them to better align store and customer service operations to address Hispanics' expectations. Moreover, it gives companies the insight to revamp operational strategies that impact areas such as HR, store hours, promotions, and locations. For example, Walgreens is seeing solid return on investment across all of its Hispanic stores by making sure that it has the right items in the right stores at the right levels. Departments that were expanded to include more Hispanic-relevant items have grown across every item, and this has resulted in strong customer satisfaction increases. Further proof are its increases across every metric, including the number of shopping trips to its stores, market share, and same-store sales in its Hispanic stores.

As well, Denny's conducts a continuous tracking of consumer sentiment to ensure that expectations are met consistently across all customers, including Hispanics. Margaret Jenkins, senior VP of marketing and franchise development and chief marketing officer at Denny's, said, "there are many more parallels with ethnic consumers than most people realize. I think that in some categories everyone looks for the same basic things, and our Hispanic customers are no different."

RESULTS

When looking at results, companies can have a variety of expectations. But as long as those expectations and the metrics are set up in the business case that top management approved, your job is to ensure that the organization implements according to plan—a plan that it helped develop. For instance, a company's plan may state that the first two years may be considered a ramp-up period operationally and a period of brand building, but not necessarily profit. The financial model may not predict profit for two or three years down the road. Having expectations clear and up front ensures that everyone is on the same track and that management can view interim results in the proper context.

BB&T believes that because it is in the market for the long haul, its emphasis for the next few years is building its relationship with the community in order to instill a sense of trust. Everything it does works toward this goal. Teresa Mackey, vice president of BB&T marketing, stressed that "the benefits, the financial rewards, and the business gains will come over the long term. Hispanic strategy managers cannot expect to target the market and see results in six months. No, what you do is for the long haul."

But as implementation is being carried out, a continuous calibration must be part of reporting. If the economy is on a decline or the industry is changing, then sales goals will be adjusted right along with the rest of the company. Ensure that as the company starts talking about "tough times ahead" you quickly quantify the external impact on your Hispanic strategy, and the impact of your Hispanic strategy on total corporate performance.

Clearly, the companies studied for this book are pleased with their results. They report Hispanic strategies that are on track with corporate strategies and growth goals. This alignment continues to instill confidence and continued support among management ranks.

11

CONCLUSION

As you begin the process of developing or refining the Hispanic business strategy for your company, use the principles and guidelines in this book to guide your own approach. They provide a jumping-off point for embarking on this journey. The resources discussed in earlier sections—and in the Appendix, Bibliography, and Resources—will help point the way to much of the information you need, and will no doubt help you discover new and more specific resources.

By now, it's obvious that the process for creating a Hispanic business strategy involves total company commitment. There are no shortcuts and no cookie-cutter approaches. While it is immensely insightful to learn about the experiences of other companies, you cannot copy another organization's Hispanic business strategy and expect to achieve organization-specific results that align with corporate objectives.

The upside is that by the time implementation of the Hispanic strategy is launched, your entire organization will be in tune with the company's decision to implement a growth strategy that targets U.S. Hispanics, rather than the company hearing about a "Hispanic program that marketing is doing." There is a significant difference in how these two scenarios will be perceived and resonate across the organization, and the results will reflect it. In the proposed scenario, the entire organization is connected to the outcome and has a vested interest in its success.

Why? Because the metrics will highlight and link every area responsible for implementation to total organizational performance, and when adjustments are necessary, those involved will be more likely to seek them rather than avoid them.

Case study companies continue to learn and work within their organizations. They recognize that evolving their strategies to align with their overall business goals means identifying opportunities for improvement on an ongoing basis and working collectively within their organizations to make necessary adjustments. In most cases, they optimize internal and external inputs and feedback to feed forward their implementation, control, risk mitigation, and measurement plans.

They consistently challenge top management to consider that if the Hispanic market is as valuable as everyone believes it is, the process and time required to build the brand and win profitable Hispanic share will be no different than that of any new business strategy. Consistency and continuity deliver not only short-term results, but long-term growth that ties into the organization's vision—though at times, it will be difficult to overcome Wall Street's quarterly watch on business performance and the "quateritis" mindset it instills.

In my work, I have seen how complete strategic integration versus a tactical approach play out numerous times. I have seen how companies that adopt the latter approach often give up because they don't realize the (misinformed) results they expected and because it's very difficult to achieve success with limited resources, limited organizational support, or worse, indifference.

And if you think about it, so many companies, perhaps even your own, are spending tens of millions of dollars to set up shop and do business in Latin America. So, consider that the challenge of achieving corporate alignment in the United States—as daunting as it may sound—is minimal when you have the home advantage. You are competing for a piece of a Hispanic nation with almost $700 billion in purchasing power in your own backyard where you won't need to deal with issues like currency devaluation, foreign exchange risks, low disposable incomes, suboptimal distribution channels, challenging supply-chain logistics, difficult foreign government regulations, and legal systems. With the home advantage, you're operating in a control environment. Here, where the opportunity is even larger, achieving success will be about strategic management skills.

I wouldn't propose this approach if the benefit of doing so weren't substantial. The benefit will come in the form of much larger (and measurable) potential returns, long-term growth and profitability, and perhaps most important of all, a Hispanic business strategy that is entirely yours—tailored to your company's unique needs and goals—resulting in a difficult-to-duplicate, future-oriented, and sustainable competitive advantage. After all, will you be able to ignore what will soon be one-quarter of the entire U.S. population, with younger, larger households? Is profitable long-term growth even feasible without a solid strategy that positions your company as a viable option today?

SECONDARY RESEARCH RESOURCES

1. U.S. BUREAU OF THE CENSUS

Go to http://www.census.gov, select American FactFinder, and then select Data Sets.

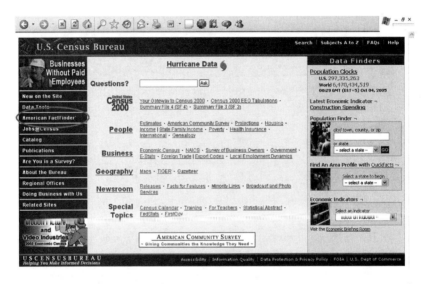

Example A. Chicago: Overall Hispanic Population and by Type

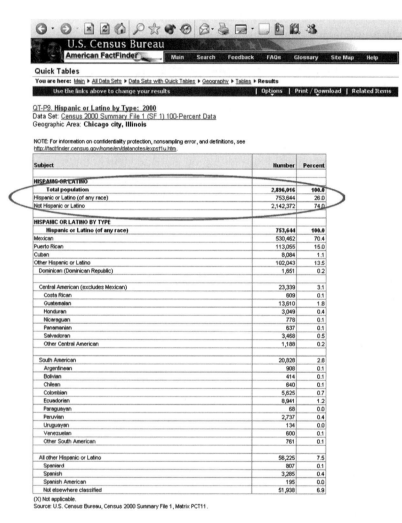

Example B. Chicago: Region of Birth and Year of Entry

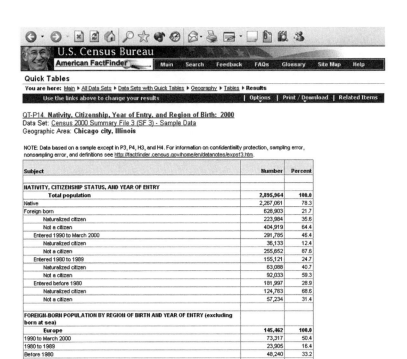

U.S. Census Bureau

American FactFinder — Main   Search   Feedback   FAQs   Glossary   Site Map   Help

Quick Tables

You are here: Main ▸ All Data Sets ▸ Data Sets with Quick Tables ▸ Geography ▸ Tables ▸ Results

Use the links above to change your results | Options | Print / Download | Related Items

QT-P14 **Nativity, Citizenship, Year of Entry, and Region of Birth: 2000**
Data Set: Census 2000 Summary File 3 (SF 3) - Sample Data
Geographic Area: **Chicago city, Illinois**

NOTE: Data based on a sample except in P3, P4, H3, and H4. For information on confidentiality protection, sampling error, nonsampling error, and definitions see http://factfinder.census.gov/home/en/datanotes/expsf3.htm.

Subject	Number	Percent
NATIVITY, CITIZENSHIP STATUS, AND YEAR OF ENTRY		
Total population	**2,895,964**	**100.0**
Native	2,267,061	78.3
Foreign born	628,903	21.7
Naturalized citizen	223,984	35.6
Not a citizen	404,919	64.4
Entered 1990 to March 2000	291,785	46.4
Naturalized citizen	36,133	12.4
Not a citizen	255,652	87.6
Entered 1980 to 1989	155,121	24.7
Naturalized citizen	63,088	40.7
Not a citizen	92,033	59.3
Entered before 1980	181,997	28.9
Naturalized citizen	124,763	68.6
Not a citizen	57,234	31.4
FOREIGN-BORN POPULATION BY REGION OF BIRTH AND YEAR OF ENTRY (excluding born at sea)		
Europe	**145,462**	**100.0**
1990 to March 2000	73,317	50.4
1980 to 1989	23,905	16.4
Before 1980	48,240	33.2
Asia	**▨▨▨,▨▨▨**	**▨▨▨.▨**
1990 to March 2000	52,972	46.9
1980 to 1989	32,323	28.6
Before 1980	27,637	24.5
Africa	**12,613**	**100.0**
1990 to March 2000	7,439	59.0
1980 to 1989	3,027	24.0
Before 1980	2,147	17.0
Oceania	**661**	**100.0**
1990 to March 2000	366	55.4
1980 to 1989	92	13.9
Before 1980	203	30.7
Latin America	**354,034**	**100.0**
1990 to March 2000	156,374	44.2
1980 to 1989	95,206	26.9
Before 1980	102,454	28.9
Northern America	**3,201**	**100.0**
1990 to March 2000	1,317	41.1

Example C. Chicago: Hispanic Foreign-Born and Country Origin

Region and country or area	Number	Percent
Vietnam	8,072	1.3
Western Asia	13,177	2.1
Iraq	5,133	0.8
Israel	1,599	0.3
Jordan	1,484	0.2
Lebanon	868	0.1
Syria	1,611	0.3
Turkey	922	0.1
Armenia	28	0.0
Asia, not elsewhere classified	1,359	0.2
Africa	12,613	2.0
Eastern Africa	2,146	0.3
Ethiopia	938	0.1
Middle Africa	295	0.0
Northern Africa	1,423	0.2
Egypt	436	0.1
Southern Africa	470	0.1
South Africa	433	0.1
Western Africa	7,391	1.2
Ghana	1,960	0.3
Nigeria	4,643	0.7
Sierra Leone	82	0.0
Africa, not elsewhere classified	888	0.1
Oceania	661	0.1
Australia and New Zealand Subregion	622	0.1
Australia	499	0.1
Melanesia	0	0.0
Micronesia	7	0.0
Polynesia	23	0.0
Oceania, not elsewhere classified	9	0.0
Latin America	354,034	56.3
Caribbean	13,014	2.1
Barbados	133	0.0
Cuba	5,317	0.8
Dominican Republic	1,541	0.2
Haiti	2,092	0.3
Jamaica	2,987	0.5
Trinidad and Tobago	435	0.1
Central America	317,740	50.5
Mexico	292,565	46.5
Other Central America	25,175	4.0
Costa Rica	790	0.1
El Salvador	3,482	0.6
Guatemala	13,699	2.2
Honduras	3,025	0.5
Nicaragua	732	0.1
Panama	864	0.1
South America	23,280	3.7
Argentina	1,226	0.2
Bolivia	347	0.1
Brazil	1,004	0.2
Chile	630	0.1
Colombia	5,378	0.9
Ecuador	9,921	1.6
Guyana	420	0.1
Peru	3,050	0.5
Venezuela	847	0.1
Northern America	3,201	0.5
Canada	3,177	0.5
Born at sea	0	0.0

Example D. Chicago: English Language Ability among Spanish Speakers

QT-P17. **Ability to Speak English: 2000**
Data Set: Census 2000 Summary File 3 (SF 3) - Sample Data
Geographic Area: **Chicago city, Illinois**

NOTE: Data based on a sample except in P3, P4, H3, and H4. For information on confidentiality protection, sampling error, nonsampling error, and definitions see http://factfinder.census.gov/home/en/datanotes/expsf3.htm.

Subject	Number	Percent
POPULATION 5 YEARS AND OVER BY LANGUAGE SPOKEN AT HOME AND ABILITY TO SPEAK ENGLISH		
Population 5 years and over	**2,678,981**	**100.0**
Speak only English	1,726,905	64.5
Speak a language other than English	952,076	35.5
Spanish	**625,240**	**100.0**
Speak English "very well"	289,847	46.4
Speak English "well"	144,080	23.0
Speak English "not well"	127,437	20.4
Speak English "not at all"	63,876	10.2
Other Indo-European languages	**212,576**	**100.0**
Speak English "very well"	107,567	50.6
Speak English "well"	54,728	25.7
Speak English "not well"	40,688	19.1
Speak English "not at all"	9,593	4.5
Asian and Pacific Island languages	**82,582**	**100.0**
Speak English "very well"	39,892	48.3
Speak English "well"	22,438	27.2
Speak English "not well"	15,046	18.2
Speak English "not at all"	5,206	6.3
All other languages	**31,678**	**100.0**
Speak English "very well"	20,595	65.0
Speak English "well"	7,387	23.3
Speak English "not well"	3,078	9.7
Speak English "not at all"	618	2.0
ABILITY TO SPEAK ENGLISH		
Population 5 years and over	**2,678,981**	**100.0**
Speak a language other than English	952,076	35.5
5 to 17 years	202,134	7.5
18 to 64 years	671,243	25.1
65 years and over	78,699	2.9
Speak English less than "very well"	494,175	18.4
5 to 17 years	80,286	3.0
18 to 64 years	364,436	13.6
65 years and over	49,453	1.8
ABILITY TO SPEAK ENGLISH IN HOUSEHOLD		
Linguistically isolated households[1]	107,870	(X)
Population 5 years and over in households	**2,619,871**	**100.0**
In linguistically isolated households[1]	293,053	11.2
5 to 17 years	63,399	2.4
18 to 64 years	199,609	7.6
65 years and over	30,045	1.1

(X) Not applicable.
[1] A linguistically isolated household is one in which no member 14 years old and over (1) speaks only English or (2) speaks

2. BUREAU OF LABOR STATISTICS

Go to http://www.bls.gov/cex/home.htm.

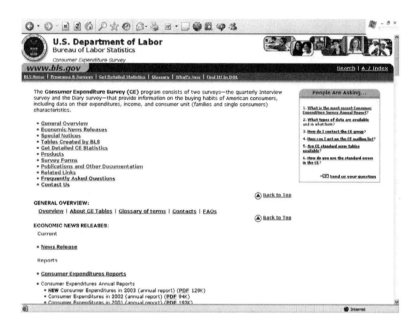

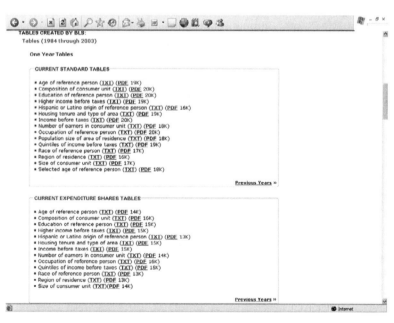

Example A. BLS: Consumer Survey, Page I

Table 2200. Hispanic or Latino origin of reference person: Shares of annual aggregate expenditures and sources of income, Consumer Expenditure Survey, 2003

(Aggregates in millions of dollars, unless otherwise indicated)

Item	Aggregate	Hispanic or Latino	Not Hispanic or Latino		
			Total	White, Asian, and All Other Races	Black or African American
Number of consumer units (in thousands)	115,356	11,727	103,629	90,019	13,610
Percent distribution of consumer units	100.0	10.2	89.8	78.0	11.8
Consumer unit characteristics (mean values):					
Income before taxes [1]	$51,128	$37,150	$52,797	$55,463	$34,537
Income after taxes [1]	48,596	36,469	50,044	52,450	33,564
Age of reference person	48.4	41.6	49.2	49.5	46.7
Average number in consumer unit:					
Persons	2.5	3.3	2.4	2.4	2.6
Children under 18	.6	1.1	.6	.5	.9
Persons 65 and over	.3	.2	.3	.3	.2
Earners	1.3	1.6	1.3	1.3	1.2
Vehicles	1.9	1.6	2.0	2.1	1.3
Percent distribution:					
Sex of reference person:					
Male	50	52	50	52	36
Female	50	48	50	48	64
Housing tenure:					
Homeowner	67	48	69	72	49
With mortgage	41	34	42	43	30
Without mortgage	26	14	27	29	19
Renter	33	52	31	28	51
Race of reference person:					
Black or African American	12	1	13	n.a.	100
White, Asian, and All Other Races	88	99	87	100	n.a.
Education of reference person:					
Elementary (1-8)	6	22	4	4	7
High school (9-12)	36	42	36	34	48
College	57	35	60	62	45
Never attended and other	(2)	2	(2)	(2)	(2)
At least one vehicle owned or leased	88	82	88	90	73
Annual aggregate expenditures	$4,706,196	8.8	91.2	82.9	8.2
Food	614,570	11.9	88.1	79.5	8.6
Food at home	360,060	12.8	87.2	77.5	9.7
Cereals and bakery products	50,831	12.3	87.7	78.2	9.5
Cereals and cereal products	17,277	13.6	86.4	75.7	10.7
Bakery products	33,554	11.6	88.4	79.5	8.9
Meats, poultry, fish, and eggs	94,890	14.3	85.7	73.5	12.2
Beef	28,257	14.9	85.1	74.4	10.7
Pork	19,634	13.9	86.1	72.2	13.9
Other meats	11,739	12.3	87.7	77.6	10.0
Poultry	16,642	14.6	85.4	71.3	14.1
Fish and seafood	14,322	14.2	85.8	72.9	12.9
Eggs	4,296	17.8	82.2	71.4	10.9
Dairy products	37,746	12.7	87.3	79.5	7.8
Fresh milk and cream	14,561	14.1	85.9	77.4	8.5
Other dairy products	23,185	11.8	88.2	80.7	7.4
Fruits and vegetables	61,614	14.3	85.7	76.4	9.3
Fresh fruits	19,664	15.1	84.9	76.4	8.5
Fresh vegetables	19,789	15.6	84.4	75.8	8.6
Processed fruits	12,473	13.5	86.5	75.9	10.6
Processed vegetables	9,688	11.0	89.0	78.5	10.5

See footnotes at end of table.

Consumer Survey, Page 2

Table 2200. Hispanic or Latino origin of reference person: Shares of annual aggregate expenditures and sources of income, Consumer Expenditure Survey, 2003 — Continued

(Aggregates in millions of dollars, unless otherwise indicated)

Item	Aggregate	Hispanic or Latino	Not Hispanic or Latino		
			Total	White, Asian, and All Other Races	Black or African American
Other food at home	$114,979	11.0	89.0	80.4	8.5
Sugar and other sweets	13,703	12.0	88.0	79.2	8.8
Fats and oils	9,865	12.7	87.3	76.7	10.7
Miscellaneous foods	56,342	10.3	89.7	81.3	8.4
Nonalcoholic beverages	30,883	12.0	88.0	79.4	8.6
Food prepared by consumer unit on out-of-town trips	4,185	6.9	93.1	89.1	4.0
Food away from home	254,510	10.6	89.4	82.4	7.0
Alcoholic beverages	45,028	8.9	91.1	86.4	4.7
Housing	1,549,166	9.4	90.6	81.3	9.3
Shelter	909,862	9.9	90.1	81.0	9.1
Owned dwellings	607,115	7.5	92.5	85.6	6.9
Mortgage interest and charges	340,765	8.5	91.5	84.1	7.4
Property taxes	155,019	5.9	94.1	87.5	6.6
Maintenance, repairs, insurance, other expenses	111,332	6.7	93.3	87.8	5.5
Rented dwellings	251,419	16.6	83.4	67.6	15.8
Other lodging	51,328	5.1	94.9	91.4	3.5
Utilities, fuels, and public services	324,316	9.0	91.0	78.7	12.3
Natural gas	45,221	7.8	92.2	78.1	14.1
Electricity	118,577	8.5	91.5	78.8	12.6
Fuel oil and other fuels	12,634	5.2	94.8	89.8	4.9
Telephone services	110,246	10.3	89.7	77.1	12.7
Water and other public services	37,639	9.5	90.5	80.4	10.1
Household operations	81,573	6.5	93.5	85.9	7.6
Personal services	33,861	8.2	91.8	81.8	9.9
Other household expenses	47,713	5.3	94.7	88.8	5.9
Housekeeping supplies	60,858	10.0	90.0	82.3	7.7
Laundry and cleaning supplies	15,223	14.0	86.0	74.2	11.8
Other household products	30,308	8.4	91.6	84.4	7.2
Postage and stationery	15,327	9.3	90.7	86.2	4.5
Household furnishings and equipment	172,556	8.5	91.5	85.4	6.2
Household textiles	13,067	8.5	91.5	85.1	6.4
Furniture	46,237	10.2	89.8	82.9	6.9
Floor coverings	5,971	3.8	96.2	93.6	2.6
Major appliances	22,566	10.8	89.2	82.0	7.2
Small appliances, miscellaneous housewares	10,107	10.1	89.9	84.4	5.5
Miscellaneous household equipment	74,607	6.8	93.2	87.4	5.7
Apparel and services	188,856	11.6	88.4	77.1	11.2
Men and boys	42,800	12.8	87.2	78.1	9.1
Men, 16 and over	32,488	11.9	88.1	80.6	7.4
Boys, 2 to 15	10,312	15.3	84.7	70.2	14.5
Women and girls	73,034	9.8	90.2	80.0	10.2
Women, 16 and over	60,844	9.2	90.8	81.2	9.6
Girls, 2 to 15	12,190	12.7	87.3	74.2	13.1
Children under 2	9,384	16.1	83.9	69.2	14.7
Footwear	33,823	14.0	86.0	69.1	17.0
Other apparel products and services	29,816	10.6	89.4	80.3	9.1
Transportation	897,513	8.9	91.1	83.4	7.7
Vehicle purchases (net outlay)	430,483	8.3	91.7	85.0	6.7
Cars and trucks, new	236,765	7.1	92.9	87.5	5.4
Cars and trucks, used	185,892	9.9	90.1	81.5	8.6
Other vehicles	7,827	[3]9.0	91.0	90.4	[3].7
Gasoline and motor oil	153,742	10.1	89.9	80.9	9.0

See footnotes at end of table.

Consumer Survey, page 3

Table 2200. Hispanic or Latino origin of reference person: Shares of annual aggregate expenditures and sources of income, Consumer Expenditure Survey, 2003 — Continued

(Aggregates in millions of dollars, unless otherwise indicated)

Item	Aggregate	Hispanic or Latino	Not Hispanic or Latino		
			Total	White, Asian, and All Other Races	Black or African American
Other vehicle expenses	$268,875	9.0	91.0	82.3	8.8
Vehicle finance charges	42,750	9.1	90.9	81.1	9.8
Maintenance and repairs	71,381	8.6	91.4	83.6	7.8
Vehicle insurance	104,428	9.1	90.9	81.3	9.5
Vehicle rental, leases, licenses, other charges	50,316	9.2	90.8	83.3	7.5
Public transportation	44,413	8.8	91.2	84.2	7.0
Health care	278,705	6.1	93.9	87.5	6.4
Health insurance	144,383	6.1	93.9	86.6	7.3
Medical services	68,155	6.3	93.7	89.1	4.6
Drugs	53,821	5.9	94.1	87.5	6.6
Medical supplies	12,346	6.5	93.5	88.8	4.7
Entertainment	237,501	6.2	93.8	88.0	5.8
Fees and admissions	57,039	5.1	94.9	91.0	3.9
Television, radios, sound equipment	84,210	8.7	91.3	81.4	10.0
Pets, toys, and playground equipment	43,580	5.5	94.5	90.7	3.8
Other entertainment supplies, equipment, and services	52,672	4.1	95.9	93.2	2.7
Personal care products and services	60,708	10.0	90.0	79.8	10.2
Reading	14,681	3.8	96.2	91.3	4.9
Education	90,347	6.2	93.8	87.4	6.4
Tobacco products and smoking supplies	33,418	6.0	94.0	86.7	7.3
Miscellaneous	69,879	7.1	92.9	84.2	8.7
Cash contributions	150,025	4.0	96.0	88.4	7.2
Personal insurance and pensions	467,798	7.1	92.9	85.6	7.3
Life and other personal insurance	45,831	4.1	95.9	87.1	8.8
Pensions and Social Security	421,968	7.4	92.6	85.5	7.1
Sources of income and personal taxes: [1]					
Money income before taxes	4,979,403	7.7	92.3	84.6	7.7
Wages and salaries	4,012,508	8.6	91.4	83.6	7.8
Self-employment income	208,249	3.7	96.3	93.9	2.4
Social Security, private and government retirement	545,459	3.7	96.3	88.3	8.0
Interest, dividends, rental income, other property income	106,877	1.7	98.3	96.4	1.9
Unemployment and workers' compensation, veterans' benefits	26,217	11.2	88.8	78.1	10.7
Public assistance, supplemental security income, food stamps	30,609	16.9	83.1	53.1	29.9
Regular contributions for support	33,396	8.9	91.1	82.2	8.9
Other income	16,088	10.4	89.6	72.7	16.9
Personal taxes	246,569	2.9	97.1	92.8	4.4
Federal income taxes	179,498	2.4	97.6	93.9	3.7
State and local income taxes	48,845	4.2	95.8	88.5	7.3
Other taxes	18,226	4.0	96.0	92.5	3.5
Income after taxes	4,732,834	8.0	92.0	84.1	7.9

[1] Components of income and taxes are derived from "complete income reporters" only; see glossary.
[2] Value less than 0.5.
[3] Data are likely to have large sampling errors.
n.a. Not applicable.

3. ACNIELSEN

Go to http://www2.acnielsen.com/company/index.shtml.

ACNielsen's Hispanic Homescan

The ACNielsen Hispanic Homescan Consumer Panel is the first household-based panel service that provides a complete view of Los Angeles Hispanic purchasing behavior and diagnostic information.

It is a truly representative sample of the entire Los Angeles Hispanic market balanced on household demographics and acculturation variables and is a continuous reporting of actual—*not claimed*—purchases from all outlets since February 1999.

ACNielsen's Target Track

ACNielsen's Target Track measures total Hispanic sales by statistically decomposing sales by store and ethnic group. It leverages Spectra's demographic and trade-area modeling expertise and ACNielsen's innovative modeling to weight UPC sales based on their development among Hispanic consumers. Target Track can provide CPG marketers with the ability to evaluate Hispanic versus non-Hispanic consumption patterns.

4. SCARBOROUGH

Go to http://www.scarborough.com/ciudad.htm.

Ciudad Hispana de Scarborough, which translates as "Hispanic City of Scarborough," is a suite of Hispanic consumer research services that provides insights into the Hispanic marketplace. Ciudad Hispana de Scarborough has a database of more than 30,000 Hispanic respondents, including more than 20,000 from its syndicated study. The suite includes two products:

1. *The Scarborough Hispanic Multi-Market Study*, which examines Hispanics across 25 of the most concentrated Hispanic DMAs with a sample of more than 20,000 respondents for in-depth analyses and comparisons across local markets, brands, media outlets, and retailers. Subscribers can explore consumer behavior in important Hispanic marketing categories such as finance, beverage, automotive, telecommunications, media, and retail shopping.

2. *The Scarborough Local Market Hispanic Custom Studies*, which is based on Hispanic oversample surveys in the ten local U.S. markets that have the highest density of Hispanic consumers: Chicago, Dallas, Fresno, Houston, Miami, New York, Phoenix, Sacramento, San Antonio, and San Francisco.

5. SIMMONS NATIONAL HISPANIC CONSUMER STUDY

Go to http://www.smrb.com/products_hispanic.html.

Simmons produces a sizeable and comprehensive database for profiling Hispanic category and brand usage. The National Hispanic Consumer Study surveys more than 7,500 Hispanic adults living in the United States and covers hundreds of product and service categories, making it a key source of information about what Hispanics use in categories such as toiletries and pharmacy, shopping, food and drink, household products, pets, electronic and home office, automotive, finance, and travel, compared to the rest of the population and across the top Hispanic markets.

In addition, the study surveys respondents on leisure activities and hobbies, sports and fitness, life milestone events, gambling and lottery, as well as attitudes, opinions, and interests across a variety of subjects including, technical, personal finance, diet and health, media, political outlook, self-concepts, and shopping behavior.

6. SPECTRA HISPANIQ™

Go to http://www.spectramarketing.com/products/docs/
Bi-Cultural_Consumers-f.pdf.

HispanIQ™ is a powerful new tool that uses Spectra's groundbreaking acculturation research, the Culture Point Model™, to help consumer packaged goods (CPG) marketers identify high-value Hispanic consumers, uncover new opportunities to reach them, and execute marketing and sales efforts at the store level. Spectra HispanIQ™ integrates local market insights from Simmons and Scarborough Research to allow for customization of Hispanic marketing plans by individual market.

7. THE YANKELOVICH MONITOR MULTICULTURAL MARKETING STUDY

Go to http://www.yankelovich.com.

Yankelovich was the first to market with a major multicultural study. Specific areas covered include general attitudes, lifestyle, demographic, and ethnic-specific questions, plus industry-specific behaviors and attitudes on a wide variety of categories and topics. The study includes a nationally representative sample of 1,500 African-Americans, 1,500 Hispanics, and 1,200 non-Hispanic whites age 16 and over, which is a 50-percent larger sample than in the past. The survey consists of a 20-minute phone interview followed by a 45–60-minute self-administered mail or online questionnaire.

Yankelovich MONITOR **Multicultural** Marketing Study

Actionable Insights into the Complex Drivers of the Multicultural Marketplace

Yankelovich was the first to market with a major multicultural study. Our methodology uses in-depth data along with expert analysis.

Robust sample

Nationally representative sample of 1,500 African-Americans, 1,500 Hispanics and 1,200 Non-Hispanic Whites age 16+. 50% larger sample this year!

High quality interviewing

20-minute phone interview followed by 45 to 60-minute self-administered mail or online questionnaire.

In-depth data collected

General attitude, lifestyle, demographic and ethnic-specific questions, plus industry specific behaviors and attitudes on a wide variety of topics.

New this year

Important supplemental marketplace information, including consumer marketing resistance measures and stronger links to MONITOR and Youth MONITOR data.

Deliverables

- Comprehensive Management Summary Report in hard and electronic copy
- Focus on key vertical markets, such as Finance, Consumer Packaged Goods, Healthcare and much more
- Complete data set via CD-ROM and web for easy access and distribution within your organization
- In-person consultation, presentation and workshop customized to your business and delivered by market experts
- Consulting available for specific projects
- Ability to run custom cross tabs of the data on your PC via separate purchase Quanvert software
- OmniPlus recontact capability available separately for collection of custom data

"ABC Speaks Spanish in Primetime." *Hispanic Business.* Submitted by editor on 10 September 2005, 15:52, *http://www.nshp.org/?q=node/1251.*

"Banks Are Still Sizing Up Opportunities in the Growing Hispanic Market," *http://www.fdic.gov/bank/analytical/regional/ro20044q/na/2004winter_05.html.*

Barney, Jay B. and William S. Hesterly. *Strategic Advantage Management and Competitive Advantage.* Prentice Hall, 2005.

"Blockbuster Converts 1,000 Stores to Hispanic Theme," Reno Gazette Journal, 20 November 2002, *http://news.rgj.com/apps/pbcs.dll/frontpage.*

"Bureau of Labor Statistics Consumer Expenditures Survey, 2000–2003," *http://www.bls.gov/cex/home.htm.*

"Chinese in Peru," *http://www.latinamericalinks.com/default.htm.*

De Kluyver, Cornelis A. and John A. Pearce II. *Strategy: A View from the Top.* Pearson Education, 2003.

De Soto, Hernando. *The Mystery of Capital: Why Capitalism Triumphs in the West and Fails Everywhere Else.* Basic Books, 2003.

"A Discussion on the Meaning of the Words Hispanic and Latin." *http://home.att.net/~alsosa/page2.htm.*

DuPraw, Marcelle E. and Mayra Axner. "Working on Cross-cultural Communication Challenges," *http://www.wwcd.org/action/ampu/crosscult.html.*

"The Echo Boomers," *http://www.cbsnews.com/stories/2004/10/01/60minutes/main646890.shtml.*

"El Pollo Loco Migrates to Chicago," 11 October 2005, *http://www.elpolloloco.com/whatsnew/press_text.asp?news_id=64.*

"Half of Online U.S. Hispanics Now Have Broadband at Home, New AOL/Roper Hispanic Survey Finds," *http://hispanicprwire.com/home.php?l=in.*

"Hispanic Spending Is Up," *Discount Long Distance Digest, http://www. thedigest.com.*

"Hispanic Television Viewing Behavior," *http://www.nielsenmedia.com.*

"Hispanic Television Viewing Trends," *http://www.onetvworld.org.*

HispanTelligence®. *http://www.hispanicbusiness.com/research.*

"Influencing the Future," *Executive Management Report,* The Yankelovich Hispanic MONITOR, 2002.

"Innovative Practices for Reaching Immigrants," Harris Bank, April 2004, *http://www.chicagofed.org/news_and_conferences/conferences_and_events/ files/financial_access_for_immigrants_heldring.pdf.*

Inter-American Development Bank—Multilateral Investment Fund, *http://www.iadb.org/NEWS/DISPLAY/issuebriefs/2004/remitt.cfm? Language=English*

"Internet and Multimedia 12: The Value of Internet Broadcast Advertising," *http://www.arbitron.com/home/content.stm.*

"Is There Such a Thing as Latino Identity?" Otto Santa Ana, PhD, *http:// www.pbs.org/americanfamily/latino2.html.*

Korzenny, Felipe, and Betty Ann Korzenny. *Hispanic Marketing: A Cultural Perspective.* Butterworth-Heinemann, 2005.

Kostin, David J. "Hispanization of the U.S.: The Growing Influence of the Hispanic and Latino Communities in the United States Economy," Global Markets Institute, Goldman Sachs, December 2004.

Nashville Hispanic Chamber of Commerce, *http://nahcc7.tripod.com/ index.html.*

The National Restaurant Association, *http://www.restaurant.org.*

"The Power of Hispanic Consumers a Compelling Argument for Reaching out to Hispanic Consumers," Arbitron, November 2004, *http:// www.arbitron.com/home/content.stm.*

Rodríguez, Dr. Clara E. "What It Means to Be Latino," *http://www.pbs.org/ americanfamily/latino3.html.*

Rodríguez, Darlene Xiomara. "Hispanic Public Health Concerns and Insurance Needs," *Eco Latino & Athens Banner-Herald,* April 2005, *http:// www.athensecolatino.com/v3n1/index.html.*

Saenz, Rogelio. "Latinos and the Changing Face of America," *http:// www.prb.org.*

Standard & Poor's Restaurant Industry Survey Report, 2005.

Slywotzky, Adrian J. and David J. Morrison. *The Profit Zone.* Three Rivers Press, 2002.

The U.S. Census Bureau, *http://www.census.gov.*

"U.S. Hispanic Use of Telecom Services 2002–2007," *http://www. insight-corp.com.*

Valdes, M. Isabel. *Marketing to American Latinos: A Guide to the In-Culture Approach, Parts I and II.* Paramount Market Publishing, 2000 (Part I) and 2002 (Part II).

MARKET INTELLIGENCE RESOURCES

Market Research Companies

ACNielsen Worldwide
770 Broadway
New York, NY 10003
Phone: (646) 654-5000
Web site: *http://www.acnielsen.com*

Cultural Access Group
445 S. Figueroa Street, Suite 2350
Los Angeles, CA 90071
Phone: (213) 228-0300
Web site: *http://www.accesscag.com/index.html*

Forrester Research Inc.
400 Technology Sq.
Cambridge, MA 02139
Phone: (617) 497-7090
Web site: *http://www.forrester.com*

Garcia Research Associates
2550 Hollywood Way, Suite 110
Burbank, CA 91505
Phone: (818) 566-7722
Web site: *http://www.garciaresearch.com/index.html*

Jupiter Research
INT Media Group Inc.
23 Old Kings Hwy.
South, Darien, CT 06820
Phone: (203) 662-2800
Web site: *http://www.jup.com*

HispanTelligence®
Hispanic Business Inc.
425 Pine Avenue
Santa Barbara, CA 93117-3709
Phone: (805) 964-4554
Web site: *http://www.hispanicbusiness.com*

IRI Global Headquarters
150 North Clinton Street
Chicago, IL 60661-1416
Phone: (312) 726-1221
Web site: *http://www.infores.com/public/us/default.htm*

marketresearch.com
38 East 29th Street, 6th Floor
New York, NY 10016
Phone: (800) 298-5699
Web site: *http://marketresearch.com*

Mintel International Group Ltd.
351 West Hubbard Street, 8th Floor
Chicago, IL 60610
Phone: (312) 943 5250
Web site: *http://www.mintel.com*

New American Dimensions, LLC
6955 La Tijera Boulevard, Suite B
Los Angeles, CA 90045
Phone: (310) 670-6800
Web site: *http://www.newamericandimensions.com*

NPD Group Inc.
900 W. Shore Rd.
Port Washington, NY 11050
Phone: (516) 625-0700
Web site: *http://www.npd.com*

Packaged Facts
38 East 29th Street, 6th Floor
New York, NY 10016
Phone: (800) 298-5294 / (212) 807-2661
Web site: *http://www.packagedfacts.com/default.asp*

Pew Hispanic Center
1615 L Street, NW, Suite 700
Washington, DC 20036-5610
Phone: (202) 419-3600
Web site: *http://pewhispanic.org*

PROMAR International
Rookery Farm Lane
Tilstone Fearnall
Tarporley
Cheshire
CW6 9HY
Phone: +44 (0)1829 731731
Web site: *http://www.promar-international.com/Content/home.asp*

Scarborough Research
770 Broadway
New York, NY 10003
Phone: (646) 654-8400
Web site: *http://www.scarborough.com/index.php*

Simmons Market Research
230 Park Avenue South, 5th Floor
New York, NY 10003-1566
Phone: (212) 598-5400
Web site: *http://www.smrb.com/index.html*

Spectra Marketing
200 W. Jackson Blvd., Suite 2800
Chicago, IL 60606-6910
Phone: (312) 583-5100
Web site: *http://www.spectramarketing.com/about/default.jsp*

Synovate Americas
16133 Ventura Blvd Suite 1000
Encino, CA 91436
Phone: (818) 380-1480
Web site: *http://www.synovate.com*

The Conference Board
845 Third Ave.
New York, NY 10022
Phone: (212) 339-0345
Web site: *http://www.conference-board.org*

The Selig Center for Economic Growth
Terry College of Business
University of Georgia
999 Brumby Hall
Athens, GA 30609
Phone: (706) 542-3000
Web site: *http://www.selig.uga.edu*

Yankelovich
400 Meadowmont Village Circle, Suite 431
Chapel Hill, NC 27517
Phone: (919) 932-0000
Web site: *http://www.yankelovich.com/index.aspx*

Web Sites

http://www.HispanicPRWire.com

http://www.Hispaniconline.com

http://www.Hispanictrends.com

http://www.Hispanicmagazine.com

http://www.marketingymedios.com

Corporate Information

Many corporate filings with the federal Securities and Exchange Commission, including 10Ks and 10Qs, are available through the commission's Edgar Web site:

http://www.sec.gov/edgar/searchedgar/companysearch.html

Government Agencies

Bureau of Labor Statistics (BLS)
Postal Square Building
2 Massachusetts Ave. NE
Washington, DC 20212
Phone: (202) 691-5200
Web site: *http://stats.bls.gov*

U.S. Department of Commerce
1401 Constitution Ave. NW
Washington, DC 20230
Phone: (202) 482-4883
Web site: *http://www.doc.gov*

U.S. Census Bureau
4700 Silver Hill Road
Washington, DC 20233-0001
Web site: *http://www.census.gov*

U.S. Food and Drug Administration (FDA)
5600 Fishers Ln.
Rockville, MD 20857
Phone: (888) 463-6332
Web site: *http://www.fda.gov*

Hispanic Associations

Association of Hispanic Advertising Agencies (AHAA)
8201 Greensboro Dr., Ste. 300
McLean, VA 22102
Phone: (703) 610-9014

Hispanic Organization of Professionals and Executives (HOPE)
1700 17th St. NW, Ste. 405-2009
Washington, DC 20009
Phone: (202) 234-2351

Hispanic Public Relations Association (HPRA)
601 W. Fifth Street, 4th Floor
Los Angeles, CA 90071
Phone: (213) 623-4200

Associations

Latin Business Association
120 South San Pedro Street, Suite 530
Los Angeles California, 90012
Phone: (213) 628-8510
Web site: *http://www.lbausa.com*

National Hispanic Corporate Council
8201 Greensboro Dr., Ste. 300
McLean, VA 22102
Phone: (703) 610-9016
Web site: *http://www.nhcc-hq.org*

National Hispanic Employee Association (NHEA)
San Jose State University
1 Washington Square
San Jose, CA 95192
Phone: (408) 924-2256
Web site: *http://www.nhea.org*

National Society of Hispanic MBAs (NSHMBA)
1303 Walnut Hill Lane Suite 300
Irving, TX 75038
Phone: (214) 596-9338
Web site: *http://www.nshmba.org*

Share the message!

Bulk discounts
Discounts start at only 10 copies and range from 30% to 55% off retail price based on quantity.

Custom publishing
Private label a cover with your organization's name and logo. Or, tailor information to your needs with a custom pamphlet that highlights specific chapters.

Ancillaries
Workshop outlines, videos, and other products are available on select titles.

Dynamic speakers
Engaging authors are available to share their expertise and insight at your event.

Call Kaplan Publishing Corporate Sales at 1-800-621-9621, ext. 4511, or e-mail nakia_hinkle@kaplan.com

PUBLISHING